salesmanship
A CONTEMPORARY APPROACH

salesmanship
A CONTEMPORARY APPROACH

FERDINAND F. MAUSER

Professor of Marketing,
School of Business Administration, Wayne State University,
and Visiting Professor of Marketing, Graduate School
of Business Administration, Keio University, Tokyo

HARCOURT BRACE JOVANOVICH, INC.

New York   Chicago   San Francisco   Atlanta

ISBN: 0-15-578042-5

Library of Congress Catalog Card Number: 72-92768

Printed in the United States of America

PICTURE CREDITS

Page 10, Culver Pictures; page 12, Mildred Rosenblatt, D.P.I.; page 14, F. Grehan, Photo Researchers, Inc.; pages 27, 34–35, 45, Harbrace; page 66, Joyce Wilson, Harbrace; pages 75, 92, Harbrace; page 99, Lizabeth Corlett, D.P.I.; pages 107, 118, 154, Harbrace; page 157, Albert Session, Harbrace; page 185, Lizabeth Corlett, D.P.I.; page 212, Butler Manufacturing Company; page 224, Dennis Martin; pages 237, 245, Harbrace.

PREFACE

"What? Another book on salesmanship?" These were my words when it was suggested that I write this book. Surely I must have sounded like a prospect determined never to buy an idea. And yet—as this book teaches students of salesmanship—"The sale begins when the prospect says no!"

Frankly, I was allowed to sell myself on the idea of producing this volume. Once I considered the proposition, I became enthusiastic about the idea of writing it. For I discovered what many buyers discover—there are needs of which we are not aware. Once we understand them, we buy.

This is a short book. The brevity and conciseness are deliberate, because I felt that students with sales-oriented personalities are inclined to be *active doers* rather than *passive readers*. There is plenty to do in this volume. Students today want personal involvement. The body of almost every chapter contains relevant personal-involvement exercises designed as self-education projects that will capture student interest. Chapter-end materials are extensive. There is a two-part Chronicle that, in serialized form, is a continuing story of John Elsworth. He is a character with whom students can identify because he starts out on a selling career by taking a summer job as a sales trainee while he is still an undergraduate. The kinds of problems Elsworth encounters in his work can and often do confront students when they get their first selling job.

The Chronicle is in two parts. The Field Chronicle deals with Elsworth's activities in the field, away from the company. The Company Chronicle describes what happens to Elsworth within his own company. It is especially vital because, as perceptive sales managers say again and again, the way in which the salesman handles himself within his own organization contributes to his success or failure.

There is a generous chapter-end supply of short cases based mostly on situations that have actually occurred. Since there is no one right way to sell, the materials are intended to raise questions rather than to provide fixed answers and solutions. The materials and ideas in this book are immediately usable. They stress resourcefulness, not formulas. The text of the book is not intended to be "taken" and filed away for later use in the conventional sense of "taking a course"—it is meant to be immediately applied by the student in his interactions with others.

Becoming professional in selling involves the absorption of hundreds of experiences and the learning from many publications and people. The writing of a textbook in salesmanship involves the same process. It would be impossible to identify and to name all those who contributed to this book. But let me name and once again thank, this time in print, those who were most generous and helpful with ideas and encouragement. Special appreciation goes to Bill Clements, Jr., who has taken great interest in the project. Lillian M. Plomley, Managing Director of Sales/Marketing Executives of Detroit, Inc.; and Phil Ruprecht, a sales and marketing veteran, former Vice President of McGraw-Hill Publications, New York, and Manager for Westinghouse Electric, both conscientiously reviewed and reacted helpfully to the entire manuscript. Gale E. Hurley of Cañada College, Redwood City, California, also diligently applied himself to reading the manuscript and provided many helpful insights, assurances, and suggestions. Alice Formberg cheerfully, expertly, and encouragingly handled the typing responsibilities.

I would also like to thank those who were most cooperative in providing illustrative material to highlight the text: Joseph Naar of The Conference Board, New York; Kenneth W. Hartwell of the Detroit Edison Company; K. A. Cruise of the Bendix Corporation, Southfield, Michigan; James W. Gordon of the Slide Chart Corporation, West Chester, Pennsylvania; Clete Beaubien of the Metallurgical Products Department, General Electric Company, Detroit; Howard W. Bacon of Michigan Blue Cross/Blue Shield, Detroit; Lawrence Stessin, Professor of Management, Hofstra University, Hempstead, New York; Arnold W. Hartig of the Chrysler Corporation, Detroit; and William Lamoreaux, Editor, *Michigan Challenge* Magazine.

FERDINAND F. MAUSER

CONTENTS

3

TYPES OF SELLING AND SALES TRAINING   42

4

THE SALES FIELD: SIZE, COMPENSATION, AND ORGANIZATION   62

5

COMMUNICATIONS AND THE PSYCHOLOGY OF SELLING   85

6

7

8

THE SELLING PROCESS: PART III
MECHANICS OF SELLING: MEETING OBJECTIONS
AND SALES RESISTANCE · 170

9

THE SELLING PROCESS: PART IV
CLOSING AND FOLLOW-UP · 201

10

THE PERSONAL ASPECTS OF SELLING: OPPORTUNITIES AND RESPONSIBILITIES

salesmanship
A CONTEMPORARY APPROACH

1

SOME DIMENSIONS OF SELLING

*I love to lose myself
in other men's minds.*
—CHARLES LAMB

SELLING IS UNIVERSAL:
IT IS OFTEN LINKED TO BOTH
PERSONAL AND PROFESSIONAL SUCCESS

The study of selling deals with many familiar matters, for selling is an inherent aspect of all human transaction. In a noncommercial sense we sell every day. We sell when we try to convince our parents that they should allow us to use the family car to visit a neighboring city over the weekend. We sell when we try to persuade the manager of a store to give us a discount on a piece of merchandise. We sell when we make ourselves attractive and pleasing to a member of the opposite sex. We sell when we appeal to a teacher to grant us an extension on the due date of a term paper. In a very real way, the successes and failures of one's efforts in life often hinge on one's ability to sell.

Clearly, these efforts relate very closely to our personal welfare. They involve the utilization of inherent talent for the purpose of achieving specific goals. Similarly, training oneself in salesmanship is largely a matter of activating one's latent talents for the purpose of influencing others. It can be said that the salesman is the humanizing element in today's mass-production society. He is the interface contact between factory and family. As John Dykstra, former president of Ford Motor Company, so often said, "We make cars by the thousands, but we sell them one by one."

Sales Skill Is a Unique Quality

"Are salesmen made, or are they born?" is a well-known if rather academic question. We also sometimes hear the statement, "He's a natural-born salesman." Clearly, everyone is born with some selling skills and talents. This does not mean, however, that everyone is a "professional" salesman. Learning to sell is a matter not only of activating the talents one may have been born with, but of adding to those talents and skills until one is exceptionally prepared to be successful at selling.

To put it another way, the unique qualities of one's particular personality can, once they are cultivated and augmented, be put to productive use in selling successfully.

Each of us, in varying degrees over the years, develops sales techniques, or selling behavior-patterns. We use them to help us exchange what we have for what we want. Those who develop the most successful selling behavior, those who are most effective when it comes to persuading others to "buy" what they have to "sell," often attain a high level of self-satisfaction and prosperity.

For Every Seller Action There Is a Buyer Reaction

The process of making a sale is a two-way street. In other words, the sales effort is a tandem act in which successful progress depends on the participation of both the buyer and the seller. The successful salesman knows the strengths and weaknesses of his own personality. In addition, he is also a keen observer and assessor of the personalities of those he seeks to influence. His objective is to conduct himself in a manner that is in tune with the personality of each prospect. If he can get on the same "wave length" as that of his prospective customer, his sales message will register. He can sell successfully. The best salesmen do this in a highly individualistic way.

Mastering Salesmanship Has Many Advantages

Because selling is universal, it is useful to understand the psychology of selling, whether or not you intend to make a career of selling. Thus, taking a course in salesmanship and studying this textbook serve more purposes than that of career preparation alone. The intent of this book is threefold: (1) to provide you with the basics prerequisite to earning your living by being a professional salesman; (2) to help you become more successful in whatever business, trade, or profession you enter; and (3) to help you discover useful concepts of applied psychology as well as those insights that can, in your daily life, contribute to your happiness and personal well-being as your persuasiveness and ability to cooperate increase. After all, the success of any business depends on sales volume and this makes selling a most crucial activity in any business, for, as successful salesmen are fond of saying, "Nothing happens until a sale is made."

Great personal satisfactions come from being a good cooperator and from knowing how to secure the cooperation of others. Inner peace of mind comes from knowing how to relate to society, cooperating in worthy causes, and influencing others to do the same.

In essence then, the major aim of this book is to teach the art of cooperating with others and the skills needed to get others to cooperate with you, through the use of the principles and psychology of selling.

PERSONAL-INVOLVEMENT
EXERCISE NO. 1–1

SELF-TEST. Following are three situations. Be as candid as possible and select the alternative you would most likely choose based on the way you usually think in everyday life. The self-test discussion below explains, in terms of your answers, whether your present natural inclinations reflect an aptitude for selling.

1. A friend whom you respect seems to be avoiding you. You are puzzled because you can think of no reason why. You would probably:
   a. start avoiding the friend
   b. wait and see what happens
   c. arrange to discuss the matter with your friend
   d. other:

2. It is January. You very much want a job for the summer. A friend of your father mentions that a neighbor of his, who has a small garden-supply business, will be hiring several students for the summer. You would probably:
   a. stop by and see the man as soon as possible
   b. phone for further details when it is convenient
   c. see or phone the man a few weeks before the summer vacation starts
   d. other:

3. While eating lunch with someone you work with, you hear his views on a controversial subject and realize that you have strong opposing feelings. The subject might be birth control, capital punishment, or the role of women in society. You would be inclined to:
   a. avoid talking about the subject again
   b. emphatically tell the acquaintance about your contrary views
   c. let your coworker know that you disagree and over a period of time explain your views on the matter
   d. other:

SELF-TEST DISCUSSION. *Question 1*—Answer *c*—"arrange to discuss the matter with your friend"—is perhaps the approach most likely to be selected by a person who has natural talents for sales. The *c* answer indicates that you are sensitive to and curious about people and are interested in finding out why they react the way they do. It also indicates that you do not shy away from face-to-face discussions and that you are probably prepared to persuade your friend that your friendship is worthwhile. The *a* answer indicates a reluctance to confront and possibly persuade others. The *b* answer indicates a tendency to postpone confrontation. Remember, a salesman enjoys persuading others while avoiding a head-on collision of ideas!

Question 2—Answer *a*—"stop by and see the man as soon as possible"—is the most reasonable action from a salesmanship point of view. It indicates an aggressive trait, a key ingredient of selling. The *b* and *c* alternatives run the risk of losing the opportunity because others with more initiative may get the job before you even get around to applying. Also, use of the telephone in a situation where personal contact may be more effective would be a definite mistake. A person with a good sales sense would realize that a face-to-face meeting with a prospective employer is the best way to sell himself because, of course, an employer wants to see whom he is hiring.

Question 3—These are difficult choices; however, *c*—"let your coworker know that you disagree and over a period of time explain your views on the matter"—would probably be most appropriate. The situation is an emotional one where risking alternatives *a* or *b* could easily alienate your friend. In a situation such as this, which involves controversy and emotion, a time lapse to cool feelings, and patience in making your views known, are called for.

SELLING AND SALESMANSHIP

Whether one thinks of selling and salesmanship as a science, as an art, or as a combination of the two, the fact remains that these terms are described in so many different ways that one can learn a lot about selling and salesmanship just by thinking about definitions that relate to selling.

Definitions of Selling and Salesmanship

Here are some of the better-known descriptions:

> Selling effects the transfer, with a profit to buyer and seller, of goods or services that give such lasting satisfaction that the buyer is predisposed to come back to the seller for more of the same.[1]

> Selling is 90 percent perspiration and 10 percent inspiration.

> A salesman is an order maker; a clerk is an order taker.

> Salesmanship is the process whereby the seller ascertains and activates the needs or wants of the buyer and satisfies these needs or wants to the mutual, continuous advantage of both the buyer and the seller.

> Salesmanship is the art of selling your goods and services at a profit.

> Selling is the process of assisting and/or persuading a prospective customer to buy a commodity or a service or to act favorably upon an idea that has commercial significance to the seller.[2]

[1] Elmer F. Schumaker.

[2] Ralph S. Alexander and the Committee of Definitions of the American Marketing Association, *Marketing Definitions*. New York: American Marketing Association, 1960, p. 21.

Think about these definitions. Notice how different each is from the other. Obviously, each is a *limited* description. It describes one way of looking at selling or salesmanship. And the almost endless number of different descriptions, or definitions, indicates the richness and the variety one finds in the subject. There are probably as many approaches to selling as there are people who are practicing it.

There is, in fact, no one definition of salesmanship, just as there is no one formula for selling. This is perhaps why those who sell frequently point out that they feel they participate in exciting and interesting activities. Each person, whether he sells as a career salesman or sells ideas or persuades others to agree with him and to cooperate with him, develops his own selling style. This style is based on his own particular makeup, his life-style, his particular abilities, and his own special potential.

We have already provided several definitions. They can be altered, dramatized, and embellished. In fact, a good salesman is creative and is an adapter. Thus, it is good practice to adapt materials and ideas in this book to suit various occasions and needs. Here are two working definitions:

> *Selling* is the process of inducing and assisting a prospective customer to buy goods or services or to act favorably on an idea that has commercial significance for the seller.
>
> A *salesman* is one who practices the profession of selling.

Note that the second definition states that a salesman is one who practices the *profession* of selling.

Professionalism and Selling

The word *profession* has overriding significance. There are a number of basic requirements for a true profession. These include:

1. An organized body of knowledge
2. A relatively long and specialized preparation
3. A structured program to train individuals who plan to enter the profession
4. An established and accepted code of ethics
5. A set of standards for admission and disqualification
6. Recognition that service to others comes before self-interest

A person in a profession is engaged in a field where there is a prescribed or generally accepted moral code. Doctors, lawyers, and teachers are professional people because they adhere to a generally accepted moral code that applies to their field of specialization. A professional salesman adheres to a moral code that includes honesty and presumes a fair exchange of values as represented to the customer. Anyone engaged in selling who does otherwise is not a professional salesman.

R. S. Wilson, former executive vice-president and sales manager of the Goodyear Tire and Rubber Company, says that "the distinguishing mark of a professional is the constant aspiring toward perfection."[3] Wilson defines the professional salesman as a person who:

1. Is constantly studying to improve his proficiency
2. Recognizes the fact that there is no substitute for hard work
3. Above all else, maintains his own self-respect, integrity, and independence
4. Puts true value on his services

The knowledge of three fundamentals—personality, product, and prospect—together with a complete mastery of the strategy and tactics of salesmanship in the sales interview, characterizes the professional salesman.

We have been considering what selling *is*. We must also consider what selling *is not*. The general public is inclined to have a great many false impressions about selling and salesmanship. The reasons for these misconceptions about salesmanship are largely historical.

Historically, the Salesman Is Colorfully American

Americans have always had a particular zest and flair for selling and merchandising. America's early history is studded with the names of bombastic hucksters and traders such as P. T. Barnum and Diamond Jim Brady, John Jacob Astor and R. H. Macy. The salesman as an American symbol is part of our folklore. The Yankee trader pushed westward on horseback and in covered wagons. He plied overseas under canvas sails in his famous Yankee Clipper, which was built for trading. Great American humorists such as W. C. Fields and Will Rogers often approached their best form when they were outrageous at the expense of the salesman. The offerings of the early music halls, old-time burlesque houses, riverboat melodramas, and minstrel shows seldom were without the characterization of the traveling salesman. The salesman was the butt of many jokes: he was characterized as flashy, brassy, and sassy while he bilked rubes, seduced fair maidens, and generally took advantage of the gullible—always just three steps ahead of the law.

This uncharitable image of the salesman is so deeply embedded in American folklore that the image of today's professional salesman is still tainted by its past. But salesmanship has changed fundamentally, despite the seeming reluctance of many to recognize these changes. Colorful, naughty, and wicked characterizations die slowly; as entertainment, they are not easily replaced by characterizations of sobriety, industry, and respectability.

INTERNAL AND EXTERNAL DIMENSIONS OF SELLING

Along with the general public's historical misconceptions of the salesman's character, there are also misconceptions about what the salesman does and how he spends his time. You will probably become aware of the many mis-

[3] "Salesmanship as a Profession." New York: Goodyear Tire and Rubber Company, 1958, p. 16.

conceptions about salesmen when you form opinions from the interviews suggested at the end of this section.

In general, people form their opinions about selling on the basis of the salesman's external activities. This is natural enough because this is what people see—the salesman calling on his accounts, talking to people in showrooms, making product presentations, writing up orders, and the like. Actually, there is considerably more to salesmanship than just meeting the public.

Consider what it takes to support one salesman who is selling a given product line. The product has to be designed, manufactured, packaged, priced, distributed, advertised, and promoted before it can be sold. These functions require many separate activities, involve many people, and demand a wide spectrum of support to back a salesman.

Once the salesman has the product to sell he must study it, determine its characteristics—the benefits it offers buyers, the advantages it has over similar products, and so forth. He must travel to reach prospects, sit in on sales meetings to learn about the product and the selling plan, and wait in reception rooms to meet with merchandisers.

For each hour that the salesman spends in face-to-face contact with customers, there is an estimated two or three hours spent in traveling, waiting, attending meetings, reading and studying, preparing for contacts, handling bookwork, and following up on orders.

It has been pointed out that the salesman is a coordinator. He is, however, much more than the liaison between his company and his customers. Of course, the salesman represents the company he works for. From the moment an IBM or Ford-dealer salesman introduces himself, in the eyes of the person he is talking to he *is* the IBM Corporation, or in the case of the automobile salesman, he *is* the spokesman not only for his employer, the dealer, but also for the Ford Motor Company. Thus you can be sure that the IBM salesman spends a great deal of time learning about IBM as a company—about its products and about its history, policies, and operations. The conscientious salesman will also learn as much about the competitors of IBM. Both the Ford Motor Company and their dealers do much to train dealer salesmen and to keep them as well informed as possible.

Because a salesman so intimately represents the company he works for, it is easy to understand why his success hinges largely on how he represents his company—how well he understands his company's operations, policies, and products. A pleasant personality, a mastery of the psychology of persuasion, both supported by a solid foundation of company and product knowledge, prepare a salesman to sell effectively.

Every salesman leads what could be considered a double life. His external life, which is his customer-contact work, is his extrovert side. Depending on the personality of the salesman, different approaches to meet the public are used. Some salesmen are "hail-fellow-well-met" types. Others are "brotherly counselors." Still others are "no-nonsense technical advisers," and so on.

Then there is the internal side of the salesman's job, his introvert side. This is the side the customer does not see, nor even know about. Significantly, the success of the salesman probably hinges as much on his internal activities as on his external activities. The sale often depends on how much "homework" the salesman has done. Whether he knows the products and policies of his company and is able to supply his customers with the service and the information they require depends on his ability to learn and absorb information at company sales meetings and study, understand, and keep abreast of developments in his field. A salesman is often referred to as the "eyes and ears" of his company and of the business world. When salesmen are good at acquiring and absorbing information and in passing it on to the company, they can be most successful. And it is in this way that they make one of their greatest contributions to society. For as products and services become more complex in an increasingly technical society, the customer's need for information in making intelligent buying decisions becomes more critical.

Unfortunately, courses and textbooks in the past have focused largely on the external or extrovert side of salesmanship. The materials in this textbook will place equal emphasis on the external and the internal aspects of the sales career. A special feature called "Chronicles" at the end of each chapter will highlight both the external and the internal aspects of selling and salesmanship.

PERSONAL-INVOLVEMENT EXERCISE NO. 1–2

OPINION SAMPLING. Select three people whom you know well enough to talk to about selling and salesmanship. Try to select three people who differ in age and background. This will give you a broader sample. Ask them the following questions and write down their answers.

1. How would you describe the work a salesman does?
2. Do you feel that selling is, or is not, a good field of work? Why?
3. Do you think that a salesman's job is easy or difficult? Why?

After you have finished your interviews with the three people you selected, read over their comments and, based on the general impressions your interviews produced, check the following list.

Their understanding of what the salesman does is:
—— Narrow
—— Biased
—— Vague
—— Realistic

Their attitudes toward selling are:
—— Favorable
—— Neutral
—— Unfavorable

They feel that selling is:
—— Easy
—— Difficult and complicated
—— Neither difficult nor easy

OLD VERSUS NEW CONCEPTS
IN SALESMANSHIP

The history of salesmanship in America can be divided into three eras: prior to 1920, between 1920 and 1960, and the period since 1960.

Prior to 1920—The First Era

In many of the countries from which early Americans emigrated, selling and trading were considered fit only for those who were relegated to the ghettos. Napoleon, when he pointedly insulted the British, called them a nation of shopkeepers. Early Americans, however, did not retain their Old World prejudices. They had chosen to come to the New World. The special charm that this continent held was its newness, and the people gravitated to it for that reason. This very newness caused people to view salesmen differently. Since they were purveyors of the new, they were accepted. The Great Seal of the United States bears the motto *Novus Ordo Seclorum* ("A New Order of the Centuries").

The history of the westward expansion of America contains many thrilling stories of the pioneer families who forged their way across the country. Some settled in friendly territory along the way. Other families pushed on in search of more promising land. Some were intent on owning their own land. Others went in search of gold. Still others sought adventure in distant fields. But whatever their goals, pioneer families were self-sufficient. They could find their own food, make their own clothes, fashion the tools they needed to survive in the wilderness.

Right along with this tremendous push westward were many people who lived, or made their living, by looking after the needs of others. These were the merchants and itinerant peddlers, the people who bought and sold goods and services. History books are full of stories of men who ran what were called "general stores" or had pack horses and wagons from which they sold a variety of merchandise. They bought what others had to sell and they sold to those who wished to buy. These hardy merchants and peddlers were good businessmen. Those who survived knew well how to buy for less and sell for more. They were the forerunners of today's salesmen.

Historically, the era prior to 1920 was identified by the Latin admonition *caveat emptor* ("let the buyer beware"). Before 1920 those who offered goods or services for sale did so without feeling any particular responsibility toward the buyers of their goods and services. It was strictly an era when each person who purchased anything was fair game for those who could "put it over on them." In other words, in the selling of goods or services, it was "each man for himself," part of the code of the pioneer. Indeed, you helped your neighbor, but you were on your own when it came to the other things in your environment.

A person who bought or traded what he had for what he wanted did so at his own risk. This was a natural outgrowth of the development of the country. If a person could not judge whether he was getting good value for his money, that was his, not the seller's, problem. In fact, those who were clever

enough to sell something for more than it was worth were considered "smarter" than those who spent their money for worthless, or nearly worthless, merchandise.

In the old days of the Yankee traders it was dangerous for the uninstructed or the uninformed buyer to venture into the marketplace. It was commonplace for an unscrupulous trader to try to sell them a "pig in a poke"—a useless or nearly useless commodity—before they discovered they had been "taken." In the early days, such "salesmen" would, for example, represent farm animals as being "sound of wind" when, many times, they would become lame when they were hitched to a plow or winded when saddled.

This was also a time when "medicines," frequently made up of sugared water and coloring matter, were sold as "sure cures" for all the ills that beset man. It was indeed a time for the buyer to beware. No warranties or guarantees protected the unsuspecting buyers. Either a buyer was wise enough to avoid making a bad purchase or he would be a victim of the consequences. The buyer had no recourse to protective statutes nor could he expect sympathy from those who were fond of saying, with P. T. Barnum, "a sucker is born every minute." Ruthless? Yes, and worse. The "good old days" in selling left much to be desired.

Because of the way selling and salesmanship started, some of the distrust that people developed toward early salesmen is still felt toward salesmen today, even though the job of selling and the techniques of salesmanship today are quite different from the crude and rude methods used by hucksters at the turn of the century and for some decades after. In fact, there are still hucksters in the marketplace—companies and their representatives who are out to make a "fast buck" and then disappear.

Fortunately buyers are, for the most part, better educated today and less apt to fall for ridiculous claims that cannot be supported. Unhappily, there will probably always be some customers who are unable to distinguish good merchandise from bad. They will be preyed upon, as always, by those who live by taking advantage of others.

Between 1920 and 1960—the Second Era

The second era of selling and salesmanship emerged as the frontier days ended and the producers of goods and services began to establish their businesses in locations on a more or less permanent basis. It then became a matter of good business to be sure that the consumer purchased goods and services that would live up to customer expectations. This was the only way to ensure repeat business and thus growing sales.

Salesmen became more truly representative of the manufacturers and/or producers of goods and services. They began to replace the "tricks" of selling, used in earlier days, with sounder selling techniques. The kind of selling style that developed, however, was singularly uninspired even by the standards existing between 1920 and 1960. Salesmen generally followed what was called a selling formula. This usually consisted of certain standardized "steps" that the salesman used regardless of what he was selling or to whom he was selling it. The second era of selling and salesmanship prevailed for forty years, and its technique still persists in less sophisticated business circles. It can be identified as the "standardized era of selling."

The following excerpt from a biographical sketch of Henning W. Prentis effectively describes the transition from the pre-1920s to the second era of selling, which lasted into the sixties. Prentis, the guiding genius of the Armstrong Cork Company and president and board chairman of Armstrong Cork from 1935 to 1959, offers these specific comments: [4]

> "In the 1920's, general practice in the flooring business was for retailers to purchase linoleum wherever they could get the best price. The price, in each transaction, depended on who could bargain the best, and CAVEAT EMPTOR was the rule of the game. It was a veritable oriental bazaar. The consumer, at the mercy of the marketplace in such a situation, found it almost impossible to be sure he was getting good value in his purchase." Mr. Prentis believed strongly in fairness, responsibility and honesty. Instead of "Let the buyer beware," he thought it should be "Let the buyer have faith."

A search of the backgrounds of business leaders who emerged in the 1920s will readily reveal others who, like Henning Prentis, believed that com-

[4] *Nation's Business,* January 1970, p. 53.

panies had to change their business policies and ensure company growth by assuming greater responsibility toward their customers through improved merchandising techniques and methods.

In the standardized era of selling between 1920 and 1960, companies were able to reduce the irresponsibility of their salesmen by insisting that they follow a standardized method of selling their goods and services. Usually a definite number of selling steps were organized into a selling presentation, and the salesmen were required to memorize the exact words of the selling presentation and deliver them verbatim to every customer. Such "canned," or memorized, sales presentations helped companies control to a greater degree what their salesmen said to prospects and customers. In this way, reputable companies tried to protect their customers from the extravagant claims, wild promises, and outright deception that too many "old-time salesmen" made in order to get sales. Even though giving the same canned sales talk to every prospect must have been frustrating both to prospects and to salesmen, it was a step in the right direction. Salesmanship began to come out of the dark ages.

The canned sales presentation then ushered in what was called method selling. The same method was used no matter what the product, the prospect, or the salesman. The idea was to cover the usual steps leading from the opening remarks to the "signature on the dotted line." Usually five or six steps made up the process. These steps included getting attention, arousing interest, creating desire, establishing conviction, moving to action, and closing the sale. Sometimes this routine was varied by demonstrating benefits, proving advantages, offering service after the sale, and many other variations.

A further "refinement" was the development of a method for "overcoming objections." This provided salesmen with answers to any questions that the prospects might raise during the sales talk. A series of possible objections were anticipated, and convincing answers were memorized for each objection. As soon as a prospect mentioned any one of the anticipated objections, the salesman was prepared to come right back with the memorized answers and then go on with his prepared sales talk. As mechanical and as phony as this technique was, it did keep even the poorest salesman on what was believed to be "the path toward a sale."

The result of this kind of selling and salesmanship was that a stereotyped kind of salesman emerged. A "good salesman" in this era was one who "followed the formula." In the era prior to 1920, the "good salesman" slapped customers on the back, told a funny story or two, inquired how the wife was, and asked for the order. The "method" salesman of the second era wore well-polished shoes and carefully pressed suits, had a ready smile, said all the right words, and led the prospect straight through a routine that was "guaranteed" to get the order. Neither kind of salesman would make a name for himself as a "good salesman" today!

The reason why these two early types of salesman—the "let-the-buyer-beware" type and the "method" salesman—would not set any sales records today is simply that buyers are far better educated and much more sophisticated. They do not accept so meekly whatever the salesman may memorize and play back like a broken record. Prospects are more likely to ask questions that have to do with materials, manufacturing methods, technological developments, consumer benefits, and warranties, to name just a few subjects. The day of the consumer is at hand. The customer is indeed "king" and he knows it. Few if any products these days can succeed in the marketplace solely on the strength of what the salesman says about them. Proof must be in evidence. With communications at today's levels and with competition at an all-time high, and with governmental requirements as well as warranties and guarantees that are widely published and supported, consumers now enjoy a stature never before accorded them in this country.

An interesting coincidental development should also be noted. It has always been possible in this country for those who wish to manufacture or build a product or promote a service to do so. Quite understandably it came about that once a man or a group of men produced more of an item than could readily be sold in the neighborhood, they needed sales help. This, as the nation became industrialized, led them to employ salesmen, men who were sent out to find customers to buy the products that were being produced.[5] The question of market, or need, for certain products apparently never concerned the builders or producers of those days. There were such great needs and such vast scarcities that whatever one made was presumed to be marketable. The question was not "What should be built?" but rather "Here is what we have made. Who wants to buy it?" and salesmen went out

---

[5] The career salesman, working for others, emerged with the industrial revolution. In earlier times, the salesman was self-employed. He was either a peddler who bought what he sold, or he was a producer who sold what he made himself. Selling for the producer in pre-industrial days was an incidental function.

to find buyers for whatever was produced and waiting to be sold. No wonder early salesmen took to "customer conning" as their modus operandi. This unsolicited production also resulted in waste, since it often turned out that what someone wanted to produce might not be what people wanted to buy! Nowadays, of course, before any product or service is put into production, market surveys are made to see whether there are enough people who want to buy that product to make it a desirable venture.

Market surveys or studies today provide manufacturers not only with figures as to how many or how much of a given product they can expect to sell in a given market, but also with information on what quality is desired, how much people will pay for the item, how it should be packaged in order to sell well, and other equally important projections. A sampling of consumers is questioned and a good deal of careful research is done before a product leaves the drawing board bound for the market. The consumer is asked what he will buy *before* production, not after.

The major shortcoming of the formula approach was that the prospect's point of view and reactions were not analyzed in terms of his needs. The prospect's requirements were actually overlooked or ignored; they were handled in terms of the seller's rather than the buyer's interests. The formula approach is now largely in disrepute in the more mature sales organizations and is being gradually abandoned, although it is still far from dead. Method selling is still practiced in many businesses today, particularly those that employ people who are not, for any number of reasons, fully prepared to be

professional salesmen when they begin to sell. Such "salesmen" may not want to spend the time it takes to really learn the profession of selling. Some may lack education—certainly they lack training—and, in many cases, they may not have the capacity for understanding, absorbing, and utilizing sophisticated sales training. In such cases, a formula, a canned presentation, or a memorized sales talk is virtually the only way they can perform as "salesmen." On the other hand, there are high-potential people in selling today who, unlike those just mentioned, have tremendous capacity for developing modern selling skills and techniques. They will have great futures in tomorrow's sales arena. Old-timers who see the old tried-and-true methods being discarded are dismayed and claim that salesmanship is dying. Others disagree: "The salesman isn't dead, he's different." [6]

After 1960—The Third Era

Salesmanship Today: The Customer Problem-Solving Era. Business is now in the third era of salesmanship: the customer problem-solving era. Pressures for adopting a problem-solving approach to selling came from executives in the more enlightened purchasing departments. This was well explained in 1960 by Wilber J. Pierce, then of the purchasing department of the Detroit Edison Company. He said:

> We once placed orders with salesmen for what we thought we wanted. Then we realized that such an approach was a mistake because oftentimes we weren't sure what we wanted. Our requisitions which we were trying to fill resulted not from a desire for a certain product but rather from a desire to accomplish a certain objective. We had always known that the supplier's salesman was a highly-specialized expert who knew a great deal about the work objective we wanted to solve. He not only knew his products far better than we did but he also spent most of his workday traveling from one plant to another studying various ways in which his product was used.
>
> The product which appeared on our requisition was only one out of many thousands which we ordered each year—chances are that our people really knew very little about the product they ordered. Certainly it was nothing compared to what the salesman and the organization that backed him up knew. Nowadays, in our complex world, only the supplier-specialist is up-to-date in his field. So now we have adopted a policy of not ordering goods per se but rather presenting the salesman with the problem we seek to solve. This takes a little more effort and creativeness on the part of the purchasing department, but it has rewarded us handsomely by improving many of our manufacturing and processing techniques as well as improving the appropriateness of what we buy. [7]

[6] Carl Rieser, "The Salesman Isn't Dead—He's Different." *Fortune,* November 1962, p. 124.

[7] Ferdinand F. Mauser, *Modern Marketing Management.* New York: McGraw-Hill, 1961, p. 186.

Professors Harper Boyd and Robert T. Davis have described the transition to the problem-solving approach in this fashion: "The traditional salesman was concerned primarily with moving merchandise; his successor starts with the entire spectrum of customer knowledge." The key to training the new salesman lies in the Charles Lamb quotation at the start of this chapter: "I love to lose myself in other men's minds." Or to express it in a more folksy manner we can quote a famous old marketing couplet:

> If you want to sell Jane Smith what Jane Smith buys,
> You must see Jane Smith through Jane Smith's eyes.

SALES AS A CAREER FIELD

Many students take a course in salesmanship so they can decide whether or not they should seriously consider selling as a career. This is wise procedure, for the selection of a career field is one of life's most serious decisions. A person's future life-style and ultimate happiness relate directly to the kind of lifework that is selected. It means the difference between getting up in the morning and anticipating the new day by looking forward to going to work and, in contrast, being bored with the prospect—or even worse, dreading it.

Selecting a career is like finding yourself a new suit of clothing. It is like searching for a garment with dimensions and style appropriate to your particular physical and taste specifications. It is most difficult to size up any career field objectively because there is so much involved that is of a subjective nature. On the one hand, it is hard to find people who are in a field, or who write or teach about it, who do not have strong opinions with which they are eager to indoctrinate others. This is especially true of selling because the man who sells will also try to sell the career of selling.

On the other hand, it is exceedingly difficult, if not impossible, for anyone to be objective about himself. The old adage "know thyself" is a feat not easily accomplished. Because it is so difficult for us to know ourselves, it is difficult for us to determine what kind of work will best suit us.

The author of this book is not trying to argue either for or against the selling field as a career. Great care is taken to present the pros and cons of selling without prejudice so that students intent on finding a career can make a balanced decision about it. It is important in any society that the skills of citizens be put to use where they will make a maximum social contribution. And people do those things best that they enjoy most or find the greatest satisfaction in doing.

Relating Yourself to the Sales Field

There is actual value in reviewing the history of the sales field in terms of the three periods discussed earlier: (1) the buyer-beware era, (2) the standardized method era and (3) the customer problem-solving era. Such knowledge is helpful in trying to understand the sales field. The development of selling, like most other evolutionary matters, has been complex and uneven.

Today there are companies that do their selling in the style of any one of the three eras. Thus, when looking over the field, you will find some used-car, encyclopedia, and insurance companies that sell in terms of "buyer beware." Their salesmen are usually fast-talking, shrewd, and quick to high-pressure prospects into parting with their money. They have little concern for the buyer's needs or ultimate satisfaction. At another time, you might stop at a cosmetic counter, listen to a sales presentation, and suddenly realize that it is memorized in the tradition of the standardized era of selling. Or perhaps you will have the good fortune to have a perplexing problem solved by a salesperson oriented in customer problem-solving—the third era. An example might be a sales representative of an airline who skillfully sets up a vacation plan that you could not possibly have developed on your own.

Since the sales field is just entering the problem-solving era, many sales jobs are still of the standardized method type. It would be advisable to examine the selling in each era and see which kind you identify with most readily. People differ widely. There are some who will find the razzle-dazzle, circus-pitchman type of selling of the earlier era exciting and stimulating. Others who are less bombastic and more routine minded will be more comfortable in learning tested sales methods according to practices prevalent in the standardized selling era. Then there are those who will agree with Charles Lamb and opt to lose themselves in other men's minds. They will perhaps find a rewarding future with a company that practices selling as customer problem-solving.

Many students, after considering all three approaches to selling, will decide that selling is not for them at all. This is progress, too! Knowing what you *do not* want brings you a step closer to finding what you *do* want. The elimination of one possibility reduces the number of remaining possibilities.

CHAPTER-END MATERIALS

Two Chronicles, a Field Chronicle and a Company Chronicle, appear as a feature at the end of each chapter.

The Chronicles are continuing narratives presented in serialized form. The first set of Chronicles tells about an imaginary character, John Elsworth, and his plans and activities as he enters the sales field. The story of John Elsworth continues at the end of each chapter and involves the reader as it describes Elsworth's sales-related experiences.

There are two parts to every salesman's job. One is the internal part that has to do with his relation with the company he works for. These involve working relationships within the company. They are described in what is called the Company Chronicle.

The other part of the salesman's job is external. This involves his relationships with the people he calls on. These activities are considered in the Field Chronicle. It is necessary to read the Chronicles in the order in which they appear because they often relate to one another.

By reading and discussing the Chronicles, the student will become familiar with both the internal and the external parts of the salesman's job. The accounts are realistic; the Chronicles are largely drawn from actual situations.

FIELD CHRONICLE

At the end of his sophomore year in college, John Elsworth wanted a summer job that would relate to the position he planned to take upon graduation. He had decided to become a salesman.

From the college placement director, John heard about B.C. Industries, a company that manufactured and distributed building materials. Since summer was B.C. Industries' peak sales season, they usually hired a number of college students for summer work. They preferred hiring students at the end of their sophomore year so that they could work for two summers before graduation.

The company observed student summer employees carefully. If they felt a student had promise as a full-time employee, the student was offered a job when he was ready to graduate.

John Elsworth thought this was an excellent plan. It gave students a chance to look over the company and also find out facts that might well be helpful in later full-time work.

Elsworth learned from his college placement office that Henry Meyer—a recruiter for B.C. Industries—would be coming to the campus soon. Meyer was interested in talking to students who were planning to go into sales.

John Elsworth asked for an appointment to talk to Meyer the next time he visited the campus.

Elsworth was determined to do his very best to sell himself to Meyer. He wanted very much to get a chance in sales so he could see firsthand how things worked in actual practice. He also wanted to get a line on the company so he could see if he would like a permanent job with them after graduation.

The following dialogue took place when the two men met.

ELSWORTH: Good morning, Mr. Meyer. I'm your 10:30 appointment, John Elsworth.

MEYER: How do you do? I'm Henry Meyer. Please sit down.

ELSWORTH: Thank you. Mind if I smoke?

MEYER: No—I can't say that I do.

ELSWORTH: Does that have anything to do with whether I get the job?

MEYER: (*Jokingly.*) I don't suppose it's required, if that's what you mean!

ELSWORTH: No. . . . I just thought you might be hung up on smoking, that's all.

MEYER: I wouldn't say that, exactly. I would say, to change the subject, that you have a beautiful campus here.

ELSWORTH: It's too damned crowded. Do you come in the fall to watch our football team?

MEYER: Can't say that I do. . . . But please tell me about yourself.

ELSWORTH: There really isn't too much to tell. . . . (*At this point Elsworth relates what he has done so far in life—where he went to school, subjects he liked best, his hobbies. He mentions that his career goal is to become a salesman.)*

MEYER: Very interesting. Why do you want to get into sales?

ELSWORTH: Oh, for several reasons. To me sales seems to give a man a chance to prove what he can do by himself. I like to stand on my own two feet. And besides, I understand the pay is very good. I saw some figures on what well-established salesmen earn. It looks like the sky's the limit and that's for me! What do your top salesmen earn?

MEYER: We can go into that later. Do you think of a sales job as the kind of work you'd like to continue in, or do you see it as a stepping-stone to something else?

ELSWORTH: Well. . . . I don't know. I hadn't thought that far ahead. I want to start earning a good income as soon as I can after I get out of college. After that, I guess I'd "play it by ear."

MEYER: Do you think that a man usually has a better future if he stays with one company, or do you see advantages to moving around?

ELSWORTH: *(Showing a little anger at being asked this question.)* As I said, when the time comes, I'll play it by ear.

MEYER: Why do you think you'd want to work for B.C. Industries?

ELSWORTH: I'm not sure I want to. Beyond the next two summers, that is. Until I graduate. After that I'll be able to tell you why I do, or why I don't want to work for your company. By the way, exactly what line of business is your company in?

MEYER: We're in building supplies. Once we decide about the possibilities for your summer employment, we can get into the details. . . . Well, since they've scheduled these interviews just fifteen minutes apart, we'll hardly have time for a longer discussion. I do want to thank you for coming in to talk to me. B.C. Industries appreciates your interest. You'll hear from us in a few days.

ELSWORTH: Thank you, Mr. Meyer. I would like to have a chance to prove myself. I guarantee you that I'll do well at anything you offer me this summer.

STOP & THINK

1. Review, either by yourself or with others, the dialogue step by step. Evaluate what Elsworth said and did at each point. What do you feel was right or wrong about his actions and his conversation? Why?

2. What better answers do you think Elsworth could have given to Meyer's questions? What might each of your answers have accomplished that Elsworth's did not?

3. List the main points that you believe Elsworth should have accomplished in the interview. Check those you think he did achieve.

COMPANY CHRONICLE

John Elsworth was hired for the summer by B.C. Industries. A few days after the interview, he was happy to receive a letter from Henry Meyer, saying that B.C. Industries would like to have him start work the first Monday of summer vacation. The letter also said that if Elsworth had any questions, Meyer would be glad to discuss them with him.

Elsworth was a little puzzled at being asked to report for work at the employment office of a B.C. Industries warehouse, rather than at the company's main office where the sales department was located. Nevertheless, he groomed himself carefully and dressed in a business suit, white shirt, and tie in order to make the kind of impression he thought was called for.

When he reported for work, he spent an hour filling in various personnel forms in a very small, dusty office located next to a large, noisy shipping dock. When he completed the forms, he was taken to the central stockroom where he was introduced to the head shipping clerk, Tex Bailey. Bailey immediately put him to work counting and restacking cases of merchandise. Within minutes, Elsworth's clothes were soiled, and before long his ungloved hands were blistered from handling rough boxes. Elsworth was bitterly disappointed.

The following day he came dressed in appropriate work clothes. For three weeks he did hard manual labor—taking inventories and shifting around stocks of merchandise. Occasionally he was given a special order to fill that required assembling bulky building supplies from warehouse stocks and, by hand truck, placing them on the shipping dock.

Elsworth was demoralized by this work. He decided to talk to Bailey, his immediate supervisor, about the situation. He told Bailey that he was a college student and that his summer job was supposed to be concerned with learning about B.C. Industries and sales work. Bailey shrugged his shoulders and said his being a college student meant nothing to him. As far as Bailey was concerned, Elsworth was just another flunky. Furthermore, if he felt he was too good to work in the stockroom, he could always quit.

Elsworth realized that talking to Bailey was hopeless. He decided to talk to the warehouse manager, Mr. Wenzel—Bailey's boss.

Wenzel listened to Elsworth more attentively than Bailey had. However, to Elsworth, he seemed no more sympathetic.

Wenzel told Elsworth to open his eyes and to think about the purpose of everything that was going on in the warehouse. He said that warehousing, inventory control, stock maintenance, order filling, and shipping were very much related to sales. He said that stocks of merchandise were the heart of the business and that Elsworth should be glad he was getting an opportunity to learn by being in the midst of these activities.

Elsworth answered Wenzel by saying that selling, in his opinion, consisted of meeting the public and here he was spending the whole summer in a dirty warehouse, completely out of touch with customers and customer problems. Furthermore, Elsworth said that he felt B.C. Industries had mis-represented matters when they told him that he would be doing work that would provide him with training valuable to a salesman.

STOP & THINK

1. Was Elsworth right in being upset about his summer job? Explain.
2. How should Elsworth view this whole experience?
3. What do you think about Elsworth's talks with Bailey and Wenzel? What would you suggest that Elsworth should have done?

DISCUSSION

This discussion section, which appears at the end of each chapter, features realistic problems for classroom discussion. The problems relate, both directly and indirectly, to the subject matter in the body of the chapter.

Each problem should stimulate you to do some independent thinking and to encourage an exchange of ideas between you and other students, as well as between you and your instructor. Each situation brings a typical problem, or controversial area, into sharp focus.

Stigmas About Selling as a Career. David Allen, a sophomore at Fair Hill College, had just finished his third week of a class in salesmanship. In a nearby coffee shop, he started talking to a group of fellow students about the course.

One of his friends asked him why he was taking the course. David answered that he was trying to decide what he would like to do when he finished college. He said he was taking the course in salesmanship because he thought he might like to become a salesman. He said he was encouraged because he found the course interesting and because the sales field seemed to excite and stimulate him.

David was surprised by his friends' reactions to his remarks. There seemed to be many different feelings about a salesman's job. On each point brought up in the conversation, there were both negative and positive views.

Jim Turner said, "What? Get into that dog-eat-dog end of business? You have to have a hide as tough as a rhinoceros's to succeed in selling."

Jim's brother said, "Yes, but Dave will never be bored because he'll be dealing with the public. No two customers are the same. Selling is a continual challenge."

Sally Miller said, "I wouldn't want to be married to a salesman. They run around and live it up too much. I want my husband home nights."

Sue Anders responded to that by saying, "The social life of a salesman often includes his wife. It would be interesting to be married to a man who is involved in interesting situations."

Vera Raney said thoughtfully, "The pace of selling is really rough. I don't want to be married to a man who wears himself out before his time."

June Weisman answered, "That can happen in any field. It's up to each partner in a marriage to see that the other takes care of himself. What wears a person out is being unhappy with his job. Hard work never killed anyone. Besides, a salesman has a lot of time to relax. He sits around offices a lot waiting to see people. During the week, I'll bet half the people on the golf course are salesmen!"

Harvey Brown said, "People don't respect salesmen." Ron White replied to this, "In any field, people respect the man, not the job. The important thing is to do a good job in whatever field you are in. People respect the winners in every field."

STOP & THINK

1. For each negative statement above, there is a positive reply. What is your stand on each set of comments?
2. What could you tell David Allen to help him understand the many seeming contradictions in his friends' comments?

The Future in Selling Compared With the Future in Other Fields. Hugh Griffin was about to graduate with a degree in business administration. He had taken courses in accounting and marketing. He was interviewed by several medium-sized companies.

One company offered him a job as a trainee in their credit department because he had taken several courses in accounting. Another company, of similar size and stature, noting that Griffin had taken some courses in marketing and sales, offered him a job as a sales trainee. It happened that the starting salary was the same for each job.

STOP & THINK

1. Which job should Griffin take? Why?
2. Which is more important when deciding which job to take: Griffin's aptitudes and interests, or the particular job and company in each case? Or would you consider other factors more important?

Social Contributions. Willis Johnson had made up his mind to become a salesman. His father, whom Willis respected and admired, was a salesman. Willis knew a great deal about his father's work, and since Mr. Johnson was happy with what he was doing, Willis thought he could be happy in sales, too.

Willis told his girl friend, who was going to be a teacher and whose father worked in a hospital, about his decision to try to get into sales. Willis was surprised when his girl friend expressed doubts about the wisdom of his choice of a career. Willis was totally unprepared for the objections she raised and was surprised by some of the thoughts she expressed.

She said she admired her father because, in his job, he was doing something more than just earning a living. She also pointed out that she was going into teaching because she liked to help children. She said that she felt that a salesman might make a comfortable living but that there was little that a salesman could contribute to others and to society in general.

STOP & THINK

1. Is Willis Johnson's girl friend justified in thinking about the social contribution of a man's job?
2. What might Willis say to help his girl friend better understand his decision?

CHAPTER REVIEW AND DISCUSSION QUESTIONS

1. Specifically, what are the personal advantages that are gained from the study of salesmanship even if you never intend to enter the sales field?
2. Is the salesman born or made? What about the "latent talent" theory, which maintains that everyone can become a salesman? Why do you agree or disagree with the theory?
3. "The salesman is the humanizing element in today's mass-production society." Does this mean that the importance of the salesman will grow or diminish in the future? Explain.
4. How would you define salesmanship?
5. Is the salesman a professional in the same sense that a lawyer, doctor, or teacher is? Explain. What should be done to professionalize salesmen more?
6. Is the reputation of present-day salesmen colored by the history of salesmanship, or is their reputation a reflection of what salesmen are today?
7. What is meant by the statement "every salesman leads a double life?" What are the two sides to his work?
8. Does the coming of the customer problem-solving era mean that the salesman will become more or less professional? Explain.
9. "Know thyself" is a well-known adage. What in particular should you know about yourself to determine whether you could succeed as a salesman?
10. What are the three eras of selling and what are the advantages and disadvantages of being the kind of salesman demanded by each era?

2

PERSONALIZED GROWTH
AND SELF-MANAGEMENT

Fools say they learn by experience.
I prefer to profit by others' experience.
—BISMARCK

YOUR UNIQUE DREAM

There Is Only One You

Every person who reads this book is a distinct individual. Just as your fingerprints distinguish you from other people, so do the facets of your physical, mental, and emotional makeup set you apart. You are unique.

As an individual, there are certain objectives or goals that are particularly attractive to you. There are accomplishments to which you aspire, things that you want to be able to do, skills you want to acquire, impressions you want to create, abilities you want to develop, desires you want to fulfill.

Your Future

Everyone—in his youth and even as he grows older—has "dreams" for the future. Most young people have enough imagination to sit back and almost see themselves in various roles—performing fantastic feats, achieving fabulous results, doing great deeds that make the rest of the world acknowledge and admire them. The good salesman probably never loses this inclination to dream. He always feels, no matter how much he has achieved, that he is going on to do bigger and better things tomorrow.

It is natural and normal for a young person to be preoccupied with fantasies about the future during the first decade or two of his life. And the nice part of it is that these dreams can very often come true—*if* the person stops dreaming soon enough and starts doing those things that can provide him with the skills, knowledge, and abilities necessary for doing what he dreams of doing.

PLANNING FOR THE FUTURE

Self-Management Is the Ingredient That Turns Dreams into Reality

Dreams are what good fortune is built on, for without dreams, which are in essence imaginary possibilities, there can be no goals. The difference between an idle dreamer and a successful planner is self-management. Hard work is often mentioned as being the most important ingredient for success. We, however, place self-management before hard work because work alone does not lead to success. The unsuccessful salesman may work every bit as hard as the successful salesman. The difference is that the successful salesman plans and directs his work effort with skill. As a perceptive observer has said most colorfully, "There is a difference between hard work and smart work." It is efficient self-management that makes smart work possible. Thus a successful salesman must be a manager of himself. If he is not first successful in managing himself in his everyday life (a smaller universe), he cannot expect to sell successfully for an employer in the business world (a larger universe).

The Fine Art of Setting Personal Goals

You must have goals on which to base your personal program for making your dreams come true. One of the best ways to make sure that you are able to achieve what you most want to achieve is to set up goals, or objectives, and a route by which you can reach these goals.

There are many different paths along which one can proceed. While each path may lead by a different route to the same objective, the route you choose should be fashioned to suit you, to fit in with the kind of person you are. There is great value in studying the routes others have followed in attaining success. You can get ideas from others and learn from their success and failures. That is why there always is value in reading or hearing about how others have attained success. However, you should consider examples from other people only as possibilities that may or may not work for your particular personality. You are an individual and the route you choose should be right and reasonable for you.

There is no one model that anyone who wants to become a salesman can pattern himself after. The salesman who tries to become something that does not suit his personality ends up being an artificial person, a "phony." This kind of person, unfortunately, exists all too often in the sales field. The development of the effective salesman means building on the traits that the individual already possesses. To put it another way—to thine own self be true.

The Myth That the Wise and Aging Salesman Is the Top Producer

There is a persistent although possibly a dying myth, that the middle-aged (and older), mature, and seasoned salesman is the most successful.

Studies made that correlate the earnings of salesmen with age do not bear this out.

A 1972 survey made by the New York Stock Exchange on security salesmen shows that they peak in production between the ages of thirty-one and thirty-five after only nine years of experience.[1] The study covered 50,950 retail-level representatives registered to sell securities by the Stock Exchange.

Median income earned for the firms they worked for was $35,200 for twenty-two- to twenty-six-year-old salesmen. For twenty-seven- to thirty-year-old salesmen, it reached $44,600. The high of $71,000 was attained by the thirty-one- to thirty-five-year-old group. Beyond the age of thirty-five, there was a marked falling off. From age thirty-six to thirty-nine, median income was $52,100; from forty to forty-nine, it fell to $51,600; and for the fifty-year-old and over, it dropped to $39,200. Methods for paying commissions varied, depending on the firm. Salesmen grossing $50,000 for their firm would probably be paid around $15,000 for selling about $5 million in securities.

It was not possible to determine why younger salesmen were more productive; however, conjecture has it that as men get older they tend to coast because they are less ambitious and more content. Other theories are that the more capable ones get promoted into management positions, or that they have made investments that help support them and enable them to retire from selling and go into less strenuous work. It is certainly true that many top executives have risen to their positions via the sales route. There is much evidence that the very nature of the sales job contributes to personal growth. Growing in the sales field is, therefore, mainly a matter of developing natural ability.

SIZING YOURSELF UP

The first step in planning a business campaign of any kind is determining what materials are available. What are the assets and liabilities of the situation? The same applies to your self-management program. What are your strengths and weaknesses? Can you accurately estimate your capacities? Do you know what your strong points are, or can become? Is this potential strength a merchandisable item? Actually, you must think of yourself as a product that you are putting on the job market. As in any market, you will compete with all the others who have prepared themselves for the same kind of work you are looking for. Thus you must ask yourself—and be prepared to answer—these questions: Why should anyone be interested in paying me for this product? What can I do? What is it that I have to offer that makes me a more desirable product than others?

Self-Assessment Is Difficult

What makes self-assessment difficult is that it is so hard to be objective about yourself. You are apt to overlook your weaknesses and failings or at

---

[1] *Detroit Free Press*, June 10, 1972.

least find excuses for them. It is quite natural to spend time trying to explain why you do not or cannot do what is expected of you. The perpetual alibi may become a way of life for people who have had parents, doting aunts or uncles, or older brothers and sisters who "overindulged" them. When others do your part for you, you miss a chance to learn, to develop your own special abilities and capacities. You start thinking you cannot or are not required to do things that you really are quite capable of doing, if you try—and try hard enough.

Another reason why many people do not know themselves very well is that their experiences are somewhat limited. For example, do you know how you would act in an emergency? Will you be able to think and act fast and in the most sensible manner? Probably not, unless you have actually been involved in emergencies that called upon you to think and act with great resourcefulness—and even perhaps with great courage.

Let us agree, at this point, that you cannot sit down by yourself and think about your strengths and weaknesses and come up with all the answers. That is impossible. What you can do, however, is to start to get better acquainted with yourself. From now on, learn to observe yourself from day to day. See how you react to the environment in which you live. Notice how wise, or unwise, you are about what you do. Is your judgment sound? Do you behave in a sensible manner? How well and how carefully do you do those things that you set about doing each day? Do you finish what you start? Or do you put off the tough jobs until tomorrow? Find out what kind of a person you really are. Some starting suggestions follow.

Observe Yourself

Do you keep your promises? Do you promise more than you know you are able to deliver? Do you forget your promises? Are you a person who can, or who cannot, be depended upon? Are you lazy, or do you work without having someone else keep after you all the time? Do you hear yourself making excuses for yourself? Do you blame your own failures on others? Are you pleasant to have around? Would you like to have someone around who behaves as you do?

Check up on your own behavior under different circumstances. See how you act and what you do under various conditions. Pretty soon you will know better what kind of a person you really are. You will know your weaknesses and be able to work on them. You will know where you are strong and begin to have confidence in these areas.

Sales Applications of Observing Others

Like most other skills, skill in observing is something you can acquire. And like most abilities, observation improves with practice. A good salesman must certainly be observant of people, not so much how they behave in groups, but rather how they act and respond as individuals. He must learn to get people to talk about themselves—encourage them to reveal details of their background, expand about their family life, explain their hobbies and other interests, talk about their likes and dislikes, and so on. It is not enough for a salesman to be merely *interested* in people as individuals; it is equally important that he *remember* what he learns and observes about them.

Few of us can recall everything of importance about people with whom we come in contact. Therefore, most salespeople keep personal notes or running diaries about the people and accounts they call on. After each call, they jot down details about the visit. Highlights of the business part of the conversation are recorded, and relevant details that the buyer revealed are noted for future reference. Typical notes might run as follows: "He plans to go to Key West on his vacation during the last two weeks in August with his three-year-old daughter and wife, Janet"; "He is registered as an independent but admires the mayor's transportation policies"; "His son, Arnold, who spent two years in the Peace Corps in Haiti, is coming home for six weeks in November"; "He has no interest in baseball but occasionally goes to the harness races"; "He had a sample of a competitor's new model X100 on his desk"; "His boss, whose name is Pete Hanel, has a degree in mechanical engineering from MIT and used to work for General Electric"; "He indicated that his company was bidding to equip a new plant the Hercules Company is building in Augusta, Georgia"; and so on.

Before making a call back, the salesman reviews the notes or running diary on the particular account. He is thus able to make the call with confidence because facts about the person he is calling on and details about the account are fresh in his mind. The customer is impressed because the salesman is able to swing into the sales call with ease and authority. He knows about the customer's background and does not waste time going over things that have been covered before. Personal relationships are strengthened because the salesman is able to make references to details he remembers from the past. For example, when he calls on the buyer mentioned above he is able to ask about such matters as how the buyer and his wife, Janet, enjoyed their vacation in Key West; whether the buyer's company got the contract to equip the plant in Augusta, Georgia; and whether Mr. Hanel, the buyer's boss, is going to the mechanical engineers' conference in Chicago—and if so, the salesman can mention that his company is going to have an industrial exhibit there that the buyer's boss should visit.

PERSONAL-INVOLVEMENT EXERCISE NO. 2–1

Start keeping a diary on two or more people with whom you will be having conversations regularly during the weeks while you are taking this course in salesmanship. Select both a male and a female. Of course, do not let the people know that you are keeping a diary about them. After each meeting, jot down highlights. Also, be sure to probe each individual about personal details—what they plan to do over the weekend; how their family is getting along; what's happening with their work, hobbies, school, and so on. Review the notes you are keeping before each new meeting. Use what you know about the person in your conversations. Study how they react when you use information they would not expect you to remember. You will find there are considerable differences between how men and how women react to information about themselves. You will learn a great deal from this experience for it will show you how valuable it is to be observant and also how to put your observations to use. You will be practicing how to bring people into focus as individuals!

THE COMPONENTS OF PERSONAL GROWTH

Growth Is a Dynamic Process

There are few things in life that are absolutely certain. An old witticism has it that only two things in life are certain: death and taxes. But this is far from the whole story. Growth is also a certainty for living things. People are born and they grow. Some people grow more than others. Some grow for a longer time than others. Some grow in desirable ways. Some grow in undesirable ways. But everyone grows—in one way or another. And each person has a great deal to do with how much, how well, and in what direction he grows.

It is true that not all people are born with the same capacities for growth, and that not everyone has the same opportunities for personal growth. But one's capacity, or lack of capacity, for personal growth is not the critical component. The important ingredients are one's own personal desire and determination to grow. If a person has the profound desire and determination to develop to the fullest extent whatever capacities he has, or can acquire, then he has the makings of a successful person. He can be a person of maximum achievement and self-fulfillment. This in itself is reason enough for making the total effort.

No person is a failure who makes of himself the most fully rounded and productive person he can possibly be. Such a person grows into a mature, constructive, positive force who has a good chance of living successfully in whatever circumstances he finds himself.

GROWTH ATTITUDES THAT ARE WORTH DEVELOPING

Like Yourself

As you get to know yourself, it is important that you discover aspects of your character that you like—features you can be glad about. This suggestion may seem strange at first. But think of it this way: If you, who know yourself more intimately than anyone else can possibly know you, cannot find something about yourself to really *like*, then how can you possibly expect others to like you?

Actually, there are always some things that are likable about every person in the world. Find out what likable characteristics you have and like yourself—appreciate yourself—for those reasons. You will grow by developing more of the things you and others find desirable. Certainly you will discover some things about yourself that even you cannot like. These are the things you need to work on, to correct, to root out of your personality. The fact is that as you work on this self-improvement—or growth—plan, you will find yourself liking yourself better. As this happens, you will find that others like you better, too. It is an easy way to make personalized growth a rewarding activity.

Know Others

Get to know other people. Study them. Observe them. See how they behave; what they say and do; how they say and do it. Watch them react when a situation is pleasant. See how they act when conditions are unpleasant or difficult.

How well are you able to get along with others? You may think you get along with other people very well, but look more closely at yourself in your relationships with others. Are you really getting along well or are others merely tolerating you? Do people have to adjust to you and your ways? Or do you see to it that you adjust to them and accommodate yourself, at least in many instances, to their wants and needs?

One way to judge how well or how poorly you get along with others is to think about the number of people you know who think of you as a desirable and worthwhile friend. Before you respond to this, give it some further thought.

You may think of any number of people as good friends of yours, but do *they* regard themselves as good friends of yours? Think about this. It will give you some important clues not only about yourself but also about others. Keeping the above well in mind, add a third and most necessary objective to your list of factors that lead to personal growth.

Develop Desirable Relationships

Develop desirable relationships between yourself and others. This is one of the most important areas of growth for a person who wishes to achieve his personal goals and objectives in life. Certainly it is the key to salesmanship.

The person who "makes a million" but finds himself without a single person with whom he can share his good fortune is really a miserable failure. He cannot be really happy. Unless you can develop desirable relationships with others, there is very little point in undertaking a program of personal growth. It cannot be done. You may get to know yourself. You may observe others and get to understand why they do what they do. But if you do not learn to develop desirable relationships with others, the rest is apt to mean very little to you or to them.

How can you learn to develop desirable relationships with others? Here again, there are many ways, but virtually all of them involve conversation.

CONVERSATION

Conversation is a major tool in the salesman's kit of personal resources. In order to understand what the tool of conversation does, we must realize that people converse for three reasons: information, entertainment, and fulfillment of emotional needs. The good salesman understands these three levels of conversation and he functions on each level. He probably converses most frequently on the information level because that is his prime responsibility —to pass along information about products and services; to provide news about recent developments; to explain new techniques and policies. He knows, however, that his success as a salesman is also tied to the other two levels of conversation, and therefore he spends time entertaining those he deals with by telling stories and passing along interesting anecdotes. He knows further that he is not "the compleat conversationalist" unless he also provides for emotional needs. So he is sympathetic when he is told about misfortune; he gives praise where it is merited; and he will on occasion massage a sagging ego when he sees someone's morale is low.

PERSONAL-INVOLVEMENT EXERCISE NO. 2–2

How can you tell whether you are a good conversationalist? Find out by testing yourself on the following questions.

	Yes	*No*
1. Are you inclined to interrupt others before they have finished speaking?	——	——
2. Do you use poor grammar?	——	——
3. Do you tend to use big words when simple ones would be clearer and sound more natural?	——	——
4. Do you have a tendency to monopolize conversations?	——	——
5. Do you speak too rapidly?	——	——
6. When someone else is talking, are you thinking about what you will say next, or do you really listen to what the other person is saying?	——	——
7. Do you ramble instead of coming to the point?	——	——
8. Do you talk too much about yourself?	——	——
9. Do you use trite phrases such as "see what I mean?" "you said it," or "man, that's cool"?	——	——
10. Do you use "ers," "ahs," and "you knows," and mumble?	——	——
11. Are you inclined to "talk to" rather than "talk with" people?	——	——
12. Do you avoid looking directly at the person with whom you are speaking?	——	——
13. Are you inclined to be a "know-it-all" in your conversation?	——	——
14. Are you inclined to talk only about what you are interested in?	——	——

The more "no" answers you have to the above questions, the better conversationalist you are. After you have tested yourself on these questions, cover up your answers with a clean sheet of paper and ask others who know you to rate you as candidly as possible on the same test. Comparing your results with those given to you by others may give you some helpful insights as to your weaknesses and the kind of conversational impressions you make on others.

Another way for you to size yourself up as a conversationalist is to get a tape recorder and actually record some of your conversations. This will enable you to study the way you converse. You can then make improvements in your speaking tempo and in the way you use your voice, phrase your sentences, and so on. Listening carefully to recordings of your conversations will be invaluable because there is no other way in which you can hear yourself as others hear you. The way you think you converse and the way you actually do are quite different, as the recording experience will demonstrate to you.

Conversation Versus Talking

The ability to converse effectively is a priceless skill. Many people regard talking as conversing. But there is a difference between talking and saying something. While one is often able to communicate with others by means of the spoken word, much more real communication takes place when one knows not only how to talk, but even more important, knows how to listen. As a matter of fact, one can often communicate more completely with another person if he does not rely entirely on words. A look, a gesture, or some other form of behavior may, on many occasions, improve communications more than additional words.

A little later we will be discussing some specific elements of communication. For now, in order to improve your communications with others and develop desirable relationships with others, start to observe, very carefully, your own relationships as well as those of others. Notice how others communicate. Listen to the words they use and the results they get. See how they behave under different circumstances. You will be amazed at what you can learn about the relationships that exist among the people you meet.

Once you know yourself, know others, and learn how to develop desirable relationships with others, you are well on your way to a kind of personal growth that can help you achieve your most cherished dreams. You can set reasonable goals for yourself and drive toward them with the best possible chance of success. You will be able to communicate with others in ways that will help you accomplish your objectives.

Communication is a form of selling in which every human being engages throughout his lifetime. Whether or not you ever intend to "sell"—as a professional salesperson—makes little difference. The main thing is that you must be able to sell your ideas, or products, or services, and, most of all, yourself, if you are ever to be a fully successful, self-realizing individual. This is the goal of every human being.

Practicing Conversation

In its most basic ABC sense, what is salesmanship? Essentially it is this:

> **A**   A human being, called a salesman,
>
> **B**   *Contacts other human beings,* called prospects or customers,
>
> **C**   In order to sell them something.

The crucial factor in the above equation is in italics. Clearly the start of all selling requires one human being to make contact with another. Thus it behooves all students of salesmanship to learn the difficult and elusive art of gracefully establishing contact with other human beings.

It is very difficult for most of us to start conversations with strangers. And yet what a wonderful attribute it is to be able to start conversations, for if it is done well—with ease and grace—it brightens both your life and that of the person to whom you have spoken. The ability to strike up conversations with strangers is a readily available remedy for loneliness and a means of broadening your life experience.

The only way to acquire skill in contacting strangers is to practice meeting people. Unfortunately most people seldom try their hand at opening

conversations. They wrongly assume that strangers will not want to talk to them or that strangers will not be interesting to talk to. Yet it is reasonably safe to assume that any stranger will want to talk to someone who is interesting and pleasant, and also that many strangers will add interest to one's own life. Fortunately, it is very easy to practice opening conversations with strangers. You can start talking to someone who rides with you in an elevator, delivers your paper, sits next to you in class, shares a table with you at a coffee shop, and so on. A serious student of salesmanship will not wait until he is hired as a sales trainee to get experience in taking the initiative in opening and carrying on conversations. It is very interesting and educational to try different conversational openings and to observe and analyze how people react to them. The most common opening, of course, is to talk about the weather. It is widely used because it takes little thought and it is so familiar. It is effective even if it is unimaginative because you can talk about something you share with the stranger you have met. The weather as a conversational opener has its limitations, of course, because it is so trite and certainly it does not give the stranger the impression that he is talking to someone worth cultivating. The best conversational openers are those that will both interest the stranger and cause him to conclude that the person who is talking to him is worth getting to know.

Following are samples of conversational openers that are improvements over talking about the weather!

A student to a girl sitting next to him on the first day of class:
"Excuse me. Do you know anything about this prof?"

A young woman talking to an elderly gentleman sitting next to her on an airliner:
"This is my first experience with this airline. How do you like it?"

One customer standing next to another in line to buy tickets:
"How far did you come to stand in this line?"

One patient addressing another patient waiting in a dentist's office:
"What would you rather be doing than sitting here waiting to see the dentist?"

PERSONAL-INVOLVEMENT
EXERCISE NO. 2–3

During the next week, open conversations with seven (that's only one each day!) or more people you do not know. Try different approaches and analyze why each did or did not work. Jot down notes about what you did and what you concluded in your analysis. At the end of your experiments answer the following questions.

1. What have you learned about opening conversations?
2. What can you do to become better at it?
3. Why should you not be discouraged if your attempt is unsuccessful?
4. What factors other than what you say relate to whether you succeed?

FIELD CHRONICLE

Elsworth completed his second summer of work for B.C. Industries and was finishing up his senior year in college. The first summer had been spent working in the B.C. Industries warehouse, as described in the Field Chronicle in Chapter 1. During the second summer Elsworth was assigned to work in the main-office credit department. He was confined to a desk next to the assistant credit manager whom he helped with the increased volume of work generated by peak summer business. Because of increased construction in the summer, the size of orders was larger than usual and the demands for credit by customers expanded accordingly. This meant that the credit department had to watch its accounts more closely because there was a tendency for some customers to overextend themselves financially. Elsworth found his work in the credit department interesting, but he also found it too confining, because he liked to be more active and more involved with people rather than with paper work.

In early February of his last year in college, Elsworth received a telephone call from Henry Meyer, the B.C. Industries campus recruiter. Meyer said he would like to set up a luncheon appointment so Elsworth could meet J. C. Spangler, the main-office assistant sales manager. Elsworth agreed to meet Meyer and Spangler at a downtown hotel restaurant. When he arrived on time he found the two B.C. Industries executives seated at a table they had reserved in a quiet corner of the restaurant. He was surprised and flattered that everything had been so carefully arranged.

After Meyer introduced Elsworth to Spangler and a few pleasantries were exchanged, it was clear that Spangler was definitely in charge. The conversation ran as follows.

SPANGLER: We are aware that you will be graduating in June. Now that you've worked for B.C. Industries for the past two summers, we wonder how you feel about the company.

ELSWORTH: I guess the company is OK. It's pretty hard to judge from just working in a warehouse and the credit department.

SPANGLER: I'm always puzzled when college students feel the work that beginners are assigned to is unimportant. Merchandise—the handling and stocking of what the company makes and sells— and credit are basic to any business.

ELSWORTH: I suppose maybe they are. But I didn't make a single decision or use my head very much in either job.

SPANGLER: You should have been using your head to figure out what each department you worked in was all about. Decision-making should be based on realistic knowledge. We assigned you so you could see for yourself how departments that back up the sales department operate. Later on, when you're out in the field, you'll be better able to understand their problems because you know about them firsthand.

ELSWORTH: Maybe I didn't fully appreciate what you were trying to do for me. Somehow the experiences of those two summers made business seem rather dull.

MEYER: Learning the ABCs in any field is bound to seem dull. But there is no escaping it if you're going to build your career on solid ground.

SPANGLER: That's true, Henry. I'm sure that Elsworth will see the value of his summer job experience later on. But now, Elsworth, let's get down to business. Are you interested in a job as a sales trainee with B.C. Industries?

ELSWORTH: Well, let me put it this way. I see no reason why I *shouldn't* be interested in a trainee job with your company. Although up to this point I also don't see why I *should* be interested in a job either.

SPANGLER: That's a good answer, Elsworth! You're asking me, as assistant sales manager, to tell you why you should buy B.C. Industries as a place to work. Frankly, I was disappointed that you didn't see the value of working for us for two summers. However, now that you've asked me to sell you on selling for our company, I can see that you like to get the facts and that you have spirit, two qualities that can help a salesman go a long way. I'd like you to visit me in my office. I want you to give me half a day there to sell you on sales as a career field and on B.C. Industries as a good company to work for.

ELSWORTH: Fair enough. That will be a day I'll be looking forward to.

STOP & THINK

1. How does the way in which B.C. Industries has handled Elsworth so far impress you? Evaluate the company and its personnel based upon the Elsworth experience to date.

2. On a step-by-step basis, review the conversation with Spangler and evaluate how Elsworth handled himself. Is it best to be perfectly frank in your answers when being interviewed for a sales job? Or will the man who is interviewing you think that as a salesman you might alienate customers?

3. Rephrase Spangler's comments and questions to reflect other topics he might have brought up to decide whether Elsworth is a good prospect as a sales trainee.

COMPANY CHRONICLE

When Elsworth graduated from college he decided to take the sales trainee job B.C. Industries offered him. He had enjoyed the half-day he spent with Mr. Spangler in his office. Spangler made the sales field come to life in a challenging way by allowing Elsworth to spend two days working with Harry Katzman, one of B.C. Industries top salesmen, who sold their building supply line to contractors and architects. At the end of the second day with Katzman, the two men had a long talk over coffee. Elsworth had grown to admire Katzman; he was glad to be able to talk freely with this experienced salesman. He decided to sound Katzman out on a wide range of subjects.

ELSWORTH: I've really been impressed watching you work these last two days.

KATZMAN: Really? What was it that impressed you?

ELSWORTH: Well, it was that I had such a wrong impression of what a salesman does. You didn't really do any selling the way I thought it would be done. You didn't put any pressure on anyone to buy. And I thought your customers didn't think of you as a salesman. You were more like an old friend and adviser. In fact, once you advised a customer to order less because you thought a new model was coming out, and another time you suggested that a different product would suit the customer better than your own product would!

KATZMAN: The customers in both cases would have found out the things I told them and then they would feel that I'd let them down. A salesman-customer relationship is a long-range relationship. Any time a salesman takes an order that earns him a quick commission now but puts his future relationship with his customer in jeopardy, he's hurting both himself and his company.

ELSWORTH: Mr. Spangler said I could start as a trainee on straight salary, or get paid like the regular salesmen—salary plus commission. The regular salesmen's base salary is less than the straight salary I would be getting, but overall they earn more than half their pay in commissions, which means their total earnings are considerably higher than what I'd get on straight salary.

KATZMAN: I'd plunge right in, if I were you. If you jump right in, you'll learn to swim quicker. Taking a straight salary for the first six months means that you'd be making it easy for yourself. Why pamper yourself? I think you should challenge yourself to make more than what your straight salary would be for those first six months.

ELSWORTH: You say that because you've got confidence in yourself which I don't have. It's easy for someone with a few years' experience to talk that way.

KATZMAN: Confidence comes from experiencing hard knocks and in overcoming them. You'd be putting off the building of confidence in yourself.

ELSWORTH: Well, I'll think about it. By the way, how come you've remained a salesman when I know you've had several chances to go into management level positions?

KATZMAN: Managers have to work through others. I'm too impatient for that. I like to do things myself. And also I like to see a payoff go directly into my own pocket for my own effort. When things go wrong or right in my territory I have myself alone to blame or to congratulate.

ELSWORTH: I can see your point, but isn't there more prestige in being a manager instead of a salesman?

KATZMAN: Prestige comes from doing what you like to do best.

ELSWORTH: I'm not sure I understand that. By the way, are there any women selling building supplies? Seems to me that the decisions to buy houses that your customers build and design are made chiefly by women. Wouldn't that mean that having saleswomen would be a good idea?

KATZMAN: Up to now, women haven't shown any interest in selling to the building trade.

STOP & THINK

1. Which remuneration plan would you select if you were Elsworth? What about Katzman's advice on not making it easy for yourself?
2. How is self-confidence acquired? Does a top salesman make a good manager of others? Discuss.
3. Review and react to the ideas that Katzman expressed in response to Elsworth's questioning.

PROBLEMS

How Should Minority Group Salesmen Be Used? Jack Allen, a black student, had the following discussion with his girl friend, Lucille Smith.

"The Marketing Club just had a guest speaker from the XX Corporation. He said that his company hired a lot of black salesmen, but that they used them mainly to sell to black customers. He was pretty frank and said that he felt it was best that whites sell to whites and blacks sell to blacks because each could best communicate with his own kind."

Lucille responded by saying, "I suppose that makes sense. Selling is a service that depends on knowing what the other person feels and thinks."

Her boyfriend had reservations and expressed them in this manner. "If someone is a good salesman, it depends on him as a person and not on whether he is black or white. When I spend my hard-earned money, I want to deal with someone who understands the product he is selling and who can advise me on how to satisfy my needs. That has nothing to do with color. I think a company should look at it in the same way, and place people on the basis of their ability alone."

STOP & THINK

1. Whose point of view do you support, Jack Allen's or Lucille Smith's? Explain your position.
2. Discuss the problems that must be faced by a minority-group salesman. How can they best be resolved?

What About Being Transferred to Different Parts of the Country? Chuck Harris was interested in going into sales so he decided to talk to his friend Jeffrey Anderson, whose father was a sales manager for a medium-sized company. He led into the discussion with the question, "What chances are there for advancement and promotion starting out as a salesman?"

Jeffrey replied, "They're darned good, but you've got to make up your mind beforehand to do whatever the company suggests. They like to rotate the men they are interested in promoting in order to give them wide experience. My dad was transferred to a different part of the country at least once every five years. He felt he always had to take the new job that was offered him because once you say No, they lose interest in you and you're stuck."

Chuck asked further, "If you decide to stay in selling, aren't you less apt to be transferred?"

Jeffrey had this to say, "I think a company likes you to do what they want no matter what your job is. Salesmen get transferred too. If you don't like to be uprooted you should pick a local and not a national company."

STOP & THINK

1. How does being transferred to different parts of the country relate to a person's future?
2. Do salesmen get transferred as much as those higher up on the executive ladder?

Nervous Tensions and Selling. Jerry Correlli was telling his mother that he was thinking of going into selling as a career. His mother, as mothers will, expressed concerns that sales work was too strenuous. She based her feelings on what she had heard from relatives of salesmen. She mentioned that there was a lot of pressure in the selling field. It was a life of worry—worry over whether a sales quota would be met, whether a certain large order would be placed, whether an important customer would switch his business to a competitor—worry that business would slack off because of an economic recession, and so on. There was the strain of constant travel, the family instability caused by being away from home so much, and the danger of developing bad habits from living off an expense account so much. Jerry was rather stunned by all the negative things that his mother mentioned.

STOP & THINK

1. Are the nervous tensions and stress of selling excessive? Explain the basis for your conclusion.
2. How do you explain Mrs. Correlli's reaction to her son's choice of careers?

CHAPTER REVIEW AND DISCUSSION QUESTIONS

1. What are the advantages of dreaming about the future? How can one overcome the limitations of dreaming so as to put its advantages to good use?
2. Why, in the study of salesmanship, would it be undesirable to teach students to pattern themselves after "the ideal salesman"? Why is it appropriate to advise "to thine own self be true"?

3. How can you develop your abilities and differentiate them from others in order to make them attractive to a potential employer?
4. How do you explain the fact that salesmen in their thirties are the top producers?
5. An employer is most interested in proven ability. If you do not yet have actual sales experience, how can you demonstrate "proven ability" to get a sales job?
6. How can you determine what your strengths and weaknesses are? What can you do to become more objective about yourself?
7. Why are some people more observant than others? How can you train yourself to become more observant?
8. Why do people like some people and dislike others? How can you identify your likable and unlikable characteristics? What value is there in identifying them?
9. What is the difference between talking and saying something? How do you get people to realize that you are saying something rather than just talking?

3

TYPES OF SELLING
AND SALES TRAINING

*A wise man will investigate what
a fool will take for granted.*

—PROVERB

When a person says he is a salesman, you really do not have much of a clue as to what he does until you ask him. This is not only because there are many classifications of sales jobs—retail, door-to-door, industrial, and so forth—but also because the salesman works in every conceivable area—aerospace, entertainment, insurance, farm supplies . . . you name it, and he's in it! This is one of the reasons why the sales field attracts people with such diverse personalities, aptitudes, and interests. Because of the great scope of the sales field, it is a key for opening doors that lead to wherever one's interests lie.

A person who develops selling skills has a career asset that is highly flexible. He can usually apply his skills to whatever selling opportunities are most promising. Thus, for example, if a young man is interested in medicine but does not want to be, or cannot complete the program of study necessary to become, a doctor, he can become a salesman for a pharmaceutical house —a detail man—and build his whole career in a professional medical environment, calling on doctors and hospitals.

A young woman who is interested in architecture can become an effective real estate agent, since this particular interest would be an asset. She will be spending her time talking to a wide variety of people who are interested, as she is, in the design and decorative aspects of buildings. She will be seeing many styles of architecture and the interiors of many different kinds of houses.

You too can capitalize on any of your interests by becoming a salesman in that field. In other words, you can select the kind of environment and associate with the kind of people you find most stimulating by getting a sales job in an area that you are interested in and enjoy most.

THE DIFFERENT KINDS OF SELLING

Through the function of selling, goods and services in our society are transferred from those who provide them to those who use them. It is the salesman who is the facilitator in this activity. He is the go-between who makes the sale. Go-between jobs can be classified in a number of useful ways, depending upon what is sold and to whom it is sold. The nature of the sales job differs according to classifications.

The broadest differentiation is based upon whether the salesman sells tangibles or intangibles. Tangibles are physical goods such as real estate, automobiles, clothing, and toothpaste. Intangibles are nonphysical, such as insurance, transportation, stocks and bonds, and electric and telephone services.

Sales jobs are also differentiated according to who the customer is. Table 3–1 lists the categories, or levels, of customers and the special terminology that is generally used when talking about them.

The classifications and titles in Table 3–1 apply in a general way. The terminology listed is not used by the public in a standardized way. At times, for example, a shopper may be called a buyer. Regardless of the name given to a customer classification, the differences between the types of customers are very real, and they markedly influence the nature of the salesman's job. Selling a luxury coat for Saks Fifth Avenue bears little resemblance to selling a tank car of chemicals for Du Pont.

Selling Tangibles Versus Selling Intangibles

The problems in selling tangibles and intangibles are quite different. In selling a tangible, what passes on to the buyer exists and can be touched, operated, examined, and even listened to, smelled, or tasted. The customer

Table 3–1

THE MAJOR CUSTOMER-CLASSIFICATION LEVELS IN SELLING

Who They Are	Their Customary Title	Where They Are Based	Whom They Buy From
Ultimate Consumers	Shopper	Private Residences	Retailer
Resale Buyers	Buyer	Retail Stores and Wholesale Houses	Wholesaler, Broker, Manufacturer
Industrial and Institutional Purchasers	Purchasing Manager or Agent	Manufacturing Concerns, Hospitals, Hotels, etc.	Manufacturer, Broker, Wholesaler
Government Procurers	Procurement Officer, Purchasing Manager	Government Offices: Federal, State, Military	Manufacturer, Wholesaler, Broker

knows that he can physically possess what he buys. He will be acquiring something that he can control and use as he sees fit—a piece of machinery, a piano, or a house.

Thus the successful salesman of tangibles is an effective demonstrator of products, an authority on the product's use and its capacities and/or capabilities. Furthermore, the salesman may advise the buyer on trading in an old model of the product for a new one. He can provide information on how to service and protect the new product. Thus a relatively tongue-tied but mechanically gifted tinkerer with machinery can be an effective salesman of equipment. Fast talk may not sell a piece of complicated machinery; a mastery of the machine's functions may be far more persuasive.

Selling intangibles is quite another matter. There is usually little that the salesman or customer can physically examine or assess at the time the purchase is made. What is sold is chiefly an idea (a ski vacation in Sapporo, Japan) or a promise (fire insurance). The salesman selling intangibles must emphasize the qualifications of the supplier and the character of what he is able to provide. He focuses on assurances that whatever is promised will be provided. Insurance policies, airline tickets, and stocks and bonds are intangibles. They involve the sale of pieces of paper that are valuable not in themselves but in what they represent. Hence the selling of intangibles is quite abstract when compared to that of tangibles. The painting of word pictures may be quite important here.

The seller of tangibles can let the merchandise talk for itself. In the case of intangibles, it is what the salesman says, or the evidence he can cite, that counts.

The "Shopper," or Ultimate-Consumer, Level of Selling

Most of what shoppers buy is purchased without the services of the salesman. This is because a large proportion of consumer expenditures is for low-cost and standardized requirements such as eggs, dry cleaning, gasoline, parking space, books, clothing, soft drinks, and so on. These are sold largely by vending machines, mail order, self-service or minimal-service retail outlets. Here the need for salespeople has largely been eliminated by retailers who display merchandise so customers can help themselves and who provide check-out counters where customers can pay for the merchandise they have selected; and by manufacturers who prepackage merchandise and provide labels that answer customers' questions.

The personnel still found in retail establishments selling standardized merchandise are for the most part *salesclerks* rather than *salesmen*. The distinction between the two is rather like the distinction between a nurse and a nurse's aide. The salesman is expected to be the well-trained professional who knows his product fully and knows how to handle uninformed customers. The salesclerk, on the other hand, usually can be expected to have only superficial knowledge about both customers and merchandise.

Salesmen are, however, used by retailers on the ultimate-consumer level when what is sold is complicated and expensive. The term "big ticket" is often applied to describe the merchandise that these salesmen sell. Big

ticket refers to the high cost of an item as noted on the price tag. Thus, in the selling of automobiles, appliances, real estate, and expensive clothing—all big-ticket items—large numbers of salesmen are employed. Such men and women are often highly trained and, ideally, are well versed in the products they handle. This type of salesman sells to everyday shoppers who are nonprofessional buyers. At the other three levels of selling (see Table 3–1) salesmen call on professional buyers who work for companies or for institutions such as hospitals and governmental agencies.

The housewives, working people, and students who are the average ultimate consumers are truly nonprofessional buyers. Very often when they buy an appliance, an insurance policy, or an automobile, it is a first-time experience for them. The salesman thus must be a counselor who can explain clearly the purchase to them in terms of their own particular requirements. Emphasis in the sales presentation tends to focus on the personal satisfactions or customer benefits that will be derived from the purchase. These are often inclined to be emotional rather than rational. That is, clothing is sometimes bought because it is the latest style rather than because it will keep the buyer warm. A piano may be purchased because it is a symbol of status to the buyer rather than because it is well constructed or produces excellent tone.

The salesman at the retail level may be less essential than he is at the other levels shown in Table 3–1. Nonetheless, sales experience at the retail level is considered by business employers to be extremely valuable. Experience in selling at the retail-store level is very basic. The everyday shopper has much to do with the level of overall business prosperity. Thus, to have experience as a part-time clerk in a retail store while you are going to school will impress prospective employers of resale and industrial sales trainees, because knowledge of retail customers is considered to be a fundamental grass-roots experience that will be helpful at all levels of selling.

Resale Level of Selling

At this level the customers are wholesalers and retailers who buy goods in large quantities because they want to resell them at a profit. Salesmen in this area are employees of manufacturers, brokers, and wholesalers.

An example of a *manufacturer* is Procter & Gamble. P & G salesmen are employees of the Procter & Gamble Distributing Company, which is the sales subsidiary of the P & G parent manufacturing company. The P & G sales subsidiary is a mammoth organization that in its domestic operations alone sells through nineteen sales offices and employs a total of 4,500 salesmen.

It is not unusual for a large manufacturer to have a wholly owned separate subsidiary company that distributes and sells its product output. The reason for this is that the selling function is so different from the manufacturing function. Selling can be more effectively done by a subsidiary company that is removed entirely from manufacturing and is totally sales oriented. On the other hand, where the manufacturing and selling functions are not completely separated, there is a real danger that the sales function may be handicapped by being dominated by a manufacturing rather than by a marketing environment. In such cases the sales function may suffer.

Brokers and wholesalers are both middlemen who sell to wholesalers [1] or retailers. A *broker* is a middleman who sells goods he does not own or physically possess. A *wholesaler* is a middleman who sells goods that he owns and may or may not physically possess.

An example of a broker is the P. F. Pfeister Company, a Detroit food-brokerage house that represents such accounts as Dole Company, Ocean Spray Cranberries, and Star-Kist Foods. This small company employs about twenty to thirty salesmen who call on food retailers and wholesalers in the Detroit area only. Brokers are almost always local; that is, they sell in only one city or sales area.

An example of a wholesaler is McKesson-Robbins, a national drug wholesaler which sells pharmaceuticals and liquors to druggists all over the United States. This huge company employs hundreds of salesmen.

Salesmen selling on the resale level deal with professional buyers who are very knowledgeable about what they buy. At the resale level, unlike the ultimate-consumer level, the salesman does not focus on the customer's emotions or on his personal likes and dislikes. Rational considerations prevail, focusing primarily on profit-making. The central question at all times is whether the goods that the salesman is selling can be resold by the retailer or wholesaler at a profit.

Salesmen on the resale level do not limit their activities simply to selling merchandise. Their success hinges on whether what they sell to the retailer is quickly resold. That is why resale salesmen often spend a great deal of time and effort helping the retailer resell the merchandise he has bought from the salesmen. They are often expected to assume the responsibility for keeping the retailer's shelf stocks in order. For example, salesmen for Gerber Baby Foods or the National Biscuit Company spend time in local supermarkets persuading the manager to give their products better display space. They build their own displays, put up promotional materials, and attractively arrange stocks of their merchandise on the store shelves. The more of their products the merchant sells, the more merchandise they can sell to him "next time around."

Organizations selling at the resale level often employ specialized salespeople in addition to their regular sales force. These are of two types— *missionary salesmen,* who work in the retail stores setting up displays and putting up point-of-purchase advertising, especially when new products are introduced or when a special sales-promotion program is launched, and *store demonstrators.* Store demonstrators are also employed for special occa-

---

[1] Wholesalers sell to other wholesalers for reasons such as transportation cost reduction. Car lots are shipped by rail to large city wholesalers. Or shiploads of, say, packaged frozen fish may be sold to a wholesaler in a Great Lakes port city. Partial truck-load lots from these large shipments are sold to wholesalers in smaller cities. Another example might be a dental supply wholesaler who finds that to round out his line he should handle medical cotton. Since the quantities would be small, it might be much more expedient and economical for him to buy from a local wholesaler rather than to go to the manufacturer directly.

sions. They pass out samples or demonstrate products for customers who come into the store. These two sales-related positions, the missionary salesman and the store demonstrator, are often used as preliminary jobs for trainees preparing for the regular sales force.

Industrial Level of Selling

Selling at the industrial level is more service-oriented than selling at any of the other levels. Goods and services sold at this level are used for manufacturing other products. Salesmanship here is highly professional, for the salesman must know thoroughly what he is talking about. Often a very high degree of technical knowledge is required in industrial selling. A salesman for a chemical company may have a degree in chemistry, a salesman for a steel company a degree in engineering, and a salesman for a computer company a degree in accounting.

The industrial salesman focuses on problem-solving and on contributing to the efficiency of a manufacturing operation instead of on offering products for the personal satisfaction of a buyer, or on reselling at a profit to a retailer, as in the case of the two previously discussed levels of selling. Most people are not aware of how large the industrial level of purchasing is nor do they consider the large number of attractive, well-paying jobs that are available in this field of selling. For example, the Ford Motor Company buys from an estimated 21,074 different suppliers, most of whom have salesmen who call on Ford. General Motors spent 47.75 percent of its $28.2 billion of annual sales (1971) for goods and services it bought from others through industrial salesmen.

A corollary of industrial selling is institutional selling. These are sales that are made to hospitals, hotels, and airlines and consist of products such as hospital supplies, cleaning equipment, linens, and bulk foodstuffs. Salesmen in the institutional field are also highly specialized and, like industrial salesmen, focus on aiding the buyer to maintain or improve the efficiency of whatever operation he performs.

Government Procurement Level of Selling

The various governments—city, county, state, and federal—are enormous buyers of all the things that communities and nations use—military equipment, streetlight poles, parking meters, office supplies, uniforms, garbage-hauling equipment, police cars—whatever is needed by a city or state to maintain its roads, public buildings, and vehicles. Much, but not all, of this buying is done on a bidding basis as required by law, where the sale is made by the supplier who submits the lowest bid. Thus, different suppliers bid on required specifications when tenders are made public by various governments.

Salesmen calling on these accounts watch for announcements and see that their companies submit bids for whatever business may be available. Frequently these salesmen will visit government procurement officials to give explanations and demonstrate the qualities of the products and services they sell that could improve the city or governmental agency's operations.

Selling One Product to Three Different Types of Customers

Following are three dialogues that illustrate how typing paper is sold to three different classifications of customers. As you read the dialogues, notice how the emphasis on what is stressed changes with each situation. Also, ask yourself how the customers' remarks reveal their primary concerns. Analyzing the customer is the chief activity of the salesman, so practice this skill as you read!

RETAIL-LEVEL SALE

Scene: A salesman is in an office supplies store. The customer is a young woman who earns extra income by doing part-time typing.

SALESMAN: Good morning. May I help you?

CUSTOMER: Yes. I want 1,000 sheets of typing paper.

SALESMAN: That's two reams you'll be needing. There are 500 sheets to a ream.

CUSTOMER: OK. It's still 1,000 sheets to me.

SALESMAN: Do you want a fairly good grade of paper?

CUSTOMER: Actually I want two kinds. Five-hundred sheets of a good bond and 500 sheets of cheap stuff for carbon copies.

SALESMAN: What's the bond going to be used for? Letters, or what?

CUSTOMER: I'm typing a final manuscript of a master's essay for a student. It should be paper that looks like good quality, slides easily, doesn't wrinkle when it's read, and erases easily without messing. I'm not the world's best typist.

SALESMAN: OK, I get it. This is a nice bond that comes packed 100 sheets to a box and sells for $2.50. A ream, five boxes, will cost you $12.50. This cheap stuff we're having a special on is practice paper for kids. It'll make good carbons. A box of 200 costs only $1.19, three boxes would be $3.57. The whole thing will run you $16.07, plus tax.

CUSTOMER: I only need 500 sheets of the cheap paper and you're trying to sell me 600.

SALESMAN: Sorry, lady, the cheap stuff only comes in boxes of 200. It's either 400 or 600.

CUSTOMER: Can't I buy some other kind that's packaged so I can get 500 sheets?

SALESMAN: Look, lady, this is a bargain. At that price you're ending up with those extra 100 sheets free.

CUSTOMER: I don't care about that. The fellow I'm doing the typing for buys the paper and he told me to get 500 sheets.

SALESMAN: All right. Here's some more expensive stuff that's packaged in 100s. Five of these will cost you 95¢ each or $4.75 and the quality isn't any better than the paper that's on sale.

CUSTOMER: Just give me five boxes of the bond and five packages of the 95¢ paper.

SALESMAN: OK, you're the boss. Glad to serve you.

RESALE-LEVEL SALE

Scene: A salesman calls on a buyer for a department store in the month of May. He talks to the buyer as he opens his sample case.

SALESMAN: We have a very fine deal to offer that you can use for a September back-to-school promotion. A 125-sheet jumbo package of pretty good quality practice typing paper that you can sell for 69¢ if you buy 100 cases or more.

BUYER: Is this the package? (*Reaches for a package the salesman has in his hand.*)

SALESMAN: Yes, it's all cello-wrapped and makes a good jumbo-size impression. It's a nice promotion-type package, isn't it?

BUYER: Looks OK. What kind of terms are you offering?

SALESMAN: In order to get the best price you have to take delivery in June or July. That's our factory's slack season, so they're running this volume special. They also want to ship during the slack months. The deal doesn't apply if you want shipment during the rush months.

BUYER: What if I want to reorder in September?

SALESMAN: Sorry, but the deal and the special jumbo package will be all cleaned up by June 1.

BUYER: If I have to order and take delivery that far ahead, what will the billing arrangements be?

SALESMAN: Our normal billing is 2 percent, ten days, net 30. For this deal we'll give you 2 percent, 30 days, net 90. So if you get delivery in June, you still won't have to pay until after September when you run your promotion.

BUYER: Well, that sounds OK to me. Is there a special discount if I order a whole car?

SALESMAN: No discount, but there is a savings in freight that reduces your unit cost about half a penny a package.

BUYER: Fine. Write me up for a car. What else do you have?

INDUSTRIAL-LEVEL SALE

Scene: A salesman calls on a buyer of supplies who works in the purchasing department of a chemical company.

SALESMAN: My records show me that it must be about time for you to reorder typing paper.

BUYER: Let me see what our inventory situation is. Just a minute, please. (*Examines some computer printouts in a book he has on his desk.*)

SALESMAN: You'll remember that we need a three-week lead time on printed letterheads. The stock items require four weeks delivery. That means you can figure seven weeks on the letterheads.

BUYER: I see we're down to a three-month's supply. You're right. It is time to reorder. Are there any changes in quotations from last time?

SALESMAN: No. We're holding the line on prices for reorders, provided you buy standard units of 20 cases, the way our pallets are loaded.

BUYER: What quantity will we need?

SALESMAN: Well, we've got a six-year experience record on your company so I should be able to estimate fairly accurately. Here's a list of what you should order to cover the next six months.

BUYER: Looks all right to me. You can write up the order on that basis.

PERSONAL-INVOLVEMENT EXERCISE NO. 3–1

SELF-TEST. Assume the following sales jobs are available when you are ready to leave college. Review each job and put a check next to the appropriate items that follow. Then rate the jobs from 1 to 6, indicating which job you would prefer first, second, and so on.

JOB 1

—— Salesman for a life insurance company at $450 a month, plus commissions—up to $2,000 a month, if you're good.

—— Intangibles Selling   —— Would consider this job
—— Tangibles Selling   —— Would not consider this job
—— Ultimate-Consumer
   Selling   Why?
—— Industrial Selling
—— Government Selling

JOB 2

—— Selling annuities [2] for a religious organization that help it finance charities. Salesmen earn a straight salary of $500 a month.

—— Intangibles Selling   —— Would consider this job
—— Tangibles Selling   —— Would not consider this job
—— Ultimate-Consumer
   Selling   Why?
—— Resale Selling
—— Industrial Selling
—— Government Selling

JOB 3

—— A sales trainee for the General Foods Corporation at $600 a month, plus car.

—— Intangibles Selling   —— Would consider this job
—— Tangibles Selling   —— Would not consider this job
—— Ultimate-Consumer
   Selling   Why?
—— Resale Selling
—— Industrial Selling
—— Government Selling

[2] An investment plan in which the investor receives monthly payments, usually starting at age sixty-five and ceasing at death. Some religious groups sell annuities, pointing out that when the investor dies, remaining funds can go to their organization.

JOB 4

———— A used-car salesman at $300 per month, plus a 10 percent commission on all sales. Salesmen in this company sell two to ten cars a week.

———— Intangibles Selling   ———— Would consider this job
———— Tangibles Selling   ———— Would not consider this job
———— Ultimate-Consumer
    Selling   Why?
———— Resale Selling
———— Industrial Selling
———— Government Selling

JOB 5

———— A salesman for a paper company selling newsprint to newspapers, at $600 a month, plus car.

———— Intangibles Selling   ———— Would consider this job
———— Tangibles Selling   ———— Would not consider this job
———— Ultimate-Consumer
    Selling   Why?
———— Resale Selling
———— Industrial Selling
———— Government Selling

JOB 6

———— A sales trainee for a chemical company selling fertilizers to farmers, at $600 a month, plus car.

———— Intangibles Selling   ———— Would consider this job
———— Tangibles Selling   ———— Would not consider this job
———— Ultimate-Consumer
    Selling   Why?
———— Resale Selling
———— Industrial Selling
———— Government Selling

TRAINING ACCORDING TO TYPES OF SELLING

The general public probably does not realize that salesmen spend a lot of time training for their jobs. After all, they are professionals—and this implies training. In the old days, salesmen learned mostly on a sink-or-swim basis. Nowadays beginners hired by larger companies go through orientation and training programs that vary in nature and duration. Furthermore, even members of the regular sales staff or seasoned individuals often continue to receive training throughout their careers. Extensive initial training and continued training are necessary because of the complexity of markets and products and because of the introduction of new products, changing markets, and ways of doing business. A salesman must be versatile. As customer needs change so he must change too. As one sales manager put it, "Our greatest problem is instilling creativity."

Duration of Initial Training

The Conference Board (formerly the National Industrial Conference Board) surveyed 276 companies about their training programs for salesmen.[3] It was found that more than 95 percent of these companies had formal sales training programs. The median period for training was six months. Table 3–2 gives detailed information about the results of the survey.

Content of Initial Training Program

The Conference Board study found that the average (median) training program involved 10 percent company orientation, 20 percent market orientation, 20 percent selling techniques, and 40 percent product knowledge. These percentages, of course, vary widely because the duration and the substance of the training program depend on the nature of the selling job, the company policy, and the products and markets to be served. Depending on the circumstances, training programs consist of formal class sessions and seminars, job rotation, on-the-job training, and home-study programs. Demanding and lengthy training programs and break-in time create problems for the trainees, who may get impatient or bored, and for the company, which may lose recruits who get discouraged or who are lured away by companies who promise them immediate responsibility. Thus, those in charge of training recruits try hard to sustain their interest and to give them a sense of accomplishment during the time that they might otherwise feel unproductive.

Examples of Training Programs

This section presents descriptions of training programs provided by companies serving different levels of customers.[4] In general, it appears that

Table 3–2
LENGTH OF TRAINING PROGRAMS—
224 COMPANIES

Under 3 months	32%
3 months and over, but under 6 months	13
6 months and over, but under 9 months	22
9 months and over, but under 12 months	1
12 months and over	32
Total	100%

Source: *Training Company Salesmen,* Experiences in Marketing Management No. 15. New York: The Conference Board, 1967, p. 7.

[3] Morgan B. MacDonald, Jr. and Earl L. Bailey, *Training Company Salesmen,* Experiences in Marketing Management No. 15. New York: The Conference Board, 1967, pp. 7–13.

[4] The training-program descriptions on pages 54–56 are from *Training Company Salesmen,* Experiences in Marketing Management No. 15. New York: The Conference Board, 1967, pp. 53–54, 61–62.

salesmen on the industrial-governmental-procurement levels are most extensively trained; resale-level salesmen dealing with retailers and wholesalers are moderately trained; and salesmen dealing with the ultimate consumer least extensively trained of all. This varies widely, of course, since an insurance salesman selling to a homeowner may be more extensively trained than a salesman selling sweeping compound to a factory.

Intangibles Sold to Ultimate Consumers

INSURANCE COMPANY. Each newly hired, inexperienced agent is sent to a three-week school at the beginning of his sales career. The school covers product knowledge and selling techniques of the various lines of insurance we sell. The agent is then returned to his district sales manager for a thirteen-week installation program that combines a field training program and close supervision of the agent's sales activities. The combination of the three-week school and the thirteen-week installation program covers the first four months of the agent's career.

We consider the salesman's first year to be his basic training period. In addition to the four months described above, he participates in the following three formal schools during his first year, each of which is supported by a field follow-up training program:

> Salesmanship workshop
>
> Basic commercial lines workshop
>
> Mutual funds training program

Tangibles—Soft Goods [5]—Sold to Retailers and Wholesalers

APPAREL COMPANY. Our current training program for newly hired, inexperienced salesmen requires approximately five weeks of training. It consists of about four weeks at the corporate headquarters in school session and one week in field training with either sales management or a senior salesman. The sixth week is then spent at regional headquarters with the regional manager, service administration, and the regional sales manager reviewing the new salesman's territory and accounts, and planning his work itinerary for six months.

The training at corporate headquarters consists roughly of the following:

> About two weeks of product knowledge taught by various product or market managers, or the director of merchandising, or his assistant.
>
> About one week to ten days learning about markets, types of buyers, order frequency, method of payment, and so on.

---

[5] In the resale field, retailers and wholesalers refer to two goods classifications; *soft goods,* which are textiles and textile products; and *hard goods,* which are fabricated metal, plastics, and glass products.

A couple of days in the factory to understand how the various components of garments are cut, stitched, finished, and packaged for distribution. A couple of hours are spent in quality control, gaining an understanding of company quality requirements.

Woven throughout this pattern are marketing orientation, selling techniques and company orientation. Included are introduction to the president, the executive vice president, and the various vice presidents of the company's divisions.

Tangibles—Hard Goods—Sold to Industrial Purchasers

METALWORKING MACHINERY COMPANY. There cannot really be a specific length of training time for the marketing of machine tools. The man chosen must indicate mature judgment, possess a general knowledge of metalworking manufacturing processes, have adequate product knowledge, and participate in salesmanship training. The time required will vary with the individual. However, let us assume the man is directly hired after graduation from a university, preferably with a degree in engineering, although this is not mandatory.

A training program could vary from three to five years, depending on the man, business conditions, and company personnel requirements during that period.

The first nine months are spent in a planned program at the technical training center. The program is designed to provide machine shop experience, operational contact with company products, and an opportunity to survey the overall operations and personnel. This provides both company orientation and product knowledge.

Upon completion of this program, the man is normally assigned to a field service organization. In this position the man demonstrates machines in customers' plants. This provides additional product mechanical knowledge, and a first exposure to customer requirements. Quite often an opportunity is provided to work with regular company salesmen, and various selling approaches—both good and bad—can be observed. No formal sales training is provided at this stage, although it certainly would be beneficial.

After one or two years of field service, the man is transferred to a sales project engineering department for one of the machine tool divisions. In this position, the man will develop machine proposals for specific customer requests that cannot be handled at the local office level. This provides product application experience in depth, develops written communications ability, and involves direct and indirect customer contact. Many times these men are called upon to accompany the salesmen when proposals are presented to the customer. This is "front-line" sales experience.

When requirements for additional salesmen arise, selected sales project engineers are transferred to the marketing personnel development department for a concentrated sales training program. (Selected men may also be chosen from other company areas.) This program takes from sixteen to twenty weeks and concentrates on product knowledge for the complete line of machine tools, marketing approaches for each type of machine, planning and operating procedures for a salesman, and salesmanship.

Separate classroom facilities are available for the concentrated sales training program. The director of marketing personnel development has the responsibility for course development and class supervision.

Before the formal sessions begin, each trainee spends a week in the field with a regular salesman. This provides him with a better insight into the job requirements and opportunities.

The trainees present many of the product class sessions. Usually an expert from the machine section involved is present to monitor the class. Certain of the more highly technical or new-process presentations are conducted completely by experts in the particular field.

After some weeks of product exposure sessions, practice sales sessions are begun. Role playing is utilized. Situations depicting all types of calls are presented, from the "cold call" through the "service-type call."

Different members of management present sessions covering their particular areas of responsibility. These sessions help to build a feeling in the trainees of being part of the team.

FIELD CHRONICLE

John Elsworth was surprised to learn that he would be a trainee for nine months before he would actually work as a salesman. He thoroughly enjoyed the first six weeks, which he spent in the company's manufacturing plants. He wore overalls and was assigned to work with a man in a different manufacturing section each week. On Friday afternoons Bruce Brady, of the manufacturing division's personnel department, would introduce him to the man he would report to on Monday morning for the next week's work-watching experience.

Although Elsworth got along well enough with the man he was assigned to in the fixture-assembly division the first week, he felt that the man tolerated him rather than welcomed him. The man would explain only sketchily what was going on, and he answered Elsworth's questions briefly and unenthusiastically. Elsworth felt he would have learned a lot more if the man had taken an interest in telling him about his work.

One Friday afternoon Brady came by to introduce Elsworth to his next week's assignment, which was in the wallboard processing division. When they arrived in the noisy, smelly, busy department, Brady had a hard time stopping the floor superintendent, Stu Wilson, long enough to introduce him to Elsworth. When Wilson finally came over and was introduced to Elsworth, he said, "For the love of Mike, don't tell me you have another one of these damned ninety-day wonders who's going to tag along with me all week. I'm paid to get out wallboard, not to be a baby sitter."

Elsworth was shaken by this reception and certainly did not look forward to the week ahead. He and Brady stopped off in the large, deserted factory cafeteria for a cup of coffee. Elsworth decided to bring up the subject of the seemingly cool reception he was getting from people he was being assigned to. He told Brady how he felt.

BRADY: Elsworth, you're too self-centered. If you're going to be a salesman who's worth his salt, you're certainly going to have to learn to think of the other person's situation. I'm surprised you don't realize that for the next year, you're largely going to have to learn from others who aren't really obliged to teach you a thing. Just as the guy in the wallboard department said, he isn't paid to baby-sit—what could be clearer?

ELSWORTH: Yes, but he works for the company. He gets paid for his job and he shouldn't make me feel he's doing *me* a favor.

BRADY: You're going to be a hell of a salesman if you can't learn that people in the real world are people who have problems and frustrations—they're not like the happy-go-lucky characters you read about in fairy tales.

ELSWORTH: All I'm asking is to be treated like a human being.

BRADY: If you'd forget about yourself and think about the other guy's problems, you'd be taking the first step toward becoming a salesman. You should look at these guys you want to learn from for the next six months as a challenge in salesmanship— sell yourself to them so they'll want to teach you what they know.

ELSWORTH: I don't get it.

BRADY: Whether they teach you something depends on you, not them. The world and the people in it don't owe you a thing. And that's the fun of it—making things pay off for you because you influence the people you meet so they'll cooperate. That's where the real satisfaction comes from—in striving for what you attain.

For some reason Elsworth was not offended by Brady's overall blast. He thought long and hard over the weekend about what Brady had said. He decided that Brady was right and that he was going to revise his attitude about his training opportunity.

STOP & THINK

1. What is the situation of the people Elsworth is assigned to for training?
2. How should Elsworth conduct himself to maximize what he can get out of training?
3. Why are beginners in any learning situation apt to be self-centered? How can they overcome this?

COMPANY CHRONICLE

At the end of his first month of training, Elsworth was asked to make an appointment to see his old friend Henry Meyer of B.C. Industries' personnel department. The appointment resulted in an hour's discussion with Meyer that gave Elsworth a lot to think about. Highlights of the discussion follow.

MEYER: Now that you're well started on your training program we want you to decide which particular phase of our business you want to specialize in. The first part of our training program is the same for all trainees. All of them learn about the manufacture of our company's products and all receive the same general overall company orientation program. During the second half of the program, trainees specialize in a particular division of our company. We'd like to know which division you'd prefer.

ELSWORTH: I didn't know there was a choice. I'd like to know something about each division before I make up my mind.

MEYER: I was coming to that. You see, as a supplier of building materials, B.C. Industries sells to three very distinct and different types of customers. We have a division that specializes in each type of customer. Our home-sales department sells kitchen, playroom, and bar-workshop-basement remodeling jobs directly to the homeowner. This is the company's fastest growing division.

ELSWORTH: Where do salesmen get leads on people who are interested in home improvements?

MEYER: All of our business comes to us through the home furnishings department of department stores and through interior decorators. We estimate the jobs and make the installations for retail stores. They bill their customers for our installations and get a percentage of whatever business we generate for them. As our salesman, you would call on customers of retail stores who asked for an estimate for a remodeling job.

ELSWORTH: I would be visiting customers in their homes at their invitation, as it were. Is that right?

MEYER: Right. It's a pleasant way to get into selling at the grass-roots level. Now, our do-it-yourself division is altogether different. If you go into that, you'd be selling our do-it-yourself home-improvement line to buyers in department stores, discount houses, hardware stores, and lumberyards. This is a volume business. All of our merchandise is prepackaged, branded, and sold in large quantities to retailers who sell it to do-it-yourself home improvers. Our brand is well established in retail stores.

ELSWORTH: That kind of selling seems rather cut and dried, if most stores handle the line. Buyers know all about it, so there can't be too much that the salesman has to do.

MEYER: Well, it isn't as simple as that. After all, the market never stands still, which means that the salesman must also always be on the move, following changes that come about in the market.

ELSWORTH: What's the third division all about?

MEYER: It's the division that sells commercial building supplies. Salesmen call on architects, lumberyards, construction companies, and building contractors. This division supplies materials all the way from building a modest home to a multimillion-dollar office building or shopping center.

ELSWORTH: Looks like B.C. Industries pretty well covers the waterfront. I'll have to think about which division I want to go into. Is it possible to start in one division and eventually end up in another?

MEYER: Oh yes, our company believes in making opportunities throughout the company available to everyone in the company. The thing to do is to build the kind of experience into yourself that will make you an attractive candidate for later, more important jobs. Usually though, once a man starts in one division he stays there.

ELSWORTH: In other words, once he's in a division, he's stuck there.

MEYER: Sometimes I wonder about you, Elsworth.

STOP & THINK

1. What are the pros and cons of starting out in each division?

2. What do you think is the best division to start out in? Why?

3. Explain what Meyer meant by his phrase "building experience into yourself."

PROBLEMS

Which Are Easier to Sell, Tangibles or Intangibles? John Barry, a veteran real estate salesman, was a guest at the home of his good friend Claude Walker, a life insurance salesman of long standing. After a pleasant dinner, the two men lit up cigars in Walker's den and started on one of their favorite debates.

BARRY: You've got it made, Claude. While I'm climbing up and down stairs selling houses I don't know too much about, you're selling the same old insurance policies you've sold all year—and you sell them without moving out of your chair.

WALKER: Are you going to start that again? You're the one who's got it made. What a pushover it must be to sell something you see, hear, touch, smell, or taste. It takes a much better salesman to sell intangibles and you know it. You always bring up the subject because your conscience bothers you when you think about how easy you've got it selling houses while I'm out there trying to sell insurance.

BARRY: If selling intangibles is so hard, how come you end up selling more insurance each year than I sell houses?

WALKER: Now we're not talking about the difference between selling tangibles and intangibles. Now we're talking about the difference between a superior salesman and an ordinary one!

STOP & THINK

1. What are the differences between selling insurance and selling real estate?
2. In general, which is easier to sell, tangibles or intangibles?

A Moral Dilemma in Changing Jobs. Harry Bellows felt he was on top of the world. He and his wife (who was an editor on a local newspaper) had been happily married for six months, and he had recently completed eight exhaustive months of training as an apprentice salesman for a large and distinguished computer manufacturer. He ranked in the upper third of the large group of trainees that had been recruited at the time he graduated from college. He was now assigned to his first sales territory and felt he was catching on reasonably well.

One afternoon while he was waiting to see a buyer, he started talking to another man who was waiting to see the same buyer. The man turned out to be the district sales manager of a small competitor. Bellows gave the man his card. That evening the man called and invited Bellows out for dinner. The upshot was that the competitor offered Bellows a job at a salary that was 35 percent more than he was making. The sales manager painted a rosy picture of the future Bellows would have if he joined the company. He assured him he would get more responsibility more quickly in the smaller company and pointed out that the way to the top was much shorter.

Bellows spent several sleepless nights deliberating with himself. His present employer had paid his salary for eight months and had invested probably as much in a fine training program. So far Bellows had contributed nothing to offset what had been done for him. Yet it would probably be five years before he would be earning what he had been offered by the competitor. The competitor was obviously saving large training costs by luring away the large company's top trainees.

STOP & THINK

1. What are the issues involved in this decision?
2. How should Bellows handle this situation?

Sales Training and the Future. Sara Emden was a very attractive young woman who worked as a fashion model during the day while she was finishing up her last year of college at night. Sara was ambitious and quite security-minded; she enjoyed her work as a model and the high income it provided. She felt her work was not mentally stimulating, but since she carried a heavy load of courses at the night school she reasoned that she could do without mental stimulation during the day.

One day a representative of a cosmetics firm she was modeling for took her out to lunch and offered her a job selling his company's well-known cosmetics line to department stores. The salary he mentioned was attractive yet considerably less than what she was making as a model. When she pointed this out to the cosmetics representative, he said that after she got training and experience her commissions could equal and surpass her salary as a model. He further emphasized that the years of a model's earning power were limited.

The argument that really caused Sara to reflect was this: Sales work is ideal for a woman. It is one job that gives her the real flexibility she needs as her family situation changes. She can stop working temporarily if she wants to have children. She can work off-hours and part time. And age is no barrier in sales, whereas in many fields older women have difficulty finding work.

STOP & THINK

1. What should Sara Emden do?
2. How valid are the cosmetics representative's arguments for women going into sales work?

CHAPTER REVIEW AND DISCUSSION QUESTIONS

1. What are the differences between selling tangibles and intangibles?
2. Describe the ultimate-consumer level of selling. Explain how it differs from the resale level.
3. What is the difference between rational and emotional sales appeals? Which are more effective in selling?
4. How does the resale level of selling differ from industrial selling?
5. What are missionary salesmen? Store demonstrators?
6. Select a product or service and explain the differences in the way it would be sold on the retail, resale, and industrial levels.
7. What is the typical duration of training programs for salesmen? Why is it necessary to have such extensive training in the sales field?
8. What is the content of initial sales-training programs?

4

THE SALES FIELD: SIZE, COMPENSATION, AND ORGANIZATION

Sales incentives? As the fellow says,
"Maybe money isn't everything,
but it's quite a long distance ahead
of whatever is in second place!"

—ANON.

In America we are inclined to judge things on the basis of size, money, and structure. This chapter provides data about the size of the sales field, and the compensation earned by those in the field. It also provides a description of the opportunities in the field, the various kinds of compensation arrangements, and the way companies organize and staff their sales activities. In other words, this chapter sketches out the general picture of the sales field.

STATISTICAL DATA

Size of the Sales Field

Table 4–1 shows the number of workers employed in sales as compared with the number of workers in the other occupational categories reported by the U.S. Department of Labor. The statistics run from 1950 and are projected through 1980. The figures indicate that the projected 1969–1980 increase for sales workers is 27.9 percent. Thus, opportunities for sales workers are higher than for "Total Employed," which will increase 22.1 percent over the same period.

Table 4–2 gives employment statistics for the business-related job cate-

Table 4–1

EMPLOYMENT BY OCCUPATION

(Millions of Persons, Except Percentages)

Occupation	1950	1960	1965	1969	1980	Percent Change 1969–1980
Total Employed	59.6	66.7	72.2	77.9	95.1	22.1
White-Collar Workers	22.4	28.7	32.1	36.8	48.3	31.1
Professional, Technical	4.5	7.5	8.9	10.8	15.5	43.9
Managers, Officials [1]	6.4	7.1	7.3	8.0	9.5	18.9
Clerical Workers	7.6	9.8	11.2	13.4	17.3	29.1
Sales Workers	3.8	4.4	4.7	4.7	6.0	27.9
Blue-Collar Workers	23.3	24.2	26.5	28.2	31.1	10.1
Craftsmen, Foremen	7.7	8.6	9.2	10.2	12.2	19.7
Operatives	12.1	12.0	13.4	14.4	15.4	7.2
Nonfarm Laborers	3.5	3.7	3.9	3.7	3.5	− 4.7
Service Workers	6.5	8.3	9.3	9.5	13.1	37.5
Private Household	1.9	2.2	2.3	1.6	n.a.	n.a.
Other Services	4.7	6.1	7.1	7.9	n.a.	n.a.
Farm Workers	7.4	5.4	4.3	3.3	2.6	− 21.0

Note: Data for 1950, 1960 and 1965 are for persons 14 years and over; later years refer to population 16 years and over. All years refer to civilian employment only.
[1] Includes proprietors.
n.a.—Not available.
Source: Department of Labor.

gories, as reported by the U.S. Department of Labor, and forecasts where the jobs will be in the 1970s. Prospects in the sales field are more attractive than for any other field that was reported.

Educational Attainment of Sales Workers

Table 4–3 shows, interestingly, that, with the exception of the Professional-Technical category, the educational attainment of sales workers is as high as or higher than that of workers in all other occupational categories. Thus, it would be fair to assume that, in general, educational requirements are high for those aspiring to enter the sales field. It is probably also reasonable to assume that the educational attainment of older sales workers is less than that of younger workers. This assumption is based on the fact that in most categories educational levels of younger workers are higher than those of older workers. It is clear that graduates from junior colleges and preferably from four-year colleges would have the best opportunities to get entry jobs in the sales field.

Table 4–2

	Latest Employment (1968 Estimate)	Annual Average of Job Openings in 1970s
Business Administration		
Accountants	500,000	33,000
Advertising workers	140,000	5,700
Marketing-research workers	20,000	2,700
Personnel workers	110,000	6,900
Public-relations workers	100,000	8,800
Managers		
Bank officers	125,000	9,900
Industrial-traffic managers	15,000	500
Hotel managers, assistants	150,000	9,500
Purchasing agents	140,000	6,700
Clerical		
Bank clerks	400,000	29,500
Bank tellers	230,000	20,000
Bookkeeping workers	1,200,000	78,000
Cashiers	730,000	69,000
Railroad clerks	93,000	2,700
Dental assistants	100,000	9,000
Computer operators	175,000	20,400
Hotel clerks	50,000	3,200
Library technicians	70,000	9,000
Mail carriers	246,000	12,200
Office-machine operators	325,000	25,000
Postal clerks	290,000	14,600
Receptionists	240,000	30,000
Shipping clerks	370,000	12,400
Stenographers and secretaries	2,650,000	237,000
Telephone operators	400,000	28,000
Air-traffic agents, clerks	37,500	2,600
Typists	700,000	63,000
Sales		
Insurance agents, brokers	410,000	16,200
Manufacturers' salesmen	500,000	32,000
Real estate salesmen, brokers	225,000	14,200
Retail-trade salesworkers	2,800,000	150,000
Auto-parts countermen	65,000	2,500
Auto salesmen	120,000	4,400
Auto-service advisers	10,000	300
Securities salesmen	135,000	7,400
Wholesale-trade salesworkers	530,000	25,200

Adapted from U.S. Department of Labor, Bulletin 1701.

Table 4-3

EDUCATIONAL ATTAINMENT OF EMPLOYEES, 1969

Median Years of School Completed
by Employed Civilian Labor Force

Occupation	Total 18 Years and Over	Sex		Color	
		Male	Female	White	Nonwhite
All Occupations	12.4	12.3	12.4	12.4	11.3
Professional, Technical	16.3	16.4	16.2	16.2 ⎫	15.7
Managers, Officials	12.7	12.8	12.5	12.7 ⎭	
Farmers, Farm Laborers	9.3	9.0	11.3	9.8	6.7
Clerical Workers	12.6	12.6	12.6	12.6 ⎫	12.6
Sales Workers	12.6	12.8	12.3	12.6 ⎭	
Craftsmen, Foremen	12.1	12.1	12.2 ⎫		
Operatives	11.1	11.3	10.7 ⎬	11.6	10.4
Nonfarm Laborers	10.0	10.0	10.9 ⎭		
Service Workers	11.3	11.7	11.2	12.0	9.8

Source: Department of Labor.

Opportunities for Women and Minority Groups

It is well known that there are more men than women in sales, and that the sales field is overwhelmingly dominated by whites.

Women have traditionally shied away from sales because of the nature of the work and its reputation. As described in Chapter 1, in the early days when salesmen were often rowdies and men of questionable character, a woman in the sales field was definitely looked upon as an oddity. Sales had such a masculine image that it probably would not have occurred to recruiters to seek out female employees, nor would the vast majority of women have considered the field even if opportunities had been available. Recently, attitudes about women in sales have changed somewhat, and today there are women who are notably successful in sales. The government's recent moves to ensure equal employment opportunities to women are helping to correct the imbalance in the field, and the number of women entering sales is rising considerably. Today, women are increasingly employed in selling insurance, investment opportunities, travel and airline services, real estate, and cosmetic lines. Women are also selling in retailing and manufacturing, two previously male-dominated fields.

E. B. Weiss, the well-known marketing executive, is quoted in *Advertising Age*, December 20, 1971, as saying that female earning power is expected to equal that of men in this country by 1985. He states that the top ten categories for women right now are secretary, saleswoman, elementary school teacher, bookkeeper, waitress, nurse, typist, clerk, cashier, and telephone operator. Note that selling is given the number-two spot in this list.

Another interesting comment made by Weiss in the same article is that

women are now acting as switchmen at Southern Bell Telephone Company in Atlanta, as tax experts at Scott Paper in Philadelphia, and as chemical engineers at Standard Oil of California in San Francisco.

In the sales field there are now women car and truck salesmen; women who sell stocks, bonds, and mutual funds; women who are active in design, industrial art, fashion, and architecture. Women have also risen so rapidly in advertising and marketing, a sales-related field, that today, as Weiss says, "There simply is not a shred of evidence to support the tradition of male dominance in advertising or marketing."

An article in the July 14, 1972 edition of *The New York Times* reported on women selling space in magazines. It mentioned that *Newsweek, Time,* and *American Home* had added the first women to their advertising sales staffs. The report stated that "they join a small but growing number of their sex in still another crumbling area of male exclusiveness." Their male customers were asked to comment. One said, "They bring more enthusiasm and idealism to the selling effort." Another said, "The top female salesman will match the best male salesman in selling ability." And still another said, "They sell differently. They deliver the message more earnestly, stick to the script, and work harder at it. They have less tendency to chat away from the subject." The new saleswoman for *American Home* had a background as a singer, dancer, and actress. She had this interesting comment about why she liked sales: "I love communicating with people. I love the freedom, the projecting of ideas—it's an extension of being on the stage."

All the statistics indicate that sales is an expanding field with expanding personnel needs. Women interested in sales should not hesitate to pursue their goals. It would be advisable for a woman to set her sights on sales areas in which women have gained acceptance and have made outstanding records for themselves, as in travel, airline, real estate, publishing, investment services, advertising, and marketing.

In the past, the sales field for nonwhites has been almost completely closed. Recently, however, nonwhites have been making considerable inroads in sales. As the figures in Table 4–4 show, there were a total of 166,-000 nonwhites employed in the sales field in 1969. While U.S. Department of Labor statistics for the 1970s are not yet available, company records show that the number of nonwhites in sales is increasing and that they often achieve outstanding success. Now, in fact, companies actively recruit members of ethnic minority groups.

College placement officials today often state that sales openings are greatest for minority-group graduates. Students who belong to a minority group would be well advised to talk to college placement directors and company recruiters about opportunities in sales. It is best not to wait until graduation to ask about job opportunities. The recruitment situation for minority groups in the sales field is changing so rapidly that it would be a mistake to rely on attitudes or opinions that you have now, for they may be out of date.

Table 4–4

EMPLOYED PERSONS BY OCCUPATION, SEX AND COLOR, 1969

(Thousands of Persons 16 Years and Over)

Occupation	Total	Sex		Color	
		Male	*Female*	*White*	*Nonwhite*
Total Employed	77,902	48,818	29,084	69,518	8,384
White-Collar Workers	36,845	19,574	17,271	34,647	2,197
Professional, Technical	10,769	6,751	4,018	10,074	695
Managers, Officials, Proprietors	7,987	6,726	1,261	7,733	254
Clerical Workers	13,397	3,422	9,975	12,314	1,083
Sales Workers	4,692	2,675	2,017	4,527	166
Blue-Collar Workers	28,237	23,263	4,974	24,647	3,591
Craftsmen, Foremen	10,193	9,854	339	9,484	709
Operatives	14,372	9,883	4,489	12,368	2,004
Nonfarm Laborers	3,672	3,526	146	2,795	877
Service Workers	9,528	3,257	6,271	7,289	2,239
Private Household	1,631	39	1,592	917	714
Other Services	7,897	3,218	4,679	6,372	1,525
Farm Workers	3,292	2,723	569	2,935	356

Note: Civilian employment only.
Source: Department of Labor.

Earnings in the Sales Field

From the perspective of earnings, the sales field is attractive. Table 4–5 shows that where the family head is a sales worker, his median income is $11,238, which is considerably above the $10,113 median income for heads of families generally. Figure 4–1, a graphic presentation of the figures in Table 4–5, shows visually the place of sales-worker earnings as compared to other groups reported by the Department of Commerce.

Table 4–5

MEDIAN FAMILY INCOME BY OCCUPATION
OF HEAD, 1968

Occupation of Family Head	Total Families		Head, Full-Time Worker [1]	
	Number (Thousands)	Median Income (Dollars)	Number (Thousands)	Median Income (Dollars)
Total [2]	50,510	8,632	34,044	10,113
Professional, Technical	5,831	12,619	4,962	13,143
Self-Employed	593	19,968	465	21,398
Salaried	5,238	12,268	4,499	12,795
Managers, Officials, Proprietors	6,148	12,143	5,576	12,478
Self-Employed	1,750	9,813	1,501	10,266
Salaried	4,398	12,979	4,077	13,205
Clerical Workers	3,128	9,103	2,606	9,562
Sales Workers	2,158	10,671	1,778	11,238
Craftsmen, Foremen	8,279	9,804	6,756	10,167
Operatives	7,901	8,459	6,171	8,855
Nonfarm Laborers	1,934	7,013	1,334	7,618
Private Household Workers	203	2,741	51	[3]
Other Service Workers	2,607	7,268	1,914	8,201
Farmers, Farm Managers	1,554	5,414	1,251	5,659
Farm Labor	435	4,359	264	5,071

[1] Year-round.
[2] Total also includes families with head unemployed, in Armed Forces, and not in the labor force.
[3] Not calculated because of insufficient numbers.
Source: Department of Commerce.

Figure 4–1
MEDIAN FAMILY INCOME BY OCCUPATION
Family Heads, Year-Round Full-Time Workers, 1968

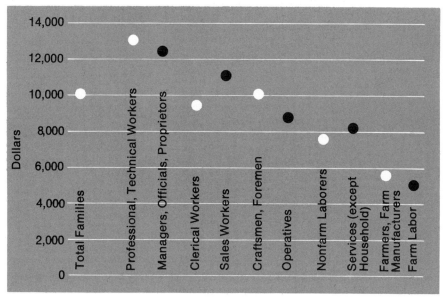

Source: U.S. Department of Labor

REMUNERATION

Methods for remunerating salesmen are quite different from those found in other occupations. This is because the salesman works largely on his own most of the time. He does best when there are incentives or extras, such as bonuses or special "spiffs."

A salesman's productivity is closely tied to his personal skill and to the actual effort he is willing to make. Consequently, incentives and motivation in the form of commissions, bonuses, contests, and so on play an important role in rewarding the salesman for his effort.

The Remuneration Mix

Basic compensation for the salesman starts with the same benefits that other company employees receive. Two sales executives participating in a recent panel discussion explained this arrangement. They were asked about the rules their companies follow in trying to design a sound incentive program that also provides security for their salesmen. One panelist put it this way:

We consider several points, commencing with a living wage. Then we provide for a satisfaction of extra wants; make possible a degree of future security; recognize length of service; and make provision for other benefits, such as training, paid vacations, group insurance, hospitalization for the man and his family, pensions as a supplement to social security, and sick leave, with at least minimum compensation during compulsory absence from work.[1]

Another panelist had this to say:

Perhaps the greatest change in salesmen's compensation plans over the past few years has been the increasing demand on the part of salesmen to be considered part of the family, and to be included, on a realistic basis, in fringe benefits, especially life insurance, hospital insurance, vacations, pension plans and/or profit-sharing. Simultaneously, salesmen have demanded some base under their earnings in terms of guarantees, draws, or salary, so that minimum economic demands can be met.[2]

The resemblance between remuneration systems for regular employees of a company and those for members of their sales department extends only to the fringe benefits discussed in the above quotations. While there are companies that pay salesmen straight salaries, these are the exceptions rather than the rule. Most companies have combinations of salaries, commissions, and bonuses.[3] Among 665 companies participating in a survey on methods of compensation, 448 (more than 67 percent) used some form of salary-plus-incentive method for salesmen's compensation. One hundred forty-three (21.5 percent) paid straight salary, while seventy-four (about 11 percent) had a straight-commission type of compensation.[4]

Incentive Plans: The Salesman's View

People not familiar with the sales field are usually surprised to discover that it is the salesmen who prefer incentive plans. Roger Bush, vice president of marketing at Ditto, Inc., had this to say about sales compensation plans.

Studies made in the late fifties indicated a very substantial trend toward straight-salary or salary-and-bonus compensation plans. More

[1] Earl L. Bailey, *Incentives for Salesmen*, Experiences in Marketing Management No. 14. New York: The Conference Board, 1967, p. 3.
[2] Bailey, *Incentives*, p. 3.
[3] *Commission* is a method of sales compensation in which payment bears a fixed percentage relationship to sales. Bonus is an amount separate from salary and commission, and is paid as a reward for special or extraordinary effort or services. Christmas bonuses, quota bonuses, and group bonuses are examples.
[4] David A. Weeks, *Compensating Field Sales Representatives*, Studies in Personnel Policy No. 202. New York: The Conference Board, 1966, p. 19.

recent studies, however, indicate that the trend is now toward more incentives and less straight salary. An interesting sidelight of one study is that employers show some increasing tendency to favor salary plans, but the same report indicated that 65 percent of the salesmen prefer incentive programs. I think that speaks for itself.[5]

The consensus of sales managers is that "a really good salesman prefers commission plans."

Table 4–6 shows the relationship between base salary and incentive earnings for average salesmen. Table 4–7 shows the same relationship for high-producing salesmen. The two tables show that both the best salesmen in the average group and the best salesmen in the top-producing group earn substantially more than their base salaries because of incentives. Thus it is quite understandable from an earnings point of view why incentive plans are preferred by the better salesmen. In addition, there is a psychological factor. People who are competitive by nature and who are stimulated by pressure gravitate to the sales field. Incentive plans are thus part of what they often refer to as "the selling game." Stars in the sales game feel that they could not perform at their best without the financial incentives of commissions on sales, bonuses for exceeding quotas, rewards for being first in attaining some sales goal, and so on.

Table 4–6

COMPARISON OF INCENTIVE PLAN EARNINGS
OF AVERAGE SALESMAN BY TYPE OF PRODUCT

	Consumer Products		
	Total Earnings	Base Salary	Incentive as a Percent of Salary
Median [1]	$10,160	$ 8,310	12%
Range of Middle 50%			
Low	8,400	7,200	8
High	11,970	9,500	22
	Industrial Products		
Median [1]	12,100	10,800	15
Range of Middle 50%			
Low	11,250	9,000	10
High	13,750	12,000	20

[1] Data based on earnings figures provided by 40 consumer goods sales forces and 45 industrial products sales forces.
Source: David A. Weeks, *Incentive Plans for Salesmen,* Studies in Personnel Policy No. 217. New York: The Conference Board, 1970, p. 73.

[5] Bailey, *Incentives,* pp. 14–15.

Table 4–7

COMPARISON OF INCENTIVE PLAN EARNINGS
OF HIGH PRODUCING SALESMEN BY TYPE OF PRODUCT

	Consumer Products		
	Total Earnings	Base Salary	Incentive as a Percent of Salary
Median [1]	$12,210	$10,000	21%
Range of Middle 50%			
Low	10,400	8,500	13
High	15,000	12,000	33
	Industrial Products		
Median [1]	16,800	13,000	26
Range of Middle 50%			
Low	15,400	11,400	19
High	20,350	15,000	40

[1] Based on earnings data supplied for 42 consumer products sales forces and 44 industrial products sales forces.
Source: David A. Weeks, *Incentive Plans for Salesmen,* Studies in Personnel Policy No. 217. New York: The Conference Board, 1970, p. 77.

Remuneration for the Beginner

It is usual to have a special remuneration arrangement for beginners and new salesmen. This is so because it takes time for a neophyte to learn about his new employer's company, products, services, sales methods, and policies. It also takes time for him to familiarize himself with a new sales territory and its customers. Most of the beginner's first months are spent learning, which means that there is little time for earning. How long the orientation and indoctrination period lasts depends on the company and on the nature of its products. The characteristics of some products—soft drinks for example—can be learned in less than a week, whereas the familiarization period for pharmaceuticals or complicated machinery can take six months or more.

Most companies have special arrangements, usually straight salary with perhaps a bonus of some sort, to motivate the newcomer to learn. These special remuneration plans are used until the beginner becomes experienced enough to compete reasonably well with the seasoned sales force. Louis J. Dubuque, III, vice president of the Dictaphone Corporation, had this to say about remunerating the beginner:

> Our feeling now concerning compensation for the new salesman leans more toward a basic salary plus commission and bonus, rather than straight-commission plus bonus. This naturally is intended to sustain the new salesman while he becomes acquainted with the territory, the products, and the selling techniques. However, after a

salesman has been with us six months, the straight-commission-plus-bonus plan still appears to us to be of greatest motivational value.[6]

Advancement and Promotion

Opportunity for rapid promotion and recognition is a prime reason behind decisions to go into the sales field. It is well known that top executives in many companies have come up via the sales route. A company prospers by pleasing customers. Learning about customers, markets, wants, and needs is the all-absorbing task of the salesman. This kind of experience is so highly valued that many companies insist that their executive trainees get experience as salesmen. Procter & Gamble requires its trainees to work as salesmen for six months. The Kroger Company requires its trainees to work in contact with customers in their stores for a year or more. Such training is considered so valuable that companies often subsidize executive trainee salaries to make the experience possible.

There are at least three alternatives open to people who enter the sales field. One is to become a professional salesman and to make the job of a salesman a lifetime career. Many choose this route because of the independence it offers. Furthermore, top salesmen know that regardless of business conditions, there is always a job for a good salesman. When budgets are cut, people working in staff positions in personnel, advertising, and production may be laid off. The salesman who has a line job rather than a staff job knows if he is good, his job is rarely threatened.

A second alternative for those going into sales is to seek promotions to executive jobs in sales work. Sales administration requires many executives, such as assistant district manager, district sales manager, regional sales manager, and sales supervisor. These jobs hold considerable prestige and often are well paid. Tables 4–8 and 4–9 show how field sales supervisors are remunerated and the amount of compensation they receive.

A third alternative for those going into sales is to leave the sales field entirely, after a period of several years, and to go into one of the many executive positions where a sales background is a definite asset. Such opportunities are widely available for those who succeed in sales. Because a salesman's work is contact work, many people in important positions are aware of his existence. This leads to opportunities. Company executives, searching for qualified people to promote, look first to their own sales department as a source of executive talent. The salesman will know the company, its products, and the market it serves—hence he becomes a logical candidate to be considered for executive responsibilities. A statement made by Howard F. Larson, vice president of marine marketing for the Outboard Marine Corporation, illustrates this point. He notes that in his company there is a policy of making every effort to promote from within the company sales force. "That a man is employed by the Evinrude Division does not mean that he won't be considered for a promotion in some other division. As a matter of fact, we switch a good deal from division to division."[7] The salesman is also

---

[6] Bailey, *Incentives*, p. 15.
[7] Bailey, *Incentives*, p. 7.

Table 4–8

BASIS OF COMPENSATION FOR FIELD
SALES SUPERVISORS

Basis of Compensation	Percent of Mentions
Salary plus bonus	57.2%
Salary only	20.3
Salary plus commission	13.1
Salary plus bonus and commission	8.1
Commission only	1.3
Total	100.0%

Based on 223 sales forces, including 141 selling industrial products, 54 selling consumer products, and 28 selling services (e.g., insurance, transportation, gas, or electricity).
Source: Earl L. Bailey, *The First-line Sales Supervisor*, Experiences in Marketing Management No. 17. New York: The Conference Board, 1968, p. 6.

Table 4–9

AVERAGE COMPENSATION OF FIELD SALES SUPERVISORS IN 1966

Compensation Averages	All Sales Forces Reporting	Sales Forces Selling:		
		Industrial Products	Consumer Products	Services
Lowest reported	$ 7,000	$ 9,750	$ 7,000	$ 9,780
1st quartile	15,000	15,500	11,000	11,450
Median	17,500	18,000	15,665	15,000
3rd quartile	20,118	21,000	20,000	19,906
Highest reported	50,000	50,000	30,000+	27,500
Number of Sales Forces reporting	209	132	51	26

Based on sales-force averages reported by survey participants.
Source: Earl L. Bailey, *The First-line Sales Supervisor,* Experiences in Marketing Management No. 17. New York: The Conference Board, 1968, p. 6.

watched and observed by those to whom he sells. Customers frequently are looking for people with executive potential. It is not unusual for a salesman to be hired by a company he calls on.

Quotas

Incentive plans in selling are designed to motivate the salesman to fulfill or exceed the sales quota that has been set up for him. *Sales quotas* are the sales goals, or objectives, that a company sets for the upcoming year. These quotas are generally based on the number of units the company needs to sell

during the year in order to generate enough income so that it can pay all its costs of doing business and have a profit left over. This is an oversimplification of the quota-setting system—a company cannot simply decide how much sales volume it needs to come out with a profit and then go out and sell that volume. There are many factors that affect the sales volume any company can expect over a year; however, insofar as the salesmen are concerned, the company's projected, and desired, sales volume is called a *quota*. It is divided up among the company's salesmen and, if each salesman makes his share—his quota of sales—the company will reach its expressed goals. To accomplish this end, companies are willing to pay handsomely.

The total annual sales quota for the company is divided up among the company's salesmen—in terms of yearly, monthly, weekly, or even daily quotas. The salesmen who sell the greatest number of items, or have the greatest dollar volume of sales, or perhaps sell the best-balanced assortment of items in the line (or achieve whatever has been designated by the company as the most desirable sales goal) receive additional compensation, or a bonus, a special trip, some attractive merchandise prizes, or whatever other incentive the company has decided to offer as a reward for the achievement of their quotas.

An incentive that is usually popular with salesmen is an arrangement that bases salesmen's additional compensation on a rising percentage computed on his sales *at and over* quota. For example, if a salesman is given a quota of X sales and achieves his objective, he may receive Y percentage of the dollar sales he has made. If he surpasses his quota by so many units, then the additional sales, over quota, are worth a larger percentage—Y and another 3 percent, or whatever the company has agreed to pay.

In some cases, each sales increment over quota achieved by a salesman is good for an additional percentage that may apply to everything sold in excess of the salesman's original quota. For example, if a salesman sells five extra units, his compensation may be 2 percent greater for the overage; however, if he sells ten units over quota, the percentage of additional income may rise to 4 percent for all he sells over quota. There are all sorts of such incentive systems devised to get salesmen to extend themselves and sell over quota.

There is also what might be called a negative incentive system. If there are, say, ten salesmen for a company and each has a sales quota set for a given period of time, it is understood that those who do *not* reach their sales quota will be dismissed. One company makes it a practice to fire the salesman who sells the least each year. It is a regular policy (though an unwritten one) to release the low man on the totem pole at the end of each sales year. This is a negative system but it apparently inspires salesmen to meet, and even exceed, their quotas!

Another incentive that is frequently used to get sales attention and results on slow-moving merchandise is to put a "spiff" on it. That is, the sales manager will announce that he is prepared to pay an extra $5 for every one of the slow-moving items that the salesmen sell during a given period of time. The spiff incentive inspires salesmen to try hard to sell the slow-movers. This accounts for the enthusiastic sales presentations that customers may suddenly start to get from the salesman who has not even tried to sell the slow mover previously! It moves merchandise.

HOW THE SELLING ACTIVITY IS ORGANIZED

The concluding section of this chapter explains territorial arrangements for selling, whom the salesman reports to, and how he is guided.

The Sales Territory

The sales areas of companies vary widely. For some companies the market area may cover the entire nation or may even be international in scope. Other companies geographically limit their business by selling within a single city or within one or a limited number of states.

Large national companies may divide the United States into regions, designating perhaps a New England sales region, a North Central region, and so forth. Regions report to a home-office sales department.

Organizationally, regions usually have an administrative rather than an operational function. They are usually subdivided into sales districts; thus the New England sales region may be subdivided into districts designated as the Boston sales district, the New Haven sales office, and others. Some companies may organize in other ways—the sales districts may report directly to the home office. In any case, in larger companies it is the district office to which the salesman is assigned. Sales offices divide the sales area they are responsible for into sales territories of optimum size for one salesman. Each salesman is expected to cover one sales territory.

The extent of a sales territory is determined by many factors. Sales potential is a prime consideration. This is influenced by the number and size of accounts, geographical distances, frequency of calls, and types of service required at each stop. Boundaries of a territory assigned to a salesman may on occasion be changed; however, changes tend to be infrequent.

When a change in a territory is made, management usually makes the change with the utmost care, for the feelings of the salesman and the customers involved must be taken into account. Changing a sales territory is a delicate matter, for a salesman is encouraged to view the market area that is assigned to him as "his territory." Thus the accounts in the territory that he calls on are "his customers," and his customers view him as "their XYZ Company salesman."

The salesman-customer relationship is usually highly personal. Best results for a company and its salesman come after good personal rapport is established between the salesman and the customers he calls on. Most managements feel that good personal relationships are a valuable asset and do all they can to keep such relationships in good order.

By necessity, of course, salesmen are sometimes shifted from one territory to another, and areas or accounts are added to, or subtracted from, a territory. It is certainly necessary to be flexible and to change with the times. As business potential increases or diminishes, sales manpower must be adjusted to fit new requirements.

Salesmen are frequently assigned territories according to their experience. Thus, beginning salesmen are inclined to start their careers in less important areas. As they mature in their jobs, they may be switched to territories where their increasing competence can be put to better use.

A good salesman should be prepared for changes in his territory or for a switch from one territory to another. Since sales work is so highly personalized, some salesmen unfortunately make the mistake of identifying too closely with their territory or with the accounts they service. Thus they are resentful when they are asked to give up an account or to transfer to another territory.

The following example, provided by Harry L. Bullock, vice president of marketing with the Skil Corporation, illustrates how changes in sales districts come about and how managers in the sales field reason. The example shows why it is necessary for the good salesman to expect changes and to be stimulated rather than depressed by them.[8]

> We now look at our salesman in the Louisville area. We will call him Gordon Moore. Our records, plus comment from the man's regional manager, indicate that he is an experienced, capable man who handles all of our product lines well. But his sales cost is $10,-800 a year, just a little over our standard. We can't afford to keep him there.
>
> In the area just west of Louisville, in Evansville, Indiana, is Frank Smith. Smith is a new man with eighteen months experience and a

[8] *Sales cost* is the annual expenses to the company to keep the salesman in the field.

sales cost of $9,100. He is familiar with Kentucky, is aggressive, and has a good potential. But he can't handle the automotive line too well. In considering Frank Smith, we must look at the type of accounts in the Louisville-Lexington territory. The majority of sales in the area comes from our industrial line. Hardware is second in importance. There are three automotive accounts which contribute about $20,000 a year in sales. One of these automotive accounts is in the Portsmouth, Ohio, area, the fringe area of this territory. We decide to put Frank Smith in Louisville and to transfer the account in Portsmouth to Gordon Moore as part of a new Cincinnati territory. Now we have a territory.

The situation in this example was highly simplified.[1] There could have been a few very bad distributors, a lot of discount houses, an abnormally high use of one product or product line, a receding market, bad local distribution, or many other influences present. If there had been, we would have considered them along with other items at arriving at territorial boundaries.[9]

[1] Note that the names and data used in the example are fictional. They have no relation at all to actual Skil salesmen or sales.

To Whom Does the Salesman Report?

The salesman is immediately responsible to a field sales supervisor. The title of the field sales supervisor varies depending upon the company. Table 4–10 lists titles from 221 companies surveyed by The Conference Board. The title of the executive to whom the field sales supervisors report also varies

Table 4–10

TITLE OF FIELD SALES SUPERVISOR [1]

Title	Percent of Mentions
District sales manager (or district manager)	31%
Regional sales manager (or regional manager)	18
Sales manager	8
Branch manager	4
Field sales manager	4
Other titles	35
Total	100%

[1] Based on responses of 221 companies. Total title mentions (237) exceed the number of companies because a few reported for more than one sales force. In certain instances, more than one kind of title is used for first-level supervisors within the same sales force.
Source: Earl L. Bailey, *The First-line Sales Supervisor,* Experiences in Marketing Management No. 17. New York: The Conference Board, 1968, p. 3.

[9] *Allocating Field Sales Resources,* Experiences in Marketing Management No. 23. New York: The Conference Board, 1970, pp. 13–14.

widely, as shown in Table 4–11. Students of salesmanship should familiarize themselves with the job titles in the sales field; they are used frequently.

Studies indicate that the field sales supervisor, the salesman's immediate boss, has an average of seven salesmen reporting to him. This number varies widely, however. It was found that field sales supervisors for industrial products tend to supervise fewer salesmen than those in the consumer goods or services fields.

Who is the field sales supervisor? Most likely he was promoted to his position from the sales ranks. Undoubtedly he was a good salesman himself; however, he does not function as a supersalesman, although he may on occasion do some selling. His prime duty is to manage the salesmen for whom he

Table 4–11

TITLE OF EXECUTIVE TO WHOM
FIELD SALES SUPERVISOR REPORTS

Title of Executive	Percent of Mentions
Intermediate-area sales executive	33%
Regional sales manager	17
District sales manager	8
Area sales manager	2
Branch sales manager	2
Regional vice president	2
Other	2
High-level sales executive	46%
Sales manager (including director of sales or sales manager for single product line or market)	18
General sales manager	10
Vice president—sales	8
Field sales manager	5
National sales manager	3
Other	1
Marketing Executive	11%
Vice president—marketing	6
Marketing manager (or director)	5
General Executive	10%
Operating division head	5
Other	5
Total	100%

Based on responses of 212 companies. Total title mentions (225) exceed the number of companies because a few reported for more than one sales force. In certain instances, there are different reporting relationships for different field managers in the same sales force.
Source: Earl L. Bailey, *The First-line Sales Supervisor,* Experiences in Marketing Management No. 17. New York: The Conference Board, 1968, p. 4.

is responsible. He does this by training and motivating his salesmen; he plans and carries out his company's sales programs and policies in the field; he facilitates communications from the company to the salesmen and from the salesmen back to company headquarters. He is the confidant, trouble-shooter, controller, and counselor of his salesmen. By spending a great deal of time in the field with his staff, he usually is able to perform these duties in a realistic manner. Much of the training that beginning salesmen receive is done in the field under the direction of the field sales supervisor.

FIELD CHRONICLE

After a weekend's deliberation, John Elsworth chose to start his sales career in the home-sales division of B.C. Industries. It was a tough decision to make. He felt that all three of the company's divisions offered interesting kinds of sales careers—selling to retail store buyers who bought merchandise to resell, selling to builders and architects who bought building materials for construction, and selling to homeowners who were improving or remodeling their homes. He decided that calling on homeowners who wanted estimates on home improvements would offer the greatest challenge and variety. He remembered what that veteran star salesman, Harry Katzman, had said about young people taking it easy on themselves, so he decided to plunge in on what so many executives had praised—the grass-roots level of selling. He thought it would be the best spot possible for learning about the ultimate consumer.

Elsworth was to work with an experienced salesman for a month, after which time he would make calls on his own. He was assigned to work with Harry Kelly, an old-timer with twenty-five years experience. He was introduced to Kelly on Friday afternoon. They arranged to meet in the company's sales office on Monday morning so they could start making calls together. Here is part of what happened that first Monday morning.

KELLY: (*Greeting Elsworth as he walks over to Kelly's desk to report for work.*) Good morning, John. Glad to see you here so bright and early.

ELSWORTH: Don't know about the bright part, but for a Monday morning this sure *is* early.

KELLY: What's the matter? Have a rough weekend?

ELSWORTH: No, not really. Just making conversation.

KELLY: A salesman's never a complainer, my boy.

ELSWORTH: (*Noting an inflection on the word* boy.) What's this "my boy" business?

KELLY: Just wondering how old you are. With your hair so long, you could be a fugitive from some high school.

ELSWORTH: I'm twenty-two, and I don't see what my hair has to do with my age.

KELLY: When people are shelling out their hard-earned cash to have their homes remodeled, it may take them five years to pay it off. They want to talk to someone they can have confidence in.

ELSWORTH: A young guy's got to start out. Besides, I'm a college graduate.

KELLY: There's only one school that'll teach you anything about selling. It's called the College of Hard Knocks. That's where I learned —the hard way. Never went further than the tenth grade, and I can sell circles around any college graduate. You'll see.

ELSWORTH: I'm sure I have a lot to learn. That's why they've assigned me to you in particular.

KELLY: You kids coming out of college don't even try to look like businessmen. Look at that hair and those bright clothes. Do you want people to look at *you*, or at what you're selling? You just make problems for yourself looking like that when you're a salesman.

STOP & THINK

1. What is bothering Kelly? Why?
2. What should Elsworth do in order to get off on the right foot with Kelly?
3. How serious is the issue about Elsworth's appearance?

COMPANY CHRONICLE

Elsworth discovered that there was more to learn than just calling on prospects in their homes. His biggest problem was learning about company procedures, policies, and products. Not only was he expected to know about matters pertaining to B.C. Industries, but because he was referred to each prospect by a department store and because billings went through the department store, people felt he should know all about the department store, too. Elsworth spent several hours each morning either in formal training sessions held by the B.C. Industries home-sales training division or in studying literature at his desk. He quickly found a confidant in another young college graduate, Bill Simmons, also a trainee, who had started six months earlier. The two young men had coffee one morning during Elsworth's second week.

ELSWORTH: Bill, I'm absolutely swamped, trying to learn everything I'm supposed to know.

SIMMONS: I know. It's really deadly at first.

ELSWORTH: Doesn't this slack off? How can you concentrate on making outside calls when there's so much inside studying and work to do?

SIMMONS: Well, after six months, I'm still up to my ears. But it does let up some. I find I don't have to read *everything* anymore. I just sort through it because a lot of it gets repetitive when you know something about it. You've got to learn how to spot what's important. You don't have time to read everything.

ELSWORTH: I didn't realize there was so much homework connected with sales work. I thought that was all over. Doesn't homework ever end?

SIMMONS: I don't see any end to it. I don't find it a grind, though. The payoff on this kind of homework comes so quickly. When I'm in a customer's home, I seem to use just about everything I know. The newer the information, the better it is to use, it seems.

ELSWORTH: Don't you learn to bluff a lot after you get experience? Right now, I'm so stupid about everything, I can't even bluff with conviction!

SIMMONS: Well, I'm not ready to bluff even after six months. Actually, I hope I never will be ready to do that.

STOP & THINK

1. Why is there so much homework connected with sales work?

2. What about bluffing? What should a trainee's policy toward bluffing be?

3. What should a salesman do when he does not have the answer to a customer's question?

PROBLEMS

A Black Graduate's Dilemma. Donald Howard, a black student, was ready to graduate from college. He wanted to get into sales work, where he felt that his knack for getting along with people could be put to good use. He had two job offers. Both offered the same starting salary. One job was to sell insurance for a black-owned life insurance company. The other was with a white-owned Chevrolet automobile dealership. Howard would be the first black sales trainee ever hired by this dealer. Present customers of the dealership where almost all white. Howard knew little about life insurance, whereas he had always had a deep interest in automobiles.

STOP & THINK

1. What factors should Howard consider in deciding which job to take?

2. What special problems would Howard have in selling in each situation?

How Does One's Own Background Relate to Success in a Territory? Geraldine Laski was born and brought up in Cincinnati, Ohio. Upon graduation from junior college she got a position with a large cosmetic firm selling their products in department stores. The company had three-week special promotions in different department stores during which their own sales staff were added to the regular department store sales staff. Miss Laski had a choice of two sales territories. She could work in New York City, selling in large department stores there, or she could work in small cities of 50,000 to 150,000 population in Indiana and Illinois.

STOP & THINK

1. What factors should Miss Laski take into consideration in making this choice?
2. Does where Miss Laski was brought up have any relationship to her potential success in a sales territory?

Is the Best Salesman the Best Candidate for the Assistant Sales Manager's Job? Tim O'Reilly was finishing up his first year as a salesman for a typewriter manufacturer. One day he had a long talk with one of the company's older salesmen, Nels Swensen.

O'REILLY: I've really got to push to exceed my quota this period.
SWENSEN: You really do push yourself hard, Tim. Why is being the district's top producer so important to you?
O'REILLY: I want to get promoted to assistant district manager as quickly as possible.
SWENSEN: What makes you think they pick the guy who's got the best sales record?
O'REILLY: I thought it was just natural that the man with the best sales record would be offered opportunities for promotion into management jobs.
SWENSEN: Not by a long shot. The best salesman could make the worst sales manager.
O'REILLY: I think it's unfair not to reward the top salesman with promotion opportunities.
SWENSEN: Being a good salesman and being a good sales manager are two totally different things.
O'REILLY: I don't see why a man who sells well shouldn't be able to be a good leader for others to follow.
SWENSEN: If you get to be too good at doing something, you don't get promoted because you're too hard to replace.

STOP & THINK

1. How do you evaluate Swensen's arguments?
2. How do the qualifications for salesman and sales manager differ? Are the two sets of qualifications apt to be found in the same man?

CHAPTER REVIEW AND DISCUSSION QUESTIONS

1. How do you view future opportunities in the sales field in general? What about the opportunities for women and members of minority groups?
2. Are customers or are employers responsible for the lack of women and blacks in the sales field?
3. Explain sales remuneration procedures.
4. Should the beginning salesman work on a salary or on a commission plan? Which would you prefer? Why?
5. Why are remuneration methods for salesmen different from those for other company employees?
6. On the basis of what you have read in this chapter, how would you say salesmen in general view remuneration plans?
7. What are sales quotas and what purpose do they serve?
8. Explain territorial arrangements for selling.
9. To whom is the salesman responsible in the company?
10. How would you describe the qualifications necessary to become a field sales supervisor?

5

COMMUNICATIONS AND
THE PSYCHOLOGY OF SELLING

A man who whispers down a well,
About the goods he has to sell,
Will never reap a crop of dollars,
As he who climbs a tree and hollers.

—ANON.

Certain words suffer when they are defined. "Communications," a term vital to salesmanship, is one such word. Modern dictionaries define communications as "the imparting, conveying, or exchange of ideas or knowledge." This definition is terribly sterile for a word so rich and vast in its implications. Older dictionaries did the word more justice with this definition: "Communications is to share." It is with a sense of *sharing* that the modern solution-centered salesman communicates.

The story is told of an auction sale at which the furnishings of an old homestead were being sold. The auctioneer sold the furnishings one by one uneventfully until he came to a dusty old violin. He held the violin high above his head and started the bidding at $5. There were no takers. He reduced the bid to as low as $1, but there still were no takers. At this point a white-haired old man who had been sitting quietly at the back of the room came up. He took the violin and placed it under his chin, closed his eyes, and played. The exquisite music of a famous sonata filled the noisy room, which suddenly became hushed. When the old man finished, he placed the violin on the auctioneer's table and left the room. The bidding started once again. This time the auctioneer started the bidding at $100. Heated bidding ensued. The instrument, which minutes before had no takers at $1, sold for several hundred dollars. The difference, of course, was communications, in the sense of sharing. A master salesman had *shared* the virtues of a product, and the sale had been made.

COMMUNICATIONS

With the advent of solution-centered selling, communications has become more important than ever. To solve problems, a two-way flow of communications is required. In the old approaches to salesmanship, being a good talker was a prime requirement. The ability to communicate *in the sense of sharing*, however, does not place emphasis on being a good or a fast talker. In fact, the person who talks too much or too fast, to the exclusion of listening, may well talk himself right out of a sale. Communications in the sharing sense is much, much more than the ability to talk. *There is a great difference between talking and saying something.* Many people talk, but only a few say something. It is *what* you say that counts.

A successful sales manager talking to a class in salesmanship not too long ago surprised the students by stating that clarity in explaining things was a major quality found in the best salesmen. A freshman student asked, sensibly, "How is clarity achieved?" The sales manager's answer is well worth thinking about. He said, "Mainly by taking the trouble to completely understand what it is that you are selling and by talking to serve people rather than to impress them." In the discussion that followed this statement, the sales manager brought out another significant point. He said, "Good salesmen should use common words to say uncommon things."

Let us suppose we could, by some stretch of the imagination, listen to a randomly selected cross-section of several hundred real-life sales presentations. Suppose further that we could count the number of words used in each presentation. Would the number of words or amount of talking done by the best salesman exceed the amount of talking done by the poorest salesman? Of course not. Obviously it is the *quality* of what is said, rather than the quantity of words that counts.

An interesting question to ask a sales manager who supervises many salesmen is, "Who talks most, a good salesman or a poor one?" A sales manager will usually think about the question for a while and then almost invariably say that *the good salesman probably talks less!* We then ask a further question: "Does this mean that better salesmen communicate less?" "Certainly not!" is invariably the emphatic reply to this suggestion. Sales managers feel that: *The better salesmen talk less but communicate more* because communicating is much more than just talking. Good communication involves many skills. Among them are the ability

> to listen
>
> to demonstrate
>
> to dramatize both verbally and nonverbally
>
> to ask questions
>
> to supply answers to questions
>
> to inspire confidence and belief
>
> to create involvement

Let us analyze input and output, two aspects of two-way communications as applied to salesmanship.

Input

The salesman must draw information from a prospect. He must act as a sponge and soak up everything possible so he can clearly understand and define the circumstances surrounding the customer's problem. *In solution-centered selling, a customer's needs are viewed as problems, and problems cannot be properly solved until they are defined.*

Let us consider the example of a young man who comes into the clothing department of a sporting goods store to buy an outfit for skiing—and we can see how a communications input flow is established so it leads to a sale. After greeting the prospect, the good salesman will tactfully find out the size required, the price range the young man feels he can afford, whether light or heavy weight in materials is preferred, whether the customer plans to ski downhill or cross country, and so on. While getting the essential information about requirements, the salesman will also probe a bit about what factors are important to the prospect so he will know what to stress when he later talks about the merchandise. This probe is known as determination of a prospect's value scale, an important subject that will be treated in detail later on in this chapter.

In the case of the skiing outfit, the value probe would attempt to determine priorities of values such as the following: Which is more important, the style and appearance of the outfit, or the quality of the materials and the workmanship? Is getting a bargain on price more important than getting exactly what one wants? Which is more important while skiing, being warm and comfortable (a bulky outfit is all right), or looking sexy and stylishly dressed (a skintight outfit is a necessity)?

It should be quite obvious that the salesman who successfully secures all this information about the customer and his problems has the sale more than half made before he even starts showing merchandise. He knows exactly what he is looking for when he selects merchandise to show the customer— this will save the customer's time and set the right mood for the sale. Armed with such information, the salesperson will show merchandise that falls within the parameters required for solving the customer's problem.

How many times have you gone into a store only to become disgusted when a salesperson started showing you merchandise that you were not remotely interested in? The reaction to being shown what you do not need is to want to walk out of the store, something that probably all of us have done under such circumstances.

Output

We have shown that the initial and most important part of the sale is the communications input of information. Input comes before output because it is essential that the salesman understand the problem and the customer's requirements *before* he goes into the second part of the sale—the output, or serious information communications flow from the salesman to the customer. Here the salesman demonstrates products and explains their features as they relate to the customer's problem and scale of values. The salesman will review all the features of the merchandise he is showing; however, he will stress those that he feels are most important to the prospect. In other words, if, in the example of the skiing outfit, the salesman has determined that fashion is most important to the prospect, he will only briefly mention tailoring and quality of materials and will emphasize such things as the name of the designer, endorsement of the merchandise by sports personalities, appearance of similar outfits in high fashion magazines, and so forth. It is clear that the salesman who has done best to draw out the prospect in terms of his needs and values can most easily and effectively present his stock of merchandise so it will sell.

> If the problem of the prospect is well told,
> The goods become more than half sold!

It is very much up to the salesman to get the prospect to state honestly and clearly what he wants. This is not an easy task. Most people have difficulty in communicating and, indeed, in understanding their own motivations. It is sometimes hard for us to know why we did or did not do something.

Customers have difficulty in being forthright because so many of their reasons for buying are based on emotion rather than on logic. The image that each person likes to present to the world is that of a logical, rational, and sensible person. Yet this image is often false. Is it logical for an older woman to buy ridiculously expensive skin cosmetics that she thinks will restore the skin she had when she was twenty? Is it rational when a man buys an automobile with more horsepower than he can ever use but that he still pays taxes on and buys gasoline for? Is it sensible for families to commit themselves to costly country or yacht club memberships because it enhances their status?

When marketing researchers interview the public, they find people who state that they bought their Cadillac because the deal was too good to turn down, or who bought their Chrysler Imperial because it was economical. A clever salesman probably provided them with these reasons so they would be more inclined to buy the cars. *Good salesmen know that in order to make customers succumb to emotional drives to buy they must provide them with logical-sounding excuses so they can later justify to others what is essentially an illogical act.* If a woman buys a dress that she really does not need, she has to be able to go home and tell her husband that it was reduced from $22.50 to $14.99! A man who bought a power lathe for $85 has got to be able to say it will reduce home-maintenance costs, even though he has never spent a dime on anything in the house involving the use of a lathe!

It is very important that the salesman establish his identity and his legitimacy as quickly as possible. Until the prospect is sure that he is speaking to a reputable person he will not give the salesman his complete attention. This is because part of his attention will be diverted to wondering about the salesman, what company he works for, the nature of his business, and so forth.

✓ At the very outset, the salesman should state clearly his name, the name of the company he works for, and its business. Handing out a business card at this point is advantageous, for it carries the authority and stability that print conveys. A calling card very often is saved and kept in the prospect's reference file, where it may be referred to for future needs.

Largely as a matter of seeking information, a salesman may often arouse suspicion during the input stage of communicating. People become wary and suspicious when they are questioned if the reason for the questioning is uncertain. Information will be withheld unless the prospect feels that it is to his advantage to reveal it. The following are examples of the right way and the wrong way to question a customer.

Scene: A salesman is selling fireproof siding for a house.

Wrong: How much do you pay for fire insurance on your house?
Right: Siding can affect the fire insurance rates on your house. What rates do you pay now?

Many people are by nature secretive and cautious. Sometimes a salesman can get information indirectly. For example, if it is necessary to establish a person's age, instead of asking about age directly, the salesman could ask when the person graduated from high school. Since most people graduate at eighteen, a fairly accurate determination of age can be made in this way. Income estimates are often essential for selling, yet it would be highly indiscreet to ask for such information directly. Questions about the kind of work the prospect does, his educational level, what the wife or husband does, where and how a person lives, all serve as bases for income determination.

ANALYZE THE PSYCHOLOGY
Which Is Apt to Arouse Less Caution?

Scene: A middle-aged woman explains to a salesman that she is interested in buying a frame for a new pair of glasses.

SITUATION A
SALESMAN: Do you want something youthful or something conservative looking?
PROSPECT: I'm not sure what I want.

SITUATION B
SALESMAN: Let me show you the styles that are selling best right now.
PROSPECT: That sounds like a good idea.

Every salesman must be acutely aware of the emotional level that consciously or unconsciously influences each person. People are largely unaware that they make buying decisions emotionally. If they are aware of emotional influences they either do not reveal them or at least are reluctant to expose them.

OVERCOMING COMMUNICATIONS BLOCKS

It is the job of the salesman to help people become good communicators. This is where applied psychology plays such an important role.

We have described communications in terms of flow. There is an input flow—information and observations about needs and values, which the salesman draws into his mind from the prospect—and an output flow—information about merchandise and services, which the salesman sends out to the mind of the prospect. Thus communications in sales depends on *flow facilitation.* How can the salesman facilitate a two-way communications flow? There are many psychological techniques that can be used to facilitate communications. Let us first consider some of the many factors that can distort or retard communications—the so-called common blocks to communications.

Suspicion of Others. People are usually distrustful and suspicious of strangers. The initial contact between a salesman and a prospect is in essence a case of two strangers meeting for the first time.

Reluctance to Disturb the Status Quo. One of the most common brush-offs the salesman gets is, "I don't want to be bothered." Even when prospects do not say it in so many words, we can assume that many of them are thinking, "I wish he wouldn't disturb me." Coupled with this thought is, "How can I get rid of him?"

To handle these thoughts we must understand why people do not wish to be disturbed. Mostly it is because they are satisfied with the status quo. They are inclined to accept things as they are because to do otherwise might create problems. Most people resist change. Therefore, they do not wish to cooperate with anyone who in their eyes threatens to change things. The problem is one of cooperation. How do you encourage cooperation? By being courteous, pleasant, and above all, interesting. Once you capture interest, people cooperate because it makes them feel pleasant to do so.

ANALYZE THE PSYCHOLOGY
Why Is One Approach More Promising Than the Other?

Scene: A salesman approaches a man looking at a camera.

SITUATION A
SALESMAN: Good morning. This spring weather reminds us that good picture-taking weather is just around the corner, doesn't it?
PROSPECT: Yes, I suppose so.

SITUATION B
SALESMAN: Good morning. May I help you?
PROSPECT: No, I'm just looking.

Fear of Looking Bad in the Eyes of Others. Prospects do not react only in terms of themselves. It is a matter of fact that *people are often influenced more by what others who are important to them think than by what they think themselves.* A woman will react to an array of shoes in a shoe department in terms of what her husband is going to say; a purchasing agent will respond to a purchasing proposition in terms of how a production foreman will view the decision; and a dress buyer will be influenced by whether the sales force in her department will be enthusiastic about a proposed line of dresses.

It is one thing for people to make a mistake that affects only themselves. However, if they make a mistake where others are involved they may be held answerable and it might be a long time before they are allowed to forget about the mistake! Thus, when a prospect is concerned about what others may think, he becomes more cautious and careful. The seasoned salesman realizes that unusual hesitation and caution may be signs that the prospect is concerned about the opinion of someone else. A probe is needed, to determine the reason for the caution. This is often tricky, because people do not like to reveal that they may not be their own master. Therefore, a great deal of tact and ingenuity is required by the salesman when he tries to determine whether there is an outside influence involved in dealing with a prospect.

One approach for the salesman is to try to guess at what the outside influence might be, so he can deal with it. From his experience, the knowledgeable salesman will know what kinds of outside influences might be affecting a particular type of prospect. The three examples given earlier are quite typical: the wife being concerned about her husband, the purchasing agent about the production foreman, and the buyer about her sales staff. The salesman in each example might probe by guessing in the following manner.

ANALYZE THE PSYCHOLOGY
How Does the Salesman Follow Up Once the Outside Influence Is Revealed?

SITUATION A (*The woman in the shoe department.*)
SALESWOMAN: Which pair do you think your husband would like?
PROSPECT: Oh, he prefers to see me in dark shoes, but I like these red ones best.

SITUATION B (*The purchasing agent considering a purchasing proposition.*)
SALESMAN: Is there anyone in your production department who would want to size up this situation?
PROSPECT: Yes, I was thinking that Bud Ashley, our production foreman, might like to take a look at it.

SITUATION C (*The dress buyer considering a line of dresses.*)
SALESMAN: Is your sales force familiar with our dress line?
PROSPECT: I'm not sure they know about it, since your line is only handled by stores on the West Coast.

Preoccupation With Other Matters. A salesman often has a great deal of difficulty keeping a prospect's attention focused on what he is saying. There frequently are so many distractions. A salesman in a retail store will find a mother trying to keep a lively youngster out of mischief while he is trying to

explain the complexities of a sewing machine. A salesman calling on a buyer for a wholesale grocer finds that the telephone rings when he is in the middle of a demonstration of a new cake mix.

In addition to these obvious distractions, there are more subtle distractions. All minds wander, just as yours does when you are listening to a lecture or to a friend tell a story. All of us are distracted at times by our own thoughts. Let us consider the kinds of personal distractions that might prevent a buyer from listening to us. Let us tune in on some of the thoughts that may be running through his mind while we are talking to him. "Why did the boss say to call him as soon as he gets back from lunch?" "What should I say when I can interrupt this salesman who is talking to me now?" "I wonder if my coughing just now means that I'm catching cold?" and so on.

What a salesman has to say is usually poor competition for the things that run through the prospect's mind; therefore, he must be extremely skillful at mastering the difficult art of holding a person's attention. Following are a few rules which help to keep attention focused on what is being said.

1. Appeal to more than just the sense of hearing. If it is at all appropriate involve one or more of the other senses—sight, touch, smell, sound, and taste. Involving more than one sense intensifies the experience and, correspondingly, concentrates the focus of attention on the matter at hand. Good salesmen augment their presentations with demonstrations and, whenever possible, try to get prospects involved by having them handle, taste, manipulate, or even smell samples or prototypes.

2. Avoid being long-winded and irrelevant. Get to the point and use changes of pace. Watch for signals that the prospect's attention may be wandering. When you notice that attention is wandering, change your tactic, shorten what you plan to say, or use some device to refocus attention on what you are doing.

3. Get the person you are talking to involved in the conversation. Ask questions that cannot be answered yes or no. Seek opinions; get the other person to ask questions, too.

4. Use human-interest devices occasionally. The good salesman realizes that there is more to a sales call than just business. Thus he equips himself with news, perhaps of competitors, that may be of interest to a buyer, stories that can get a laugh, and anecdotes that relax and enlighten. One of the reasons salesmen are given expense accounts to entertain customers is so they can be free to pursue a prospect's undivided attention—which is often likely to result over a cup of coffee, or at lunch or dinner.

ANALYZE THE PSYCHOLOGY
How Should an Interruption Be Handled?

Scene: A buyer with whom it is difficult to get an appointment had his boss come in and for 15 minutes interrupt an important new-product presentation being made by an office machine salesman.

SITUATION A
SALESMAN: Your boss sure seems to have a lot on his mind. Do you want me to come back some other time to make this presentation?

SITUATION B
SALESMAN: You will remember that I was just explaining the third step on how this machine works. May I continue?

SITUATION C
SALESMAN: Let me review the highlights of what we have covered so far.

Unwarranted Assumptions. Salesmen sometimes assume too much knowledge on the part of the prospect. This is an erroneous assumption easy for both teachers and salesmen to make. Since both talk about their subjects day in and day out, they may get to a point where they assume that certain basic things are so elementary as to be common knowledge. A salesman is in many ways a teacher—a large part of his business is to inform or teach people about his product or service. You have been a student for most of your life, so you know a great deal about the receiving end of teaching. If you are a serious student of salesmanship, you might begin to ask yourself about the characteristics of a good teacher and then apply the relevant traits of good teaching to salesmanship. By doing this you will find you can make some helpful adaptations from the teaching field to the selling field.

Sometimes communications blocks arise, although the salesman may not be aware of it, because the prospect is lacking information. Many people are reluctant to admit their ignorance of something that the salesman treats as elementary. Also, as soon as a gap in knowledge occurs, there is a break in the prospect's chain of thought and his attention may be lost for the rest of the presentation. Another danger with a gap in knowledge is that the prospect might make a wrong guess about what he does not know and so distort his general reaction to a presentation.

There is also a danger, of course, in being too elementary. A listener will become irritated or let his attention wander when the salesman is dealing with what is obvious. It is often difficult for a salesman to judge the level of competence of the person to whom he is talking. He can interject questions into his presentation from time to time, to attempt to determine the understanding level. When the prospect seems hazy as to what he understands, points can be repeated but at the same time new information should be added to the old so the prospect is not offended by sheer repetition.

ANALYZE THE PSYCHOLOGY

Scene: A salesman in a nursery is selling plants and shrubbery to a weekend gardener who expresses an interest in doing some landscaping.

SITUATION A
SALESMAN: Do you want flowering shrubs or nonflowering shrubbery?
PROSPECT: I really don't know.
SALESMAN: We have a good selection of Douglas fir and some fine yews, if you want nonbloomers. There are forsythias, lilacs, and bridal wreath on sale, if you're interested in those.

SITUATION B
SALESMAN: I'll be glad to show you what we've got. There are nonbloomers like yews that grow slowly and keep their shape well with little care. Then there are bloomers like forsythias, which are covered with beautiful yellow flowers very early in the spring.
PROSPECT: Oh, I think I know what they are. Let me take a look at them.

Use of Emotion-Triggering Words and Subjects. Words are powerful. They are also the stock-in-trade of the salesman, so he must learn to use them with care and discretion. Words and the ideas they express can trigger emotions. Skillful use of words can pave the way to a sale. Clumsy use can lose a sale.

Obviously coarse or crude language should be avoided. No one is ever condemned for using proper language; when using crudities there is always the danger of offending. Why take the chance?

Examples of emotion-triggering words are integration, Democrat, Republican, Catholic, Jew, stupid, and hippie. Examples of emotion-triggering subjects are the women's liberation movement, abortion laws, birth control, and U.S. foreign policy.

Because they are emotion-triggering, such words and subjects are avoided, for as soon as emotion enters into the sales picture communica blocks appear. Once a salesman hits a customer's emotional sore spot, he jeopardizes his chances for doing future business. This does not mean that the salesman has to give up the right to express his beliefs. This is something he is encouraged to do—but *not* when he is working as a salesman! The salesman should express his views in his nonworking hours.

ANALYZE THE PSYCHOLOGY

Scene: A salesman enters the office of a customer he calls on regularly.

SITUATION A
CUSTOMER: Did you hear the President's speech last night?
SALESMAN: Wasn't he the perfect moron? What he knows about economics my five-year-old son could improve on!

SITUATION B
CUSTOMER: Did you hear the moronic speech the President made last night? What he knows about economics, my five-year-old son could improve on!
SALESMAN: Yes. It really was quite a speech. He sure covered a lot of ground. His talk could have been interpreted as being inflationary. That's a reason you should be keeping your stock inventories up.

THE PSYCHOLOGY OF SELLING

Salesmanship is a matter of establishing relationships with people. In order to maintain a relationship, it must be desirable for both parties. The better the give-and-take balance between the two parties, the more likely it is that the relationship will flourish and continue. A basic characteristic of human nature is the tendency to seek what offers us the greatest amount of personal satisfactions.

If you have difficulty establishing and maintaining friends, it means that you are not giving satisfactions to others. It means that you have a blind spot concerning the needs of others or that you are not interested in relating to others. If you expect to become a salesman or a saleswoman you must become interested in the needs of others; you must remove the blind spots and develop an awareness of what people want from relationships. Unless relationships promise satisfaction they will be discontinued.

Persuasion by Doing for Others: The Material Level

What do people want from each other? They have wants on two levels— the physical or material level and the emotional or nonmaterial level. Salesmen are perhaps more aware of the material than they are of the nonmaterial level. Better salesmen may have a deeper understanding of the emotions. Salesmen generally are aware that what they have to sell must be competitive in price and quality, and that the money that they are asking the prospect to part with must yield returns in satisfaction and efficiency equal or superior to spending the same money for other purposes. Thus on the material level people respond to receiving exceptional value for their money. Whether they actually do receive superior value or not is beside the point: they must believe that they have received exceptional value—this is what is important. Often when they believe they are responding on the material level they are actually responding on the emotional level. This particular point is a strange one indeed, yet it is very true. It is easily proved in marketing research by use of the so-called blind test. Housewives who maintain that one brand of vegetable shortening or detergent is superior to all others are given a selection of brands to use. Each brand is packaged in exactly the same unlabeled container. In the blind test, housewives are extremely unreliable in selecting their favorite brand as the one that they feel is best. Men do no better in blind tests when they are asked to select motor oils, beer, or cigars that they swear by. This all helps to prove that the sales effort is often more important in creating satisfaction than the product itself. A useful thing to know in sales is that *people buy and use images of products and services instead of the products and services themselves.* Thus the salesman who instills in customers the most satisfying *images* has the most satisfied customer.

On the material level, customers respond to the receiving of favors. Salesmen are often very active in this area, depending upon the nature of their product and the customs of their particular industry. In the kind of selling where the salesman calls on the same buyer at least once a month, doing favors for the buyer becomes quite an art and sometimes a necessity. Studies show that buyers in the resale goods area and in industrial purchasing are most concerned with showing their superiors that they are doing their jobs well (as compared with shoppers, who seek only personal satisfaction). Many salesmen who call on them know this, so they concentrate on providing them with information, ideas, gifts, and special greetings.

Passing Along Information

Here is an example of how the passing along of information works. A salesman hears that a competitor of a buyer's company is getting bids on machinery that is going to double the competitor's productive capacity at its Elkhart, Indiana, plant. The salesman passes the information on to the buyer as a favor. The buyer in turn will pass the information on to his boss, who will be very interested in knowing this—thus the buyer is made to look good in the eyes of his boss. The salesman has facilitated the buyer's prime ambition—to look good in the eyes of his superior. Since relationships tend to maintain a two-way balance, chances are that this salesman will be favored with future orders.

Passing Along Ideas

Here is an example of how the passing on of an idea works. A salesman covers the buying offices of food chains in the states of Ohio, Indiana, and

Illinois. He knows that one of the chief problems of food-store buyers is thinking up imaginative, sales-creating "specials" for the weekend newspaper grocery advertisements. In talking to a food buyer for a chain in Toledo, Ohio, he hears that a Memorial Day weekend special that featured—all for $1.65—a pound of hot dogs, a dozen hot dog rolls, and a special map of the state of Ohio showing all bicycle trails in the state, was a sellout success. When the same salesman talks to a buyer in Fort Wayne, Indiana, he tells him about the exceptionally successful Toledo Memorial Day promotion, suggesting that the buyer consider a similar promotion in Fort Wayne for the Labor Day weekend. The Fort Wayne buyer might well consider such a suggestion and run a similar promotion over Labor Day. The success of the promotion will make this buyer look good in the eyes of his superiors. Certainly if the promotion is a success, and chances are that it will be because it is a tested idea, the buyer will remember the salesman who provided him with it and will be inclined to be partial to him in passing out future orders.

Gift Giving

Here is an example of how the giving of a gift assists in the sales effort. But before we get into the example, let us consider the whole idea of gifts. Whether gift giving is good or bad is highly debatable. It has been debated for years and the problem will probably continue to be unresolved as long as people sell to one another! Unfortunately gift giving is, in many selling areas, a fact of life that salesmen must live with whether they like it or not. In some industries, regrettably, gifts often amount to bribery for getting an order. The question of the ethics of gift giving is discussed in Chapter 10.

Many sales departments have policies against giving gifts to buyers. Indeed, it is against the law to offer one customer something that you do not offer all other customers. The law is easily circumvented, however, because the salesman who gives the gift and the buyer who receives it are not going to publicize the fact. Many companies have policies that prohibit their buyers from accepting gifts. Some even go as far as to send letters to sales departments of supplier companies in November stating that their buyers are not allowed to accept Christmas gifts. The whole area of gifts in selling is a sticky one. Fortunately, sales supervisors are very much aware of the problem so they usually establish policy for the individual salesman to follow. In other words, if you get a job in a sales area where gift giving is an issue, your supervisors, who are experienced in such matters, will advise you on how to handle such matters.

When a gift is an individualized effort intended to be of help to a buyer, and where the cost is minimal, there may be justification for the practice, as in the following example. A salesman once heard a buyer complain that he had trouble in limiting salesmen who called on him to thirty minutes a call. Later the salesman brought the buyer an hourglass that contained sand that dropped for thirty minutes. The buyer was so pleased that he used it on all salesmen who called on him—except the one who gave him the glass!

Using Western Union

A number of salesmen take advantage of special services offered by Western Union. In some cases they give WU a list of customers, including their dates of birth, anniversaries, and special occasions to be remembered. When the dates roll around, Western Union sends a special greeting signed with the salesman's name. One salesman, for a change of pace, from time to time leaves a special "thank-you gram" on file with WU. At the end of each day he phones in a list of customers who placed significant orders. The very next morning these customers find a thank-you message in the familiar attention-getting yellow envelope on their desks. What is probably the most popular WU promotion service used by salesmen is Telegram-Plus, a service that consists of the simultaneous delivery of an item and a telegram message at a specified time. The sales material or product samples to be delivered with telegrams are sent to the appropriate WU offices in advance and are stored until delivery day. Western Union is also used to awaken salesmen at a given hour or to start the day off with reminder or encouragement messages an alert sales manager may have specified!

Persuasion by Doing for Others: The Nonmaterial Level

On the nonmaterial level there are human needs for responsiveness, understanding, approval, encouragement, and sympathy. These needs are filled largely by interaction between two individuals in communication—mainly by conversation. If conversation does not provide fulfillment for the nonmaterial needs, human relationship will not flourish. A salesman whose conversation does not provide for human needs will find that customers will give him little time or attention.

The Importance of Respect

The starting point for providing for the human needs in conversation is the quality of respect. If the speaker does not have the respect of the person he is talking to, his approval or sympathy will be meaningless or perhaps will even serve to irritate. Therefore, any salesman must work hard to be a person whom others can and will respect. Respect stems from courtesy, a sense of fairness, integrity, honesty, and sincerity. Once these are established, conversation will begin to provide human satisfactions for others.

When to Stay and When to Go

A salesman who has a quota of calls to make each day cannot, of course, spend an inordinate amount of time on any one call. From an efficiency point of view, what he would like to do is to give his sales pitch, get his order, and get on to the next account as quickly as possible. But this approach, while practical, is not solution-oriented. This is doing things from the salesman's point of view and harks back to the older eras of selling,

where emphasis was on pushing products on customers without concern for their needs. This is not communications in the sharing sense nor does it provide for human needs.

Admittedly, the salesman cannot spend unlimited amounts of time on each call. His time is his most precious resource; therefore, he must manage it and use it so it will produce maximum results. He must learn to judge when to linger and listen and when to wind things up and leave. One study of industrial sales showed that it cost a company $40 for each call that a salesman made. Clearly this kind of cost means that each call must substantially further the sales effort.

Deciding when to leave is a matter of sizing up the mood of the customer.

If the mood is social and the customer merely wants an audience so he can replay the seventh hole of yesterday's golf game, or explain what the dentist did when he put in that new crown, it is clearly a time to cut things short without being rude.

On the other hand, if deeper emotions are involved, it might be best to sit back and listen even if the conversation has nothing at all to do with the salesman's business. If the buyer is talking about a problem he had with someone in the accounting department that morning he probably is looking for sympathy—reassurance that the way he handled the accountant was right. He may be looking for suggestions on what to do next. A salesman should view a customer's willingness to share a problem—be it personal or business—as a sign of definite progress, for he has evidence that he has won a customer's respect. People are inclined to share problems only with those whom they respect. The salesman should also sit back and listen when a customer starts telling him about a victory. If he starts talking about how his company won a coveted contract in competition with three other firms or how he outsmarted another salesman who tried to put something over on him, it is time to listen. In such instances, the customer is trying to impress the salesman. He needs someone to brag to and he is selecting someone who he feels is worthy of knowing about his or his company's sterling qualities!

The Essence of Listening

When the salesman is listening he should be a good listener and give the talker the feeling that he has an exceptionally good audience. If the salesman has done a good job of listening, when he leaves, the customer will think: "My, what a fine fellow Mr. X is. What a good conversationalist." (This will happen even if the salesman has not said a word, for often when people say someone is a good conversationalist, they mean that he is a good listener!)

Being a good listener is a matter not only of being attentive; it is also a matter of appearing and acting attentive. Nodding occasionally as you are listening, interjecting words of agreement, asking a question for a clarification from time to time—all serve to establish a person as a good listener.

Conclusion

The subject matter of this chapter can and should be put to immediate use. You do not have to wait until you are a sales trainee to practice psychology in dealing with people. You can learn to draw people out and create an information flow to provide input for you to think about in your private study of people and how they think. There is a laboratory for you to study in whenever you are around people.

At this stage of learning about people, you should be absorbing observations and impressions. Notice how children endlessly ask questions when they are very young and are learning how to cope with the world. Nature undoubtedly provided undeveloped human beings with this trait of questioning and searching for answers because the child must learn to deal with other people and the environment.

So remember, you are growing old whenever you do more than fifty per-cent of the talking. Mature conversation is a fifty-fifty proposition, depend-ent equally on talking and on listening. Remember also that all knowledge and growth come from the *listening* part of the conversation, for the talking part consists only of what you already know!

FIELD CHRONICLE

John Elsworth was happy when he finally could start making calls on his own. He was exhilarated by the knowledge that whether he succeeded or failed rested solely on how he handled himself in the presence of a pros-pect. He was glad that he had chosen a sales career because he felt it was one of the few places in modern society where a man could continuously test himself on the basis of his own personal ingenuity. It was Monday evening. He had scheduled two sales calls, both with homeowners who had phoned the department store because they wanted their basements remodeled. Let's tune in on sections of each call.

THE FIRST CALL

ELSWORTH: This wall paneling comes in three styles: simulated oak, maple, and pine. It's fireproof and easy to wash off—you can even hose it down—a fine feature in a basement.

CUSTOMER: Yeah, and it also cracks and warps. I know all about that plas-tic stuff.

o o o

ELSWORTH: We can put a ventilating fan in the laundry room so that when the washing machine or dryer is being run steam and fumes don't go into the recreation room.

CUSTOMER: I thought about that and decided against it.

o o o

ELSWORTH: We can put a real, instead of an artificial, fireplace down here for you—at just a little extra cost.

CUSTOMER: My brother has one of those things in his basement and they never use it.

THE SECOND CALL

ELSWORTH: We can put folding shutters or venetian blinds on the windows. Here are pictures of both kinds.

CUSTOMER: They're both nice. Which do you think we should get?

o o o

ELSWORTH: There are different kinds of bar stools. Some have cushioned seats, others have backs on them, some have swiveled seats, others are stationary.

CUSTOMER: Which kind are the most popular?

o o o

ELSWORTH: We can divide the space you have into a bar area, a lounging area with a group of easy chairs, and a game area for a pool table or dart boards.

CUSTOMER: How do people usually allot the space in their recreation rooms?

STOP & THINK

1. What is Elsworth's problem in each of these calls?
2. What psychology would you use in dealing with each situation?
3. Is one call easier to sell than the other? Explain.

COMPANY CHRONICLE

After Elsworth had worked on his own for a couple of months, he started to wonder about the calls that were being assigned to him. He began to notice that most of the calls that were assigned to him were in the less desirable and poorer sections of town. He started asking the other salesmen which calls they were getting. He soon decided that the better calls were going to the more experienced and top-producing men. This really upset him. He stomped over to Alice Mays, the woman who sorted out the call sheets as they came in from the department store.

ELSWORTH: (*With a scowl on his face.*) Do you handle the call sheets that come into this office?

MISS MAYS: Yes, I do.

ELSWORTH: Do you assign them to the salesmen?

MISS MAYS: No, I don't.

ELSWORTH: Well, who the devil does?

MISS MAYS: That's usually Mr. Carter's job. He's the sales manager's assistant.

ELSWORTH: So he's the villain. I'm going to talk to him about this right now.

MISS MAYS: That's your privilege.

Elsworth stomped over to Mr. Carter's office. He was busy talking to someone, so Elsworth waited for twenty minutes until he was free.

ELSWORTH: Good morning, Mr. Carter. There's something that's really bugging me.

CARTER: Oh, what is it?

ELSWORTH: It's the unfair way the sales calls are assigned to the men. I seem to be getting all the lousy calls. Is someone playing favorites around here?

CARTER: Oh, I thought you understood that. Perhaps we forgot to explain it to you. The beginning men always get the less desir-

ELSWORTH: able accounts. Once we feel you're experienced enough, we start assigning you more important calls.

ELSWORTH: That seems highly unfair to me. The top men who need it least end up with the gravy and I'm left with the dregs.

CARTER: We don't run the company from your point of view—we run it in terms of what's good business.

ELSWORTH: Being fair is good business.

CARTER: That's true. Our system is fair to the salesmen and to the company. Fairness is a two-way street. Everyone has to be considered—the men who have been here a long time as well as beginners like yourself.

ELSWORTH: How is my getting the worst of the deal fair to me?

CARTER: You've got something to work for. You know that once you prove yourself you'll be rewarded with more attractive calls.

ELSWORTH: This is a case of playing favorites, pure and simple.

CARTER: No, it isn't. It's a case of good business. Look at it from the company's point of view. Would it be smart for management to assign the calls with good potential to inexperienced men? If you louse up a call that doesn't have so much potential, there isn't so much lost from the company's point of view.

ELSWORTH: The whole policy is designed only for the company's welfare.

CARTER: Depends on how you look at it. You're getting a wide variety of experience calling on less desirable accounts. You'll be working harder to make these kinds of accounts productive, if you know that by doing so you'll get more desirable accounts later on. If the company sets things up so you'll improve yourself—that's to your advantage as well as the company's.

STOP & THINK

1. How do you evaluate Elsworth's conduct in this matter? What would you have done differently? Why?

2. Selling goes on inside as well as outside of the company. How could Elsworth have used sales psychology to handle this internal matter?

3. What do you think of this particular company policy? Does it make sense to you?

PROBLEMS

A Supervisor Making Calls with One of His Men Creates Problems. Carl Soller, a young man of twenty-three, was in his second year of selling for Midwest Chemicals, Inc. He sold fertilizers to rural coöps and farm-supply stores. His immediate supervisor was Fred Bates, a man of twenty-eight. Bates had four years of successful selling experience behind him and had been appointed a sales supervisor about a year before. Every six weeks, Bates would spend an entire week making calls with Soller. Eventually

Soller noticed that sales were always materially higher during the week that Bates spent with him. Soller mulled over what was being done differently during the Bates visits. He could not determine that his conduct was any different whether or not Bates was with him. The only difference was that Bates was physically present during the calls, and occasionally he joined in on the conversation with the customer. Bates made it a point never to interfere with the conduct of the sale itself. If he had anything to say about how the sale went, he discussed it later in the car. Soller began brooding about the fact that Bates could influence sales by his mere presence. He began wondering about his appearance and his personality and began to get depressed.

STOP & THINK

1. What influences that were covered in the chapter are at work here?
2. How should Soller handle this matter?

Difficulties in Getting Out of an Office. Sol Weller was a time salesman for a television station located in Des Moines, Iowa. He was calling on Dave Blake, the media director for Chappel & Smith, an advertising agency. Weller had scheduled himself for six calls that day and was running behind. The sales presentation was finished, he had an order, and wanted to leave.

WELLER: Thanks for the order, Dave. I'll have to be running along.

BLAKE: Say, my daughter, Mary, is interested in getting into television. Is there any chance of getting her a job with your station for the summer?

WELLER: I'll see about it and let you know. I'm on my way to see the station manager right now so I'll take it up with him. (*This was not true.*)

BLAKE: Well, let me tell you a little about her. She's quite gifted, if you'll excuse a father's pride.

WELLER: I'll just get her an appointment with our personnel people and they'll go into what she can do. I'll get the station manager who I'm on my way to see to put in a good word for her.

BLAKE: Who is your station manager? I'm pretty serious about this. Would it help if I took him to lunch? After all, I swing a lot of business to his station.

STOP & THINK

1. Has Weller's daily appointment schedule influenced him unduly? Evaluate how he has handled getting out of the office.
2. How do you think Weller should handle this matter?

A Special Problem for a Woman in Sales. Sally Moore was a saleswoman for a company that sold packaging materials. She made a first call on an older purchasing agent, Mr. Whittier, who was not used to the idea of women having responsibility in business.

WHITTIER: How long have you been selling for your company, young lady?

MISS MOORE: Long enough to know our line thoroughly. If you'll tell me what particular problems you have, I'll prove it to you.

WHITTIER: Do you like the idea of selling and sitting around in waiting rooms with a bunch of men?

MISS MOORE: I find the work very stimulating. It really doesn't matter whether you're a man or woman sitting in a waiting room. Let me show you a new line of plastic bottles.

WHITTIER: It seems to me that if you're going to go into selling you ought to be selling cosmetics or ladies' ready-to-wear.

STOP & THINK

1. What, if anything, can Sally Moore do that she hasn't already done to get Whittier to get on with business?
2. What factors discussed in the chapter relate to this situation?

Note: This is an actual situation. The decision the company made was to transfer the account back to a salesman. What do you think of this decision?

CHAPTER REVIEW AND DISCUSSION QUESTIONS

1. Is the feeling of insecurity related to how much a salesman talks? If he is insecure, would he talk more or less?
2. What factors are included in good sales communications?
3. Why is it so important that the salesman be a good listener?
4. What is meant by "determination of a prospect's value scale"? How can a salesman probe to find out what a person's value scale is?
5. What is meant by the input and output parts of communications flow? Why is it necessary that input come before output?
6. Why is it difficult for people to speak clearly and honestly? What can the salesman do to help them communicate honestly?
7. What is the logic behind supplying rational reasons to explain irrational conduct?
8. What are the psychological factors that detract from communicating effectively?
9. What is involved in persuading on the material level? On the nonmaterial level?

6

THE SELLING PROCESS: PART I PREPREPARATION, PROSPECTING, AND QUALIFYING

*Opportunities do not come with
their value stamped on them.*
—MALTBIE BABCOCK

Selling is a process rather than an isolated act. "Process" means that there is much preparation and activity that precedes the making of a sale. Also, there is a lot that follows after the sale is made. This chapter deals with the things the salesman does *before* he actually meets the prospect. The salesman's odds for making a sale increase according to the caliber and amount of homework he does. Effective prepreparation sets the stage for, and immeasurably facilitates, success.

Prepreparation means providing support for yourself by maintaining good habits: systematizing routine activities and responsibilities; taking care of yourself physically so you have the energy required to take the strain of a full week's work; getting enough sleep and exercise so your mind is alert to meet the challenges that will test it; disciplining yourself to make plans and to stick to them; keeping caught up on your reports and other paper work; and so on. Your good habits are the backup team that helps you execute effective plays on the selling field.

HOW THE SALESMAN PREPARES HIMSELF

The smart salesman will not start making a sales call without first determining what demands will be made upon him in the call. He will visualize beforehand each step in the sales call. In the process of doing this he will ask himself what he will need to meet all the circumstances that could

occur. Sales calls require both physical and mental resources. The mental resources are information and human understanding, which will be discussed later. A discussion of the physical resources follows.

Use of Physical Props

The physical resources needed vary with the type of selling. The salesman selling intangibles, such as stocks and bonds, insurance, or transportation, will carry a minimum of equipment—perhaps only a briefcase with a few charts, some reference books for technical information, an order book, and various folders. A salesman selling tangibles, on the other hand, is often required to carry a great deal—actual samples or, if the product is large, miniature models of it—and advertising tear sheets, sales manuals, and visual aids such as film strips, photographs, and diagrams.

Calling Cards

All salesmen have calling cards and usually reference folders that they leave wherever they call. This seemingly small detail—leaving a business card or folders that describe the line that the salesman sells—is important in selling both tangibles and intangibles. One of the most difficult things for a salesman to do is to time his call to the exact moment when a prospect is ready to buy. The odds are against his timing his call exactly all the time. However, this does not mean in the slightest that his effort has been wasted. If the salesman makes a good presentation and leaves a folder and business card, very often orders will result days or even weeks or months after the call is made.

This practice applies to the retail field as well. Retail salespeople of big-ticket items such as men's suits, women's coats, or appliances, often hand out cards to prospects, knowing full well that such effort can lead to future business.

Supplier Resource Files

Professional buyers, who work for companies and public institutions, maintain reference files called "resource files" into which they put business cards and folders from salesmen who call on them. When they have a pur chase request for a certain item that is not routine, they go through their supplier resource files to see whom they have purchased similar items from in the past or who has called on them who can supply the needed item. Indeed, getting a business card and reference folder into a buyer's resource file is an important goal for the farsighted salesman.

It is noteworthy that purchasing departments consider their supplier resource files a valuable asset. Such well-maintained files simplify buying procedures immeasurably, for when the buyer receives a purchase requisition from someone within his company—an order for a gross of electromagnets for example—he can consult his files for notes and information about an electrical supplier with whom the company has dealt before or whose salesman has called to explain such a product line. It is understandable why these files are so essential when one considers that purchasing departments of even small companies are responsible for the purchase of thousands of different items, some of them ready-made, such as carbon paper and sweeping compound; many more of them custom-made components, such as axles and dynamos; and materials used in processing, such as wallboard or barrels of plating acid.

Think of all the products that are bought for use in your home each year. These are consumer goods, meaning that they are ready for use when they enter your home. The manufacture of each ready-to-use product in your home required hundreds of other products and services. Take the number of different products purchased for your home each year and multiply it by the conservative figure of 3,000—the number of things that were bought, made, and packaged for each item in your house! Now you can begin to grasp the size, variety, and complexity of the items that are purchased by purchasing departments of the companies that provide the needs of *just your home.* You can also appreciate the importance of the salesman as the main source of information that enables buyers to perform their complicated jobs.

Because of the huge spectrum of needs that a purchasing department is called on to supply, it relies heavily on the supplier resource files that it develops and maintains. A buyer index card is typed up and maintained for each supplier or potential supplier. Information may be added after a salesman calls. Information is added after each order is placed to provide an experience history on active suppliers with whom the company does business.

Two methods can be used in filling out the buyer index cards, as shown in Figure 6–1. Type A, used by the Detroit Edison Company, is one that the buyer fills out and maintains himself. Type B, used by the Bendix Corporation, is one which the company asks the vendor to fill out. Kenneth W. Hartwell, director of purchases, the Detroit Edison Company, had this to say about buyer's index cards. "We have used this type of card for many, many years and find it quite suitable. The buyers have an alphabetical file of these in their desk drawer that is one of their working tools. Some prefer to arrange them by supplier category rather than alphabetically."

Planning for the Week

There are usually considerably fewer than forty hours a week during which a salesman can make calls. He can see prospects only when they are willing to make themselves available. Many professional buyers will not see salesmen before 9:30 or 10 A.M.; they are inclined not to be available until at least 1:30 or 2:00 P.M. after lunch; they often do not care to see anyone when they are winding up the day after 4 P.M. Salespeople selling in retail

Figure 6–1
BUYER'S INDEX CARD TYPE A

FIRM	B. R. Thomas Co.	PHONE	215-245-6104
ADDRESS	P. O. Box 5907	REP.	R. Perkins
	Philadelphia, PA 19006	"	W. Paulson
F.O.B.	Barkingtons, PA TERMS Net 30	"	R. Battell
HOME OFFICES	Sanderville, Oklahoma	PHONE	918-814-5000

OFFICERS B. R. Thomas - Chairman - C. D. Goldston, Pres.
G. A. Martin, VP, Pipeline Div., J. M. Buddin, VP, Coating Div.

MATERIALS	PLANT ADDRESS
Pipe Coating Div	612 Farway St. Philadelphia, PA
	S. Thredd 215-637-3182
Thermal Insulation Coatings	B. R. Thomas Co. P. O. Box 416
	New Brunswick, New Jersey
	201-528-6400, M. N. Fisch, Mgr.
BUYERS INDEX	

Courtesy of The Detroit Edison Company.

Figure 6-1

BUYER'S INDEX CARD TYPE B

Company Name (1)			P. O. Box	FSSEI No.*	TWX No.
Street Address (2)		City		State	Zip

This Firm is an ☐ Affiliate ☐ Subsidiary or ☐ Division (3) of		Overland Route		Air Freight Route
Factory Contact (4)	Phone No.	Geog. Code	Vendor Code	Catalogue File No.
			Bendix Use Only	
Name and Title of Top Ranking Official at Above Location (5)		Terms	F.O.B.	
Salesman (6)	Phone No.	Address (If Different From Line 2).		

☐ Manufacturer # Employees (7) ☐ Jobber _____	Classified as Small Business Under Small Business Administration Regulations	☐ Yes ☐ No
Do You Have a Labor Union? ☐ Yes ☐ No Union Name _____ (8) Date Union Contract Expires _____	Does Your Plant Close For Annual Vacation? ☐ Yes ☐ No From To	

List Items Normally Stocked or Manufactured (Use Reverse Side if Necessary)

(9)

Bendix	VENDOR INFORMATION *Federal Social Security Employee's Identification Number	Buyer
		BC 200

Courtesy of Automotive Electronics Division, Bendix Corporation.

stores are limited, too, for they can see people only when the bulk of them come in to shop—a narrow span of hours. Indeed, the actual working hours during the week in which the salesman can be face-to-face with prospects are quite limited. Figure 6-2 gives the results of a study made of the way in which salesmen spend their time.

The Value of Time

In selling, the old axiom "Time is money" most certainly applies. There are few fields where effective use of time relates more closely to earnings than it does in sales. It is a good idea for a salesman to learn to think of himself as a very valuable piece of capital equipment. He should think of himself as a Boeing 747 of his company. In the airlines industry there is a saying, "The only time an airliner is earning money is when it is in the air." When the plane is on the ground, it eats into profits, for while it is parked on expensive runway space or is being serviced, it costs the company money. The same may be said of a salesman. The only time he is making money is when he is talking to a prospect. Parking himself in waiting rooms, covering ground traveling, and servicing accounts cost him money!

Figure 6–2
HOW SALESMEN SPEND THEIR TIME

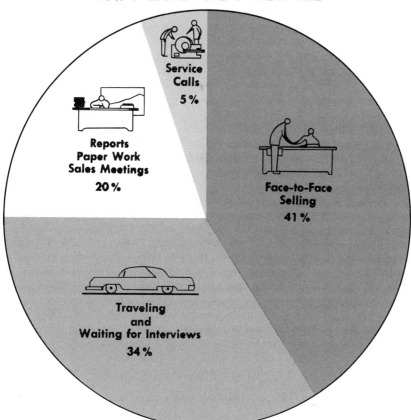

1,890 industrial salesmen were asked to keep an hour-by-hour diary of a typical work day. Here's how their time actually broke down:

1. *The reporting salesmen averaged 9 hours and 22 minutes working time. (Many worked through lunch.)*

2. *59% of their day, or 5 hours and 56 minutes, was spent in meetings, travelling, waiting for interviews, doing paper work and making service calls.*

3. *41% of their day, or 3 hours and 52 minutes, was spent in face-to-face selling.*

The salesmen averaged 8.4 completed calls per day, and stayed 28 minutes per call.

Courtesy McGraw-Hill Research.

Figure 6–3

TOTAL CALL FREQUENCY GUIDE

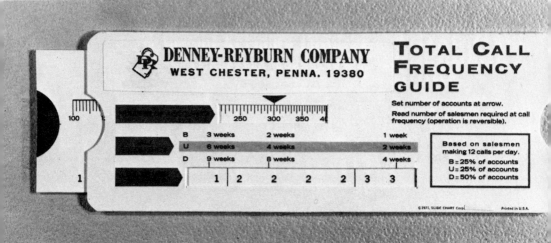

Manufactured by Slide Chart Corp. P. O. Box 527, West Chester, Pennsylvania.

This slide rule device is one way in which the salesman can determine the frequency of calls according to the number of accounts he is responsible for.

Studies of the operating costs of sales departments tell us that a company invests anywhere from $1,000 to $35,000 in the hiring and training of each of its salesmen, with an average cost, according to the Sales Executives Club of New York, of $8,731 per man! Furthermore, at forty hours a week, if you plan to earn $100 a week, your time is worth $2.50 an hour; if you plan to earn $200 a week, your time is worth $5 an hour. Clearly, plans for using time of such high value must be carefully made. When schedules are not made or followed, there is a tendency for the salesman to squander time aimlessly, wasting his most valuable resource. This is something that is all too easy to do in selling where there usually is no direct supervision and where so many enticing alternatives to working present themselves. A salesman is a man who makes a plan and then works his plan.

A study that is typical of findings of why salesmen fail indicates that most of the weaknesses relate to planning, or rather to the lack of it. Significantly, you will note that many of the weaknesses in the following list are tied to the lack of prepreparation effort on the part of the salesman.

1. Not utilizing time for working
2. Not organizing work
3. Not planning work

4. Not using enough available time to sell

5. Not having enough product information

6. Not using enough effort

7. Not prospecting for new business

Use of the Law of Averages in Planning

In planning for the week, the salesman prepares a schedule of what he is going to do. He plans for both his selling and his nonselling activities, such as filling out reports and servicing accounts (putting up displays, checking out inventories, making collections, and so on). His prime concern in planning, of course, is to determine which calls he is going to make and the order in which he intends to make them. Included in his plans is a checklist of things he must take with him when he makes each call. There is nothing more self-defeating for a salesman than waiting to get in to see a busy buyer and then searching a briefcase for something that is not there. An "Excuse me while I run out to the car" may retrieve a missing advertising tear sheet or a specifications list but it will retrieve neither the lost respect of the buyer nor the time that was wasted.

The whole approach to planning for the week is to use the law of averages to raise the salesman's sales volume and dollar income. This is also sometimes called "playing potential." The following points should be kept in mind in applying the law of averages to the salesman's schedule of weekly activities. The problem is similar to one of setting up a budget, but here, instead of allocating money, time is allocated to accomplish activities. Here are some principles that improve on the law of averages as it relates to time:

1. The more calls made, the greater the chances for sales. Hence, as many calls as can be reasonably handled are scheduled.

2. The more time that is used for nonselling activities, the less time there is for selling. Thus, emphasis is placed on reducing time devoted to nonselling purposes, and on expanding the time devoted to selling.

3. Reduction of travel and waiting time provides more time for calls. Careful routing of calls (avoiding backtracking in driving), study of traffic conditions (considering traffic conditions as they relate to where accounts are located), and judicious use of the telephone to make and verify appointments conserve waiting time and broken appointments. (The telephone can help cut down on unnecessary leg work and travel.)

4. Not all hours of the day have equal value. The value varies according to the type of selling. An example of a rating established by a salesman calling on supermarket managers might be: Class A hours (hours apt to be most productive): 9 A.M. to 4 P.M., Mondays through Thursdays; Class B hours (apt to be less productive for selling): before 9 A.M. and after 4 P.M., Mondays through Thursdays, and all day Fridays and Saturdays. Nonselling calls and activities or calls on less promising accounts should be scheduled during Class B hours. Class A hours should be reserved for calling on the most promising prospects.

Customer Call Records

A good salesman will keep a record on each customer. This record will be reviewed when the weekly schedule of calls is set up and again just before the actual call is made. As soon as the call is completed, notes as to what happened during the call are entered on the customer's record. Customer call records are kept on file cards and the file is kept in the salesman's car. A typical call card kept by a salesman for a sporting goods wholesaler is shown in Figure 6–4. (Note that the card is organized and worded so it would be understood by another salesman or by the sales supervisor. This is necessary in case an emergency arises and someone has to fill in for the salesman.)

Salesmen may keep call cards in one of two files, an alphabetical file or a tickler file. A tickler file is one that is set up by dates. Any customer who needs special attention on a certain date has his card placed in the tickler file. Each week the salesman pulls the card for the week's dates so he can integrate the special things that need to be done that week into his regular call schedule. For example, the card in Figure 6–4 would normally be kept in the alphabetical file. However, since there is a special reason why this account should be contacted on March 1, it is kept in the tickler file so it will come to the salesman's attention in time for him to act on the suggested follow-up.

In fields that are highly technical, the sales call report (see Figure 6–5) is more than a record for the salesman and his immediate supervisor. It serves the very important function of keeping key personnel throughout the sales-

Figure 6–4
CUSTOMER CALL RECORD

Claxton's Sporting Goods Store
1421 So. Main Street   Phone: 873-9385

Owner and buyer: David Emery (short, thin man, about
                            40, bald, wears glasses)
Credit rating: AA—orders over $2,000 must be OK'd
Call schedule: Call every three months

Jan. 17, 197-. Got an order for $1,750, see invoice #1456. Likes special deals for month-end sales he can feature in newspaper advertising. Left display rack for tennis balls. Check it out next time call back. Manages local high school baseball team. They will be interested in new uniforms in March. About 20 needed. Follow-up March 1st.

Figure 6–5

SALES CALL REPORT

GE SALES CALL REPORT	METALLURGICAL PRODUCTS DEPT. CHEMICAL & METALLURGICAL DIV. GENERAL ELECTRIC COMPANY	CALL DATE	DATE WRITTEN	DATE REC'D	DATE SCREENED	SCREENED BY
		7/3/72	7/7/72			

COMPANY......... *J. N. LENTZ CO.* REPRESENTATIVE.......... *P. SOMERSET*
DIV/DEPT......... *STEED WORKS* ACCOMPANIED BY:.................
STREET......... *BARROW*
CITY......... *GRAND RAPIDS* ......STATE *MICH.* PERSONS INTERVIEWED ☐ PHONE ☐ FACE-TO-FACE TITLE
MANUFACTURES......... *TRACTORS*

PERSONS INTERVIEWED	TITLE
S. SAMUELS	*TOOL STORES*
H. PISON	*FOREMAN*
R. TOMPSON	*TOOL CRIB*
K. RITTER	*CH. TL. DES.*

OBJECT OF CALL ("10 MINUTE THINK")
NEW PRODUCT OPPORTUNITY FOR AUTOMATIC SCREW MACHINES

ROUTE TO (SURNAME) CIRCLE NAME AND DIRECT ARROW TO SUBJECT IF ANSWER OR ACTION REQUIRED.

F. SHAITZ
W. CLIPPER
B. STILLTON
R. HOWARD
J. MICHAELS
T. LIPSON
L. BARKER

REPORT OF CALL: BE BRIEF, BE SPECIFIC. GIVE FACTS AND FIGURES ON VOLUME, PRICE, COMPETITIVE ITEMS. WHAT BUSINESS ARE WE LOSING? WHAT ARE APPLICATIONS FOR OUR PRODUCTS? WHAT NEW PRODUCTS ARE REQUIRED, PROPERTIES? PERFORMANCE?

(7-14-72)
TOOL HOLDERS: DR 97269* & WC-23901-W4 PER Q75688 - RICHARD
"NO QUOTE"
INSERT: DR-76902* GEM II PER Q76418 - (6-4-72) - RICHARD
*PURCHASED BY LENTZ FOR NATIONAL AUTOMATICS
AT 95 S.F. .010/.020 FEED, 1/8 D.C. ON 7592
4140, 1119, & 5472, GEM II OUTPERFORMED
CONGO (M-3) @ $3.59 GROUND STOCK (5/8" SQ.)
20 PCS/EDGE (1 EDGE) TO 1000 PCS/4 EDGES
NEEDLESS TO SAY, LENTZ IS EXCITED WITH (25)
MACHINES & (3) HOLDERS/MACHINE.
1. 13° TO 15° POS RAKE REQUIRED
2. MOST SCREW MACHINE COMPANIES USE M-3
OR M-2 AS IT'S EASIER TO REGRIND
3. TOOL RESETTING SAVINGS AT LENTZ - 1½ HRS/8 HRS
4. SCREW MACHINES, GENERALLY SPEAKING, AN
OPEN TERRITORY - POTENTIAL SHOULD
BE "GREAT"?!
NEEDS: ½ & 3/8 I.C. SQUARES & TRIANGLES WITH POSITIVE
RAKED ROLLER TURN HOLDERS ½" TO ¾" SHANK
FOR NATIONAL, CONES, R. & S. ETC.

FORECAST DATA	CURRENT FISCAL MO.			NEXT FISCAL MO.			NEXT FISCAL MO.			NEXT FISCAL MO.			NEXT FISCAL MO.		
	WHAT	HOW MUCH	WHEN	WHAT	HOW MUCH	WHEN	WHAT	HOW MUCH	WHEN	WHAT	HOW MUCH	WHEN	WHAT	HOW MUCH	WHEN
DUE FIRST FISCAL WEEK															
☐ YOUR STIMATE															
☐ CUSTOMER ESTIMATE															

MAILING LIST—CHECK DURING OR IMMEDIATELY AFTER CALL IF ADDITIONS, CORRECTIONS OR REMOVALS REQ'D CHECK HERE ☐ AND ATTACH CARD TO REPORT.

NEXT ACTION BY SALESMAN
KEEP ORDER WITH LENTZ
WATCH FOR INTEREST BY DETROIT
KEEP GEM II ALIVE

MPD 59 2-58

Courtesy Metallurgical Products Department, General Electric Company.

man's company aware of what is going on in the field. Because the salesman meets customers face-to-face at the point where buying decisions are made, alert companies feel that what goes on there should be shared widely so executives in branch and home offices will remain in touch with reality.

Flexibility in Planning

The salesman must be realistic in scheduling his appointments. Planning eight calls in a day is not a matter of scheduling an appointment each hour. Driving time, the nature of the account, and what is to be accomplished during the call all must be taken into consideration, so one call will be scheduled for thirty minutes, another for ninety.

Any schedule must be flexible, for it is impossible to judge the time that will be required for each call. While it is very important to try to adhere to the schedule, it would be foolhardy for a salesman to stick to it slavishly. The good salesman "plays things by ear." The purpose of making calls is to use time where it will produce the best long-run results. Whenever the use of more time on a call promises a worthwhile sales dividend, the necessary time should be taken, of course, and if necessary, the schedule for the day's calls revised accordingly.

Salesmen who call on accounts regularly do not expect an order each time they call. The purpose of making scheduled calls when there is no prospect for an immediate order is to further some long-range objective or simply to maintain a conspicuous profile—to remain visible. Before calling on a regular customer, the salesman carefully reviews the past record. If the record for the last call indicates that it is probably too early to expect a reorder, it would be unrealistic of the salesman to spend time trying to get a reorder. He should be prepared with a number of alternative ways to use the allotted time. These alternatives might be to:

1. encourage the buyer to consider other products in the salesman's line which have never been tried.

2. divulge information that will help the buyer in his job. This serves to strengthen the relationship between the buyer and the salesman's company.

3. bring the buyer up-to-date on developments among his competitors that may be of interest.

4. discuss plans for new products, future advertising campaigns, trade shows, and the like.

5. advise on price increases, business outlook with possible supply shortages.

6. make suggestions on future ordering so that orders may be timed to best advantage for the buyer.

THE INFORMATION DIMENSION
OF SELLING

Most people would agree that knowledge is a kind of power. Indeed, knowledge is the salesman's main source of power. The salesman is primarily a purveyor of knowledge and information. People who have all the information they need about a product can order by phone or through mail order, without the use of a salesman. The salesman is needed for what he knows. Therefore the person aspiring to success in sales must focus on developing means of being well informed.

What Knowledge Accomplishes

Knowledge helps a salesman in many ways. There is a great deal more to being well informed than merely being able to answer questions after a sales presentation. The power that comes from knowledge goes far beyond the mere supplying of information. People react to a salesman on the basis of the confidence they have in him. *It is knowledge that gives the salesman confidence in himself.* And his confidence gives him enthusiasm, for a person cannot help but be enthusiastic about something about which he knows a great deal. Confidence and enthusiasm are passed on to those to whom the salesman sells. They help build up the empathy between the salesman and the prospect.

What Knowledge Is Needed

When you ask a seasoned salesman what he needs to know in order to sell his product, he is not being facetious when he answers "everything." What he means is that you can never know what people will ask. If you argue that "everything" is pretty broad, he will probably give you examples of how the possession of some unusual knowledge on his part facilitated the making of a sale. He will be sure to say at some point in the discussion that a salesman can never know too much.

The nature of the particular selling job, the kinds of customers who are contacted, and the kinds of goods and services that are sold, of course, determine what information is most essential. A retail salesperson in a shoe department needs knowledge that is quite different from that needed by one working for a motorcycle distributor. A salesman selling insurance to members of the American Medical Association will be prepared to answer questions that are different from those handled by a salesman who sells the same insurance to members of the Teamsters Union. A man selling steel will be equipped with knowledge that differs markedly from that possessed by a woman selling cosmetics.

In determining exactly what facts and knowledge are needed, it is best to return to the idea of a system that was introduced earlier in this book. No salesman sells an isolated product or service. For as John Donne commented about man so many years ago, "No man is an island unto himself";

the same applies to goods and services—they are not separate entities, either. Any product or service relates to a system. The salesman who tries to learn about both what he sells and the system that surrounds what he sells is well on the way to becoming a well-informed salesman, a person truly knowledgeable. Let us briefly consider the parts that make up any system.

Knowledge of the Company

Fortunately or unfortunately, depending on how you look at it, most products, especially complicated ones, are not judged on their own merits. The value of a wristwatch, a cosmetic, or a hotel room is judged by the name of the company that provides it. This is easy to prove—just switch the name on a wristwatch or cosmetic from one that is well known to one that is unknown and you will find that the product will not sell or, if it does, at a fraction of its usual price. Consequently, salespeople who sell these products must be very company-oriented. We must always remember that the salesperson *is* the company in the eyes of the person to whom he is selling.

Any training program for sales trainees will include orientation about the company—its history, present resources and status, the location of its facilities, and so on. Frequently sales trainees will visit or work for short periods in manufacturing and distribution facilities of their companies for familiarization purposes.

Students who aspire to go into sales would do well to start reading about the industries and companies in which they feel they may be interested.

Such knowledge will certainly help them when it is time to look for a job. The student can get the "feel" of an industry by reading about it. The *Wall Street Journal, The New York Times* financial section, *Forbes, Barrons, Fortune,* and *Business Week* regularly feature articles about companies and biographical sketches of leaders who head them. These articles are not only highly informative but also fascinating to read. Later on, should the student become a salesman working for General Motors, for example, he may be able to entertain a customer with a story that he has read about Henry Ford II, thus demonstrating that he is knowledgeable about his industry as well as about his own company.

The Special Difficulty in Getting the First Order

An experienced salesman will tell you that one of the more difficult and challenging parts of his job, especially in the field of industrial sales, is to get the first order from a firm that has never dealt with his company before. This is important enough to bear rephrasing. *A buyer is very reluctant to try a new supplier when he is satisfied with the one he has.* Let us analyze why this is so.

Once a buyer is satisfied in his dealings with one supplier, he is very reluctant to switch, even if others offer better prices, discounts, or payment terms. This phenomenon applies widely in all kinds of sales situations. The key factor here is loyalty—loyalty based not so much on price as on confidence. The original supplier is known to be reliable and trustworthy. That is why he is so hard to dislodge. The buyer fears failure—actually he is afraid to change! What relieves fear and gains a supplier company a reputation for reliability and trustworthiness? It boils down to what are known in the field as the four P's—product, policies, procedures, and personnel. The four P's of sound policies and procedures administered by competent personnel delivering quality products spell customer confidence.

Knowledge of Product, Policies, Procedures, and Personnel

Because the four P's are the foundation stones for customer confidence, the salesman must be sufficiently knowledgeable about them so he can convince those he calls on that his company is to be trusted. If he wants to get the first order so that he can get future orders, he must not only be able to give assurance that his company is as reliable as others but he must also demonstrate that there are additional advantages for the buyer in switching to his company. "Me-tooism" is never enough. To prove that your company can do what another company can do is not enough—you must prove *that dealing with you has advantages*. Thus it takes an excellent command of information to build a case that is convincing enough to cause a buyer to switch suppliers. The salesman must know the strengths and weaknesses of his own company's four P's. He must also know the strengths and weaknesses of the four P's of his competitors. It is only when he is armed with such knowledge that he can sell with real authority and confidence.

The reason buyers are so wary of dealing with untested suppliers is that the failure of suppliers to make deliveries when promised, to supply the quantities ordered, to provide goods that meet specifications, and so on, can be disastrous for them. In the industrial field, a component-product defect or delivery failure can shut down an assembly line. In the resale field it can mean an out-of-stock on a planned-for item. These are examples of two serious consequences for which buyers are held directly responsible. *The buyer's employer blames the buyer, not the supplier, for delivery and product failures.* It is the buyer's job to keep the company properly supplied with its needs. When supplier foul-ups occur, the buyer's reputation suffers and his job may even be placed in jeopardy. This is why buyers are careful and insist on dealing with salesmen who are reliable and who know what they are talking about.

The salesman trying to make a first sale must be both persistent and not easily discouraged. Buyers, like other people, have their moods. The salesman who optimistically and creatively calls on a buyer who continually says "no" may hit that buyer on a day when he is in the mood for a change. As a veteran salesman pointed out, "Even if a competitor has an account sewed up, there comes a day when something goes wrong—when the other guy gets a chance. And this can mean you, *if* you've asserted yourself."

If the salesman is truly knowledgeable, he can back up what he says with action. After all, what makes a company reliable? Its employees, of course. It is not companies that foul things up or do things right—it is the people who work for a company who are responsible for its actions. This means that the words "salesman's knowledge" must be defined broadly. If the salesman's knowledge is more than merely superficial, he will know how the customer's order is routed through his company. Furthermore, he will probably know the people who are in charge of handling the order each step of the way. Thus if the deeply knowledgeable salesman makes promises, he checks when necessary to be sure that his company is performing as promised. Where delays occur, he takes steps to expedite matters; if failures occur he keeps the customer informed and tries to ease inconveniences.

Part of a salesman's knowledge is knowing where inventories of his company's merchandise are located in his territory. It is not unusual for an alert and conscientious salesman to borrow needed merchandise from one customer and lend it to another to help a customer who is short. A truly knowledgeable salesman can do a great deal to keep his business running smoothly. Competitors of such a salesman will have a difficult time getting orders from his customers.

A veteran sales manager in the industrial field, reflecting on what causes sales success, said that the two best salesmen he had known built their success by being able to provide the information needed by industrial buyers. The two salesmen studied carefully to determine what information each purchasing agent they called on needed to perform effectively his job of purchasing. They knew that what any purchasing agent wants most is to look good in the eyes of those for whom he works. The salesmen avidly read technical and business journals, clipping things that related to the interests and needs of those they called on. Purchasing agents soon learned to tell these helpful salesmen about their problems. The substance of these problems was the input communication needed by the salesmen to operate at their peak efficiency as salesmen who were customer solution-oriented. The output of helpful information given by the salesmen to the purchasing agents included, of course, all relevant information about their own products, too. And this yielded orders that enabled them to be top performers.

Knowledge of Product

Product knowledge is becoming more essential because (1) products are becoming more complicated and sophisticated (compare the adding machine with the computer and the radio with color television) and (2) customers are better educated and more demanding (employees in purchasing departments used to be high school graduates at most; today they have degrees in engineering or business administration; a large percentage of retail store customers also have had at least some college education).

What the salesman needs to know about his product is encompassed in these questions: What can and what can't my product do? How do my products compare with those of the competition? How can the products that I sell solve customer problems? How do my products relate to other products and systems? What nonproduct facts are related to what I sell?

What Can and What Can't My Product Do?

Performance of the product is of course one of the prime customer concerns. Salesmen should anticipate questions about performance beforehand and have the *facts* ready to present in a convincing way. All too often questions about performance are answered with generalities. For example, the question "How does this motor hold up?" Might be answered: "Oh, just fine. It's a long-lasting motor—they seem never to wear out." An answer such as that is not convincing because it is too general. It is the kind of answer that the prospect would expect from any uninformed salesman. Certainly no salesman is going to admit that his motors are not sturdy. *Answers about performance create confidence when they deal in specifics that are documented.* A much better answer to the query about the motor would be: "Our test engineers placed twenty-five motors from our regular stocks with users doing many kinds of jobs in different parts of the country so they would get a good range of weather and working conditions. Here's a copy of the test results which shows how many hours each motor ran before it needed servicing. . . ."

It does not require much analysis to understand why one answer is effective and the other is not. The salesman should arm himself with as much specific information and documentation about performance as he can get.

Frank admission about what the product cannot do, along with documentation of its limitations, also builds confidence, for the prospect is inclined to trust a salesman who does not brush over limitations.

*How Do My Products Compare With Those
of the Competition?*

Knowledge about competitors' products, terms, policies, and the services surrounding them gives the salesman the upper hand. Customers are frequently quite knowledgeable about the products of others because, especially if the contemplated expenditure is large, they will have made price comparisons, or they will have shopped around, to use a phrase from the consumer goods field.

Knowing about competitors boosts the salesman's confidence in himself. Lack of knowledge about competition seriously undermines his confidence.

Consider the differences in the following examples of what can happen when a potential customer makes claims about a competitor.

PURCHASING AGENT: Darby's lift trucks use less electricity because their batteries are larger.

INFORMED SALESMAN: Yes, but the greater costs of the larger batteries and their increased weight which increases maintenance cancel out any savings in electricity.

UNINFORMED SALESMAN: Those savings on electricity don't amount to much.

＊　＊　＊

RESALE BUYER: Acme Products Company offers a 25¢ per case advertising allowance.

INFORMED SALESMAN: I talked to my last customer about that and he told me that the Acme allowance applied only to fifty-case lots. That's a six week supply for you. That wouldn't help your turnover picture. You shouldn't have your money tied up like that.

UNINFORMED SALESMAN: You won't want your store cluttered up with those merchandise displays.

＊　＊　＊

RETAIL STORE CUSTOMER: Sears has the same sheets on sale for 15¢ less.

INFORMED SALESMAN: Our sheets have three features their sheets don't have. Ours have a 5 percent higher thread count per square inch; they're reinforced with extra-heavy thread in the hems; and ours are treated with a patented finish Sears doesn't have that makes our finish feel smoother to the touch.

UNINFORMED SALESMAN: Their quality isn't as good as ours.

How does the salesman keep up on competition? It is a continuing and relentless job, to be sure. He can do it by carefully reading competitor advertising, by pumping his supervisor and the home office for all they know about competitor activity, and by keeping his ears open when he talks to customers and middlemen who handle competing products. The salesman's customers are not necessarily reluctant to talk about the salesman's competitors. In fact the salesman often will use customers with whom he has a special rapport as a news source about competitors. In such cases the salesman will ask: "Well, what's new with XYZ these days?" The customer knows that it is important that the salesman keep up with his competition, so often he will oblige with accurate reports. The development of reliable sources of information, wherever they may be, is important in keeping up with competitors' activities.

How Can the Products That I Sell Solve Customer Problems?

It has been emphasized that the new sales era is solution-centered. Solutions are the result of the communication (sharing) of knowledge, analysis, and creativity. The applied values that result from information come only when information is used. In other words, information lying in some file is of no benefit. The conscientious salesman will have a large reservoir of information at his disposal. He will add to it almost automatically because information-gathering becomes a habit and an interesting way of life for the salesman. Professional buyers are people who, by nature and training, are intensely curious and inquisitive. It can be said that curiosity is their stock-in-trade. In order to buy well they must be informed. A major source of information for buyers comes from the many salesmen who call on them. Buyers also read widely, attend meetings and conferences, and talk to customers. Industrial purchasing agents talk extensively to engineers and other production people in their plants. Resale buyers visit markets and have meetings with their staff, who are on the front line—that is, who sell to the ultimate consumer. The adroit salesman soon learns that the exchange of information is a two-way process, since his customers are as anxious as he is to keep up with what is going on. Both are aware of the mutual value that comes from a two-way flow of information.

Here is an excerpt from a conversation that is typical of thousands that occur during any business day.

SALESMAN: How are things going, Joe?

BUYER: I'm up to my neck in reading engineering feasibility reports for that addition we're thinking about building. I don't have time to study them as carefully as I should because I've got to keep ahead of my regular work.

SALESMAN: What do you look for in those reports?

BUYER: I'll be responsible for buying the site and then for equipping the building once it's built.

SALESMAN: Bill Akers—the buyer I call on at Bell Brothers—just went through an expansion for his company. I know he's got a lot of information on sites that they considered but didn't use. I see no reason why he wouldn't be willing to talk to you about his experience and perhaps give you his old files. Why don't the three of us get together for lunch and see what happens?

BUYER: That sounds like an excellent idea. Why don't you see whether you can arrange it? Maybe I could help him out with some of their equipping problems, since that's my specialty.

A salesman cannot solve a problem or provide information that is related to the problem unless he is aware of the existence of the problem. Furthermore, problems must be clearly defined to avoid needless waste of time and effort. What will cause customers to share their problems with a salesman? It depends on the rapport that they have with the salesman and largely on whether they respect him. People share problems only with those they respect. Problems are serious business. In the example just cited, the buyer's reputation is at stake as he decides on a site for a plant expansion. The salesman who can assist a buyer to enhance his reputation in solving such a problem will be developing a relationship that could mean a great deal of future business.

How Do My Products Relate to Other Products and Systems?

An excellent way for a salesman to alert himself to what knowledge will be helpful to him comes from training himself to think of what he sells as part of a system. Chances are that the salesman who effectively relates his product to the system of which it is a part will be ahead in the selling of his product. Let us take a real estate salesman as an example. A couple come to see him about buying a new house. Whether the salesman sells them a new house depends on whether he can help them sell their old house and whether he can arrange financing for the new one. In addition, he should be able to supply the couple buying the new house with all sorts of information, such as location of schools, tax rates, driving times to various parts of the city from the new house, insurance availability, and so on. The salesman who knows people at financing agencies, insurance companies, and tax offices will consummate a sale with a minimum of obstacles and a maximum of helpfulness.

A salesman for industrial diamonds used for cutting metals has to know not only his product but also the products of companies that make the holding devices for the diamonds while they cut, and the machines that are needed for production operations involving the use of industrial diamonds. If one of his customers who has a machine using diamonds reads an article in an engineering journal describing the use of a computer in this operation, whom can he ask about "blue collar," or industrial computers? The salesman for the industrial diamond company, of course. The alert salesman will find out which trade journals and newspapers the buyers in his field commonly read and then subscribe to them and study them carefully himself. People who read similar newspapers and magazines have a great deal in common. The salesman who reads general business publications such as the *Wall Street Journal* or *Business Week* and the specialized journals in his field such as the *Tea and Coffee Journal, Sweet's Architecture File,* the *Real Estate Forum,* or *Non-Foods Merchandising* is well on his way to understanding the system that surrounds his products.

What Nonproduct Facts Are Related to What I Sell?

In extending our concept of selling a system rather than an isolated product or service, let us examine the social side of selling. We have traced the evolution of selling from the times of "buyer-beware," through the formula-selling period, up to the present time of solution-centered selling. *There is every reason to believe that business responsibility in the future will go beyond customer problems and will extend very much into the area of overall social needs.*

We are referring here to systems as they are related to ecology. Ecology is the science that studies the mutual relationships between organisms and their environment. Ecology refers to cause-and-effect balances among products, nature, and society. *Ecology raises all sorts of questions about things that people buy. The salesman is expected to know the answers!* For example, housewives are raising many questions about the environmental effects of the detergents they use. It is the salesmen of the soap companies who are expected to know the answers. What happens after a detergent enters a sewage system? Does it pollute and upset the ecological balances in our lakes and rivers? Let us take the example of a chemical company. Not so long ago one of the large chemical companies was accused of allowing a mercury runoff from one of their manufacturing plants to contaminate one of the Great Lakes. You may be sure that the salesmen from the company had a major part in explaining that situation to buyers and to the public everywhere.

The systems idea in the sales field will expand to a point where the salesman will become the expert who relates his product to the environment and who will be expected to understand its social consequences. The job of the salesman will have more and more social overtones. Let us take the case of a beverage salesman. His product may be packaged in returnable bottles, throw-away plastics, or waxed paper; or it may be sold in bulk. The salesman will be expected to know the social impact of each kind of packaging. Which form of packaging causes the greatest waste disposal problem? Which cause the fewest problems? Which containers can be recycled most easily? Which contaminate least while they are being manufactured? There is every indication to believe that the rise of consumerism and the emphasis on ecology will raise the status of the salesman. It will also put greater demands on him as a source of information for dealing with problems of the environment.

Sources of Information

The range of information with which the salesman is expected to be equipped is both impressive and astounding. It is evident that the salesman can never stand still. He must constantly be up-to-date in his quest for knowledge. He is the one whom people depend on for information about new developments.

Accomplishing this is neither boring nor a chore. This is one of the things that makes the sales field so alive and exciting. The salesman is always on the forefront of what is new. Realizing how people depend on him for information boosts his ego and makes him realize his importance. It becomes the good salesman's second nature to soak up information so he can pass it along to others.

The salesman usually has plenty of help in keeping himself informed. He invariably has an organization behind him: the industrial salesman has his home office and sales supervisor; the retail salesman has the buyers in his department, the store's training department, and the manufacturers of what he sells. These sources devote a lot of energy and effort to keeping the salesman up-to-date and well informed. In addition to the salesman's initial training courses, there are often refresher courses of various kinds. These are largely devoted to providing the salesmen with information. Many companies bring their salesmen into the home offices from their territories one or more times a year for meetings and training sessions of various kinds.

Most salesmen receive a steady stream of sales information bulletins and other literature from their home offices. Every salesman probably has a sales manual that serves as a reference book and is constantly updated by inserts sent to him by his company. New product or model introductions invariably call for a lot of briefing effort on the part of home offices. Furthermore, salesmen often attend noncompany meetings and conventions that are held for people in their industry. These are important, for here salesmen learn about what is going on in a broad sense. They meet salesmen and other employees of their competitors and they listen to a wide range of speakers and panelists talking about matters related to their interests. Much of the information a salesman needs relates to the industry he serves rather than to his particular product or brand. For example, a salesman in the transportation industry will attend conventions dealing with such things as how to reduce damage claims in freight handling, the legal obligations of shippers, insurance-claim collecting, developments in containerized shipping, and so on.

Information is the salesman's chief commodity. Great pride and personal satisfaction come to him from being a master of information in his field. He has many sources of information at his disposal. The only limitations that are placed on him in securing information are self-imposed—his own lack of imagination and ambition. A veteran in the sales field made this interesting comment: "One of the salesman's greatest limitations is that he doesn't realize his own importance when it comes to supplying information."

PERSONAL-INVOLVEMENT EXERCISE NO. 6–1

How Good Are You at Researching Information? Read through the situations below. For each one jot down on a piece of paper the title of the book you would consult to get the information needed. Then compare your answers with the sources listed on page 129. Mark your answers "right" or "wrong." (In some cases there may be more than one source for the same information. If you can verify that your source is also valid, of course, mark it "right." In each case we have given what we feel is one of the handiest sources.)

After you have taken this self-test and have scored yourself (see how you rate at the end of this assignment), go to the library and get the facts called for. Write a report in which you supply what is needed for each situation. All the details discussed in the situations are real—all names of companies will be found in standard references.

As you work, be sure to look beyond the information needed to do this assignment. Be sure to make the search of the library shelves yourself— do not ask for assistance, for if you do, you will be defeating the purpose of this assignment. The main purpose is not so much to get the information that you are looking for as to create an awareness in your mind about references so that later on, perhaps when you are a salesman, if a question comes up, you will remember a source in the library that provides the answer. *Knowing where things are is a personal asset of great value which will serve you no matter what you do.* It is stimulating to comprehend the wealth of information that others have assembled over the years and to which you have easy access. This is a fine heritage which we should cherish and learn to use to our own and to society's advantage. Do you realize that we who read English have automatic access to more of the world's information than do all the people who do not read English? This is what we mean when we ask whether we are taking full advantage of our vast heritage.

1. You have forty large training manuals that you want to package and send via parcel post to a customer in another state. They weigh eighteen ounces each. You know there are size and weight limits set by the Postal Service that you will have to know so you can package the manuals properly for shipping. Very often a salesman has to ship or mail things on his own, without the help of a home office, so knowledge of shipping information is part of his stock-in-trade.
I would look:

2. A florist and nursery supply customer of yours who bags fertilizers for which you sell him some chemicals has a scale that is used in weighing 100-pound sacks. One of the legs of the scale has broken off, reducing its efficiency. You would be doing your customer a great favor if you could procure the spare part needed to repair the scale. You feel you could assure yourself of his complete order—which he usually splits with another supplier—if you could see to it that this problem scale was fixed. The scale bears this metal tag: "Howe Richardson Scale Company, Clifton, N.J." Where could you find the home-office address, zip code, telephone number, and credit rating of this company?
I would look:

3. You feel that since you sell custom-built automotive trailers, you should know more about flashers and automatic turn signals. You work out of Cincinnati, Ohio, and would like to contact a nearby supplier of these products so you could visit his plant and get some firsthand information. Where would you look for this information?
I would look:

4. You are upset because a check you cash for a customer bounces. It isn't the customer's check—it is one he received from someone else. Within hours

you get a telegram from the bank telling you that they have made a mistake in bouncing the check and apologizing for the error. You are so impressed with this thoughtfulness that you'd like to write a letter to the president of the bank. Where would you find his name and address? The check was from the First National Bank in Duncan, Oklahoma.

I would look:

5. You and a customer of yours are impressed with a line of desks manufactured by Virco Manufacturing Corporation. The customer says he thinks it would be a good company to invest in. You would like to get some information about the company so you can talk further about it the next time you are in the customer's office. You feel you can get this buyer to give you more time if you have information in which he has expressed interest. Where could you get background information on this company—the value of its stocks, earnings record, dividends, and so on?

I would look:

6. A question has come up as to who is liable for a fraudulent claim in the registration statement for some securities you have been selling. Where could you find out about this?

I would look:

7. A question comes up as to the location of the generating plants and high voltage transmission lines of the American Electric Power System. Where could you find a map that showed this and the information required?

I would look:

8. A customer of yours in Texas has a warehouse insured with the Western General Insurance Company, 1903 Hennann Drive, Houston, Texas 77001. He is building another warehouse in California. The question arises as to whether the same company can insure the California warehouse. Where can you find out about the territories covered by insurance companies?

I would look:

9. Your company offers you either the state of Maine or the state of Nebraska as your sales territory. You feel you should compare the population (by education, occupation, etc.) and per capita income of the two states before making this important decision. Where would you find the most current information on this?

I would look:

10. You sell roofing and gutter installations. You notice a warehouse that needs new gutters and find that it is owned by an absentee owner. How would you find out who owns the building?

I would look:

Right answers: How you rate as a researcher. 0–2 poor; 3–4 fair; 5–6 good; 7–8 excellent; 9–10 sheer genius! These scores can be improved by using the library from time to time!

Here are sources for the information you needed to solve the above problems:

1. The front section of the Yellow Pages telephone directory of most large U.S. cities carries Postal Service information.
2. *Thomas Register of American Manufacturers,* Volume 7.
3. *MacRae's Blue Book, Automotive Materials, Equipment, Suppliers, and Components.*
4. *Polk's World Bank Directory,* North American Section.
5. *Standard & Poor's Corporation Records.*
6. *Topical Law Reports,* Commerce Clearing House, Inc. Volume 1, Federal Securities Law Reporter, No. 1.
7. *Moody's Public Utility Manual.*
8. *The Insurance Almanac.*
9. *The Statistical Abstract of the United States.*
10. The City Directory.

PROSPECTING

If Horace Greeley, when he talked about where opportunity could best be found, had been a sales manager instead of an editor, his advice would have been different. He would not have said: "Go West, young man, go West." He would surely have said: "Go prospecting, young man, go prospecting."

Prospecting is the growth element of sales. A most important measure of a salesman's proficiency and sales health is his record of new business or new accounts. If new accounts are not added regularly, a salesman either stagnates or regresses. In the industrial field it is estimated that each year 20 percent or more of old accounts either move from a salesman's territory, go bankrupt, merge, or go out of business. Sales managers are very much aware of the importance of prospecting and of the need to add new accounts. In many companies the salesman's weekly or monthly sales report requires the filing of a separate report that identifies new business. Sales reports will ask this sort of question on prospecting: "How many first calls were made?" or this sort of question on new business: "How much of your total volume came from new accounts?" Sales managers try to stimulate their salesmen to prospect and to develop new business. Some companies even go as far as to pay a higher commission on first orders or on the first year's sales from new accounts.

What Prospecting Is

Prospecting may be defined as *identifying and calling on those who may become customers.* Prospecting is the first step in the selling process. After all, even old established accounts were once prospects.

Well-organized companies assist their salesmen with the prospecting function. Frequently, the prospecting stage is a systematized process. Good companies check carefully how their salesmen follow up leads. Leads come in to companies from advertising, telephone calls, catalogs, and suggestions from other departments. These are sorted by sales territories and are sent to the appropriate salesman. Figure 6–6 is an example of a computer printout that provides salesmen with the names and addresses of inquiries that come in to the Eastman Kodak Company. Note the blanks on the printout that ask the salesman to indicate what happened when he called on the prospect. Figure 6–7 shows the front and the back of an inquiry form also used by the Eastman Kodak Company.

The amount of time that the salesman spends prospecting depends on what kind of selling he does, the nature of his territory, and on the extent of his ambition. Salespeople in retail stores do virtually no prospecting in the sense of locating prospects outside of the store, but they may encourage people to come back to the store by handing out their business cards or by sending out notices of special merchandise offerings. This is usually a matter of encouraging old customers to come back, not a matter of prospecting.

However, there is a resemblance between prospecting and the retail salesperson's practice of sorting out the people who come into a department.

Figure 6–6

PROSCPECT REPORT

FEB. 23, 1972

THE FOLLOWING NAMES APPEAR ON OUR INQUIRY STATUS RECORDS AS ACTIVE PROSPECTS. IF THEIR STATUS HAS CHANGED, PLEASE UPDATE AND RETURN TO YOUR SALES MANAGER WITHIN SEVEN DAYS

—FRED WILKMAN, BSMD ADVERTISING

DISTRICT: BALTIMORE, MARYLAND
TERRITORY: 181

INQUIRY# 03693 DATE 02/02/71 DEPT# 71000	J P SIMMONS EMC PO BOX 141 TIMONIUM MD 21093	KODAK SALE I_I $ VALUE _____ KODAK RENT I_I $ VALUE _____	NO PROSPECT I_I BOUGHT OTHER I_I
INQUIRY# 03724 DATE 02/02/71 DEPT# 71000	S L DRUCKER OFFICE OF ED RES 6901 N CHESTER ST TOWSON MD 21204	KODAK SALE I_I $ VALUE _____ KODAK RENT I_I $ VALUE _____	NO PROSPECT I_I BOUGHT OTHER I_I
INQUIRY# 03786 DATE 02/02/71 DEPT# 70029	F R GLADSTONE MARYLAND NATL. BK. 225 N. MAPPITT ST. BALT. MD 21202	KODAK SALE I_I $ VALUE _____ KODAK RENT I_I $ VALUE _____	NO PROSPECT I_I BOUGHT OTHER I_I
INQUIRY# 04627 DATE 03/01/71 DEPT# 70029	T M FLYNN BLACK & PODELL DATA CTR TOWSON MD 21204	KODAK SALE I_I $ VALUE _____ KODAK RENT I_I $ VALUE _____	NO PROSPECT I_I BOUGHT OTHER I_I
INQUIRY# 05190 DATE 03/09/71 DEPT# 71102	J R THOMPSON BOARD OF EDUCATION 45 E GRANDE ST BEL AIR MD 21014	KODAK SALE I_I $ VALUE _____ KODAK RENT I_I $ VALUE _____	NO PROSPECT I_I BOUGHT OTHER I_I

Courtesy of Eastman Kodak Company.

Consider this: there is definitely a difference in the effectiveness of retail salespeople. The top sales producers will sell three or even four times as much as the poorest producers. Why is this, when it is the same department and the same merchandise? It is because the top retail salesperson practices a form of prospecting. Or rather, he is skilled in identifying real prospects. When he approaches people who come into his department, he sizes them up and decides whether or not they are genuine prospects. He asks himself: Are they serious shoppers, or are they just passing the time of day? The top salesman is a more accurate judge and thus he puts his time to use where it counts most. The poor salesman uses poor judgment and thus wastes his time by talking to people who are really not serious about buying.

PERSONAL-INVOLVEMENT EXERCISE NO. 6–2

WHICH TURNDOWN SHOULD BE FOLLOWED UP? One of the trickiest judgments any salesman has to make is deciding whether the prospect who says "no" really means it. In retail selling a salesperson can waste a lot of time talking to people who really do mean "no." Top salesmen do not necessarily take "no" for an answer, but this does not mean that they waste time on those who mean "no" when they say it. Veteran salesmen know that there is a vast difference between what people say and what they mean. A "no" can indeed mean "no." A "no" can also mean "Perhaps," "I'm not sure," or "Show me." And a "no" can mean "I'm interested."

Judge the following cases. In making your judgments remember this basic rule for making judgments in salesmanship: *Listen for the meaning in what people say; do not be misled by the words they happen to be using.* Assume in each case that a housewife in her late twenties enters a drapery section of a department store. Suppose she could give any one of the answers indicated. Rate each answer according to how much prospect it seems to hold for making a sale. Place a "1" in front of the most promising answer, a "2" in front of the second most promising and so on. Be prepared to explain your rankings. On a separate sheet of paper put your follow-up statement to each of the customer's answers. Your follow-up statement should be an attempt to discover immediately whether the customer is really a prospect. Your follow-up statement should be designed to get a response that will help you decide whether to continue the sales attempt or to conserve time by dropping the matter.

SALESMAN: (*Approaching a woman who is looking at a display of draperies.*) Good morning. Don't you think these sunfast colors are cheerful? [1]

ANSWER A: Yes, they are nice, but I'm only looking.

[1] Progressive retailers now recommend use of a topical approach such as the one used here instead of the approach that was used for so long—the old "May I help you?" contact opener. STOP & THINK. Why is a topical approach (one where the salesperson relates the merchandise or customer to something current) better than "May I help you?"

Figure 6–7

COMPANY INQUIRY FORM—FRONT

INQUIRY NO. 00000

EASTMAN KODAK COMPANY
BUSINESS SYSTEMS MARKETS DIVISION
ROCHESTER, NEW YORK 14650

TO: Mr. William O'Day
President
Clover Industries
2820 Holley Road
Yonkers, N. Y.   10875

Tel: 914-639-7890

RETURN POSTAGE GUARANTEED

Kodak

BSMD ADVERTISING

LITERATURE SENT A-2014, A-1765, A-1732

INQUIRY NO. 00000

DEPT. NO. 2213   DATE SENT 4/11/72

MKTG. CNTR. Yonk. 156

SALESMAN REQUESTED   [X]

☐ PROSPECT   ☐ NO PROSPECT

☐ SOLD   ▶ $_____

☐ RENTED   ▶ $_____

☐ BOUGHT FROM
   OTHER VENDOR

TERR. NO.	SALESMAN

1 FOLLOW-UP PLEASE REPLY IMMEDIATELY
   KO 3757 9-70

Courtesy of Eastman Kodak Company.

Figure 6–7

COMPANY INQUIRY FORM—BACK

ACTION REQUEST FOR PANORAMA MAILING LIST
ALL DATA MUST BE SUPPLIED. PLEASE PRINT.

ACTION	DATA		RECEIVE MAILINGS
☐ ADD NAME	☐ CUSTOMER	☐ USES MICROFILM	☐ MICROGRAPHICS
☐ CHANGE DATA	☐ NONCUSTOMER	☐ DOESN'T USE M/F	☐ IT/COM
☐ DELETE NAME	SIC CODE	FUNCTION CODE	☐ BOTH

NEW INFORMATION

NAME OF ORGANIZATION				DIVISION
FIRST NAME	INITIAL	LAST NAME	MR-MRS-DR-ETC	TITLE
STREET ADDRESS	CITY	STATE	ZIP	BSMD TERRITORY #

OLD INFORMATION RELATING TO CHANGE

NAME OF ORGANIZATION		CITY	ZIP
FIRST NAME	INITIAL	LAST NAME	STREET ADDRESS

Courtesy of Eastman Kodak Company.

ANSWER B: Are they really sunfast? I've never had colored draperies that didn't eventually fade. So I'm not interested in colors as bright as these.

ANSWER C: The time to buy draperies is in the fall. I like to brighten up my house when the dreary weather is on its way.

ANSWER D: Wish I could buy, they are so pretty. But my husband's work has been cut to three days a week and I can't afford them.

ANSWER E: We go away in the summer so there is no point in having new draperies if you're not home most of the summer.

Prospecting by salesmen who are out in a territory rather than in a retail store is also a matter of identifying those who might buy. However, since prospects do not come to the field salesman as they do to the retail salesman, the process of finding people who might become customers is much more difficult and time-consuming. The largest amount of prospecting is done by salesmen who are expected to find their own customers. Examples are door-to-door salesmen, insurance salesmen, and salesmen who are given a territory of perhaps one or two states and have to find, say, all the pharmaceutical processors who could use gelatine capsules for the packaging of drugs. In some instances prospecting is pretty much hit-or-miss, as in the case of brush salesmen going up and down streets knocking on doors. In

r instances the search is made quite carefully and as scientifically as
ible, as in the case of a chemical salesman looking for food processors
use food additives.

Identifying Prospects

Study and analysis are the keys to successful prospecting. Creativity and
ingenuity in deciding how to go about prospecting are also required. It is up
to each salesman to develop a custom-made plan to suit his own particular
product and circumstances.

One successful mobile-home-supply salesman uses a battery-operated cas-
sette recorder for prospecting. Mobile-home parks, like many apartment
complexes, shield tenants from salesmen. This salesman drives slowly
through a mobile-home park and dictates into his recorder: "Space number
forty-two, name R. M. Phillips on the mailbox, space number forty-three,
sign Sara and John Andersen above the door." The salesman has the names
and addresses transcribed from the recorder. Then he sends each addressee
a personalized letter. The salesman says, "The only way I can get in to see
prospects in a trailer park is on an appointment basis. With this technique, I
get more appointments than I can handle."

The expenditure of time and energy in knocking on doors and in making
cold-turkey or hit-or-miss calls may be commendable as a mark of ambition
but can be wasteful of the salesman's most valuable resource—his time. Interestingly, an excellent clue to where to look for prospects is found by analyzing present customers. That approach is based on this set of assumptions.
Present customers are known buyers of the product—let us take cemetery
lots as an example. Where are there more people like those who bought the
present lots? The salesman making the study for prospects can develop what
is called a profile of present owners. The first step in developing a profile
study is to make a list of the key factors that would identify present owners.
In the case of cemetery lots the following would probably be considered key
factors: age of present owners at the time they made the purchase; religion;
address (where they live in relation to the site of the cemetery will be plot-
ted on a map); home ownership (whether they live in apartments, own their
own homes, or live in retirement facilities); occupation (whether they are retired or working; what kind of work they do or did before retirement;
whether they are blue-collar, white-collar, or professional people); family
situation (whether they are married or single; how large their families are).

A salesman can probably get this information by means of a telephone
survey of present lot owners. As he gathers this kind of information from
fifty or more present owners, he will soon find a pattern or profile of present
owners emerging from his data. Thus if he finds that present lot owners are
blue-collar labor union members who bought their lots when they were
around forty-five years of age and who are members of Catholic families
and live in their own homes within an eighteen-mile radius of the cemetery,
the salesman can next ask himself how he can find nonlot-owners within this
eighteen-mile radius who fit this profile. In other words, the salesman now
knows whom he is looking for. Thus, the time spent on the survey prevents
the salesman from wasting time on prospects that offer little potential.

When the salesman finds people who fit the profile category, he can be confident that he has excellent prospects because the law of averages indicates that this is so. He also can plan his sales presentation with confidence and authority because he now knows to what kind of person he should be appealing and he can gear his presentation accordingly. He can now figure out how to go about getting leads. He can do such things as advertising in trade union and church newspapers; he can attend union and Catholic social functions; he can contact officials at trade union locals or at Catholic churches and explain what he has to offer. Getting such opinion leaders on his side by inviting them to see the cemetery and by taking them out to lunch or dinner to become better acquainted can do much to further the salesman's goal, which is to find prospects.

Qualifying Prospects

After the salesman identifies the kind of prospect he is looking for, he must qualify the individual prospects. For example, if a Buick dealership determines that physicians rate high as prospects for their automobiles, the salesman who calls on a physician must qualify him before he spends a lot of time on the call. If the physician does not have a driver's license or if his brother owns a Mercury dealership, he is disqualified—that is, it would be a waste of time to consider him as a prospect.

Another qualifying element is whether a prospect has the authority to make the buying decision. Often a wife will not make a buying decision without her husband. The matter of who makes buying decisions in industrial companies or in the resale field is quite complicated. Quite often the buyer called on by the salesman does not make decisions on major purchases. In the industrial field the salesman may have to submit his product for a *value analysis* review. Vastly simplified, value analysis can be described as a system whereby whatever a company purchases is scrutinized to increase efficiency or reduce costs.[2] The method is also called known-cost buying, value improvement, and value engineering. Wherever buying is done for components and parts that go into a company's products, the salesman can expect to have what he sells subjected to value analysis. This means that engineers and production experts of the buyer's company will carefully analyze, test, and evaluate whatever is purchased for incorporation into what the company produces. An extension of the system is for a purchaser to set up what can be described as a supplier-suggestion system. Certain progressive companies provide questionnaires in the reception areas of their buying offices. Salesmen and suppliers are thus encouraged to submit suggestions for improvements. The Bendix Corporation, for example, has a Supplier Incentive System. A communication to their suppliers states: "A supplier who submits a recommendation which is approved by Bendix and which reduces the cost of the item to us, is entitled to——% of the net savings resulting from such change." Figure 6–8 is a reproduction of the Bendix Corporation's Value Analysis/Value Engineering Check List. These methods

[2] For a detailed discussion, see K. A. Cruise, "Learning the Basic Technique of Value Analysis. *Electronic Procurement*, July–August 1963; or Ferdinand F. Mauser, *Modern Marketing Management*. New York: McGraw-Hill, 1961, pp. 187–89.

Figure 6–8

VALUE ANALYSIS/VALUE ENGINEERING CHECK LIST

In order to insure that our competitive position in the industry is continuously maintained, Bendix Corp. has developed a very active V.A./V.E. Program. Our goal is to obtain the required performance and reliability at the lowest possible cost. It is therefore requested that the following questionnaire be carefully and completely answered as the questions apply to the items upon which you are furnishing quotations. You are encouraged to freely recommend new, untried, or revolutionary ideas. If space is insufficient to adequately detail any recommended change, additional sheets, drawings, sketches, etc. may be added to this check list.

Part Nomenclature _____ Part No. _____ RFQ No. _____

1. Do you have a standard item that might be adapted for this requirement that would reduce the cost?   Yes _____   No _____

   Explain: _____

   _____

   _____

2. Do you recommend material substitutions that will reduce the cost?

   Yes _____   No _____

   Explain: _____

   _____

   _____

3. Is there any part of this item or assembly that can be produced by some other means in order to reduce costs? Yes _____   No _____

   Explain: _____

   _____

   _____

4. Do you recommend changes to finish requirements which might reduce costs?   Yes _____   No _____

   Explain: _____

   _____

   _____

Courtesy of Automotive Electronics Division, Bendix Corporation.

5. Does it appear that test or quality control requirements are too stringent or especially expensive to maintain? Yes _____ No _____

Explain: _____

_____

_____

6. Do any tolerances appear to be unreasonable or especially expensive to maintain?   Yes _____ No _____

Explain: _____

_____

_____

7. Do you have further suggestions for cost reduction? Yes _____ No _____

Explain: _____

_____

_____

8. Does your company have a formal Value Analysis/Value Engineering Program?   Yes _____ No _____
   If not, do you think it is advisable?   Yes _____ No _____

9. For information on all aspects of an organized VA/VE Program Bendix suggests Department of Defense Handbook No. H-111 of 29 March 1963 entitled, "Value Engineering."

U. S. Government Printing Office publication No. 1963 0-685239.

Approval of the above recommendations will result in the following estimated cost reductions:

	UNIT	TOOLING	TESTING	COST OF INCORPORATION
1.	$_____	$_____	$_____	$_____
2.	$_____	$_____	$_____	$_____
3.	$_____	$_____	$_____	$_____
4.	$_____	$_____	$_____	$_____
5.	$_____	$_____	$_____	$_____
6.	$_____	$_____	$_____	$_____
7.	$_____	$_____	$_____	$_____

Company _____

Signature _____

Title _____

Date _____

highlight a creative side of salesmanship that is seldom understood in the nonbusiness world.

In resale companies, such as those in the retail food chain business, use of the buying committee is quite common. Buying committees consist of various merchandisers, buyers, and advertising and materials handling experts. They review and decide on all new product additions. Usually the salesman is not allowed to appear before the committee. Instead he is expected to furnish all relevant data and to stand in the wings in case further information is needed.

An essential part of the qualifying activity is determining specifically who has the authority to make the buying decision.

An interesting dimension of prospecting is the matter of need and value. It is not enough to establish that the prospect needs the product or service. More important, how he *values* the product must be determined. Let us consider the matter of house paint. Logic would tell us that houses that have not been painted for over ten years have a greater need for painting than those that have been painted from five to ten years ago. Yet chances are that there are more qualified prospects for a house-painting job among the five- to ten-year group. How people *value* house painting is much more important than need. Therefore neighborhoods where houses need painting most do not offer nearly as good a prospect source for paint jobs as neighborhoods where houses are well maintained.

Most important is whether the means for buying exists. People who qualify as prospects yet do not have money or credit can be a great waste of time for the busy salesman. Many people who are poor credit risks are very anxious to buy and will often waste a great deal of a salesman's time. They figure that once the salesman has spent a lot of time on a presentation he will push an order through the credit department because he is committed to making the sale. In order to save time and frustration, once the salesman sees that he has an interested client he should quickly bring up the matter of credit and payment. In the case of commercial accounts he can ask about the Dun & Bradstreet rating. Dun & Bradstreet and other mercantile agencies provide credit information on businesses which they publish in information source books which are subscribed to by practically all companies of any size. *Salesmen would do well to check out credit ratings of prospects before making calls.*

SOURCES OF PROSPECTS

Consumer Prospect Sources

As has already been pointed out, each salesman, according to his particular product or service, must develop a prospecting system suited to his particular situation. Here is a list of ways of meeting prospects in the consumer-goods field.

1. Joining organizations. For example, printing salesmen are inclined to join organizations to which people in the advertising industry belong. Surveying and engineering firms have their salesmen join organizations where real estate men, builders, and contractors assemble.

2. *Cultivating people who call on your type of accounts.* Many mutually beneficial arrangements can be worked out. A laundry and linen supply salesman will "bird dog" for an insurance salesman. Bird-dogging is the name given to the practice of paying others for leads that result in sales. This is common practice in some fields. A real estate salesman will make referrals to a moving company salesman, and so on. The salesman who takes the time to think about who would logically know about leads in his field can work up some attractive arrangements that lead to business.

3. *Consulting public reference sources.* Careful reading of news items and want ads provides news about people moving in and out of town and may suggest leads of certain kinds of goods and services. Membership lists of organizations such as Rotary, the PTA, and so on provide contacts for possible business.

4. *Following up on customers and business associates.* Present customers are good sources for leads. You may be sure that a customer who has just purchased an electric organ will spend a lot of time showing it off and bragging about it to friends. He is in a way selling the electric organ that he has just bought. Thus a salesman who makes a phone call to the customer after he has owned the organ for a few weeks might easily get a few good leads on people who might be interested in or who already have been partly sold on the organ by their friend. It is often said with justification that one satisfied customer leads to another.

It is common practice in some fields to offer a finder's fee for new business. For example, in certain service fields, such as public relations, marketing research, business consulting, publishing, salesmen sometimes let it be known that it is a policy of their company to pay, say, a 5 percent fee (which is the customary amount for a finder's fee) on all referred business. Thus a salesman for a public relations firm who belongs to a press club frequented by newspaper reporters will let it be known that his company has a finder's-fee arrangement. Reporters in their daily contacts will watch for situations that could generate business for this company. They will make occasional referrals. Thus if $10,000 worth of business results, the reporter will receive 5 percent of $10,000—a powerful incentive which can generate large amounts of business. Finding prospects is difficult; therefore, companies are willing to pay accordingly. This is an accepted and legitimate business practice.

5. *Canvassing door-to-door.* A tried-and-true method that can always turn up customers is house-to-house canvassing. This is hard and often discouraging work; yet for those who are ambitious and clever it can produce results.

Commercial Prospect Sources

Salesmen selling nonconsumer products usually get help with prospecting from their companies. Leads from advertising inquiries and telephone calls are turned over to them. The salesman usually is given a territory where the company already has contacts and accounts. The salesman calls on old customers and in addition spends time prospecting so he can build up his list of customers. Some of the things he does to further his prospecting efforts involve the following:

1. Current customers. The salesman usually takes care to create rapport with present customers. Where the contact develops into a sound personal relationship, the salesman usually can ask for and receive suggestions for more business.
2. Directories and trade registers. There is a rich supply of references that list companies, names of their buyers, and other information. Probably the most complete are *Moody's Industrial Manual* and Dun & Bradstreet's *Million Dollar Directory*, which give detailed information about thousands of companies. Standard & Poor's *Industrial Surveys* is also an invaluable source.
3. Trade magazines and newspapers. The *Commercial and Financial Chronicle*, the financial sections of local newspapers, and trade magazines such as *Office Products*, *Hotel and Motel Management*, and *Chain Store Age* give much information about specific fields.
4. Cold canvass. In the commercial field, as in the consumer-goods field, cold canvassing can work if it is done with determination and skill.

The salesman who keeps his eyes and ears open can learn much through personal observation. For example, one successful real estate man, in pursuit of listings of houses to sell, makes it a point to cultivate the friendship of town gossips. He maintains that there are people in every neighborhood who know much of what is going on. Checking with them from time to time can lead to many real estate listings, according to this very successful real estate agent! Who says that gossip can't be constructive?

COMPANY CHRONICLE

John Elsworth was beginning to gain confidence in himself and in his sales ability. He found himself exhilarated by the challenges that selling offered. He had just had the best week ever and was pleased by how it was reflected in his paycheck. It was payday and he was in high spirits, so he looked around the office to find someone to whom he could brag a bit. He spotted Harry Kelly in his office. Kelly was supposed to be Elsworth's "big brother," the man to whom he had been originally assigned to "to learn the ropes." But Kelly had given Elsworth a hard time (see Company Chronicle, Chapter 4), so since then both of them, without discussing it, had decided to forget about the big brother arrangement. The two men had virtually ignored each other for the two months since Elsworth started selling on his own.

Elsworth, feeling cocky, decided to brag a bit to Kelly. Without realizing it, Elsworth probably wanted to let Kelly know that he was doing all right without his help. So he sauntered into Kelly's office.

ELSWORTH:	Good morning, Mr. Kelly. Long time no see.
KELLY:	Where have you been hiding?
ELSWORTH:	If working hard is hiding, I *have* been hiding.
KELLY:	Oh, keeping on the move, eh? Got anything to show for it?
ELSWORTH:	Yep. Had my best week yet. Made 55 percent over my base pay in commissions last week.
KELLY:	Not bad for a beginner. I've been watching your pay record and you're improving right along. How come you're only getting 5 percent commissions? Aren't you interested in 10 percent commissions for nonreferral business?
ELSWORTH:	What do you mean 10 percent commissions for nonreferral business?
KELLY:	You've been selling only to people who are referrals from department stores—that's 5 percent commission business. Don't you know that if you dig up business on your own you get a 10 percent commission because the company bills nonreferrals direct without going through a department store?
ELSWORTH:	This is the first time I've heard about that.
KELLY:	Everybody on the sales staff knows about that. Besides, it's explained in your Employee's Manual.
ELSWORTH:	I've been so busy reading what I need to know to sell that I didn't pay much attention to the stuff that referred to me as an employee.
KELLY:	Well, I'm supposed to be your big brother. If you had come over to see me once in a while instead of ignoring me, I might have told you a few things.
ELSWORTH:	I wasn't really ignoring you. Guess I just wanted to show you that I could make out without your help after you made those cracks about the way I dress and my being so young.
KELLY:	You youngsters today seem to distrust anyone over thirty. Maybe my trying to sharpen you up a bit was my way of trying to help you. What am I supposed to do if I think you're hurting yourself because of how you dress? Congratulate you? Or put some beads around your neck?
ELSWORTH:	The way I look was good enough to turn in a pretty nice week's work last week, wasn't it?
KELLY:	If that's your idea of proving that your dress is OK I can't argue against it.
ELSWORTH:	Well, anyway, thanks for telling me about the higher 10 percent commissions on nonreferral business. I'll see if I can play ball in that park, too.
KELLY:	I like to see somebody in there pitching. Why don't you see how another uniform will help your batting average?
ELSWORTH:	Boy, you don't give up, do you?
KELLY:	Maybe that's why I'm the number one salesman.
ELSWORTH:	Could be. Good-bye.

STOP & THINK

1. Review the dialogue step by step and discuss the issues.
2. From what was said, do you think Kelly is to be trusted? What about his preoccupation with Elsworth's clothes?
3. What do you think of Elsworth's ignoring Mr. Kelly for two months?
4. How should Elsworth handle Mr. Kelly in the future?

FIELD CHRONICLE

Elsworth found that the matter of the 10 percent commissions for nonreferral business was very much on his mind. As he thought about it he felt that he had really been making sales the easy way—by making calls on people who had asked a department store to send a salesman out to see them about a home-improvement project that they already had in mind. In a moment of frankness about himself he thought, "I really won't be a salesman in the true sense of the word until I can drum up my own business. A salesman isn't a salesman until he does his own prospecting."

With prospecting as a self-set challenge, he started to think about how he could develop nonreferral business. He wanted both to test himself and to shoot for the 10 percent nonreferral commissions. As he thought of how to develop a plan for prospecting, he decided that his best leads could come from his present satisfied customers. He decided that he would make it a policy to telephone a customer approximately three weeks after his home-improvement job was completed. He would ask the customer how he liked the job that had been done and whether he could drop around and see how it looked. He felt that after three weeks his customers would have shown their improvements to their friends, relatives, and neighbors. He reasoned that if he too dropped around to admire it he could then get new business leads from present customers. He planned it this way because he remembered an adage he once heard: "One satisfied customer leads to another."

In implementing his plan he found he had no difficulty at all in getting back into his customers' homes to see the completed projects. In fact, customers were flattered to think that he was interested enough to see them and take a look at their completed recreation room, modernized kitchen, or added bedroom. Much to his surprise he found that customers with completed projects often wanted a few additional things done! This led to some unexpected business. However, he still got only a 5 percent commission on this business because it also came from referrals. It was additional rather than new business.

Elsworth found that his biggest problem occurred once he got into a customer's home: he had difficulty switching the subject gracefully to ask who among those who had seen the improvement would be a good prospect for him to call on. He experimented with a couple of approaches. Let us tune in on several of the approaches he tried. (Please assume that considerable conversation has taken place before we tune in.)

APPROACH NO. 1

ELSWORTH: This really is one of the nicest recreation rooms we've put in. It really turned out beautifully. I imagine when you show it to people, they are anxious to come over and help you enjoy it.

CUSTOMER: Oh, yes. Especially the kids want to use the ping-pong table.

ELSWORTH: Are any of the kids' parents interested in doing a recreation room?

CUSTOMER: I haven't talked to any of them about that.

APPROACH NO. 2

ELSWORTH: These new kitchen cabinets must really save you a lot of footsteps.

CUSTOMER: Yes, I like the way it's all laid out to make the kitchen efficient to use.

ELSWORTH: Have you gotten any reactions from people you've shown your new kitchen to?

CUSTOMER: Oh, yes, they all like it.

ELSWORTH: Are there any that liked it especially well?

CUSTOMER: Oh, they all like it.

ELSWORTH: Do any of them want to remodel their kitchens?

CUSTOMER: I didn't talk to any of them about that.

APPROACH NO. 3

ELSWORTH: This new room in your attic really has provided you with a luxurious new guest room.

CUSTOMER: Yes. My husband's mother came over from St. Louis for a couple of days. It's the first time I've ever seen her happy with anything.

ELSWORTH: Have you shown the room to people who visit?

CUSTOMER: Oh, yes, everyone who comes over gets a Cook's tour!

ELSWORTH: I'm interested in getting leads on new business. Would anyone you've shown your new room to be interested in a remodeling job of any kind?

CUSTOMER: I don't know.

STOP & THINK

1. Do you think Elsworth was right in going after nonreferral business so vigorously? He seemed to be wasting a great deal of time making calls that produced no leads, let alone sales. When he limited himself to referral business, he wasted little time and always had a bona fide prospect. Discuss.

2. Was Elsworth right in saying that the test of a salesman comes in finding his own prospects? Discuss.

3. Analyze each of the three approaches. What was right or wrong about each? Make improvements in what Elsworth could have said.

4. Should Elsworth disguise the fact that he is looking for leads, or should he come right out with it and say what he wants?

SITUATIONS

Planning Your Week. Managing time effectively is especially essential for salesmen, since their earnings relate directly to the amount of time they spend with prospects. The salesman's and the student's problems of managing time are very similar because both have rather unstructured responsibilities. Therefore, if you start managing time effectively as a student you will already have developed a good habit in the event that you become a salesman. Over each weekend draw up a plan for how you feel you should use your time each day of the coming week. List first the fixed obligations such as meals, sleep, going to class, part-time job, and club meetings. Then put in the special things to which you are committed and that cannot be changed —a dance on Friday night, the dentist between 2 and 3 P.M. on Wednesday, an appointment with the dean between 9 and 10 A.M. on Thursday. Whatever time is left is your discretionary time—the time segment that can be wasted all too easily. Start planning to use it. Allocate it for constructive purposes—two hours a week for a workout in the gym, twelve hours for studies (when you plan your studying, be specific; for example, read history between 6 and 8 P.M. on Tuesday), two hours for bringing order out of chaos in your room, and so forth. At the end of a week compare the plan with what actually happened. Such a comparison of plan versus actuality will reveal the chief drains on your time. Simply working out a plan and reviewing it will make you more conscious of the value of your time and will cause you to use it more effectively.

Practice Listening for Meaning. Listening to what people mean rather than to what they actually say is a talent that every good salesman should cultivate. You can practice this art in your daily life. Following are six examples of what people say. A possible meaning is provided for the first two. To give you practice in determining meanings, describe what you believe the meanings could be for the last four. Compare your answers with those of other students who do this exercise for interesting insights as to how human mentalities work.

SITUATION No. 1   *A fellow sitting next to you in class says:* "I'm not going to be able to be here for next Friday's class. I hope I won't miss anything that's too important."

Possible Meaning   "I hope you will offer to take extra careful notes and let me have them."

SITUATION No. 2   *Your girl (boy) friend says:* "Bills are really high at the beginning of the school year, aren't they?"

Possible Meaning   "Let's do something cheap this weekend."

SITUATION No. 3   *Your friend talks to you about a mutual acquaintance.* "Have you noticed that Susan has been treating people rather coolly lately?"

Possible Meaning

SITUATION No. 4   *A friend you ride to school with in the morning says:* "I went out with Phil last night. He drinks too much, and keeps me out too late."

Possible Meaning

SITUATION No. 5   *Your best friend tells you:* "I haven't been writing home lately. I wonder if the folks are all right."

Possible Meaning

SITUATION No. 6   *A girl you know says:* "I didn't want to go to that party. That crowd is just a bunch of bores."

Possible Meaning

Providing Specific and Documented Information. We have emphasized in this chapter that specific and documented information is the most effective answer to specific comments. Following are three comments that were made to salesmen. Write in the kind of specific information that should be provided in replying to these comments.

SITUATION No. 1   (*Comment made to a printing salesman*) "These manuals weigh almost two pounds. I wonder if the shipping costs are going to raise costs beyond what we can afford?"

SITUATION No. 2   (*Comment made to a broker selling stocks*) "If I put $2,000 into savings bonds, I'd probably be ahead."

SITUATION No. 3   (*Comment made to an automobile salesman*) "I think it would be cheaper for me to keep my old car another year —it's only three years old now."

CHAPTER REVIEW AND DISCUSSION QUESTIONS

1. What is a purchasing agent's resource file? How does it relate to the salesman's goals?
2. Prove the statement "Time is money."
3. What is meant by using the law of averages in planning? What principles can be applied to improve the law of averages in planning?
4. What is a customer-call record? How does a salesman use it? What information is mentioned on it?
5. What is meant by flexibility in planning? What goals other than making an immediate sale might a salesman have in making a call?
6. Knowledge is power. Explain what this power accomplishes for the salesman.

7. What are the special difficulties that go with getting the first order? Why are buyers so reluctant to change suppliers?
8. Select a product bought by an industrial purchasing agent. Indicate the kinds of information you would collect in order to be knowledgeable about the product.
9. It has been pointed out that salesmen of the future will be more concerned with social needs. Explain.
10. Describe how salesmen keep themselves up-to-date.
11. What is prospecting? Why is it so essential? How does a retail salesman prospect?
12. Explain the present customer-profile method of prospecting.

7

THE SELLING PROCESS: PART II
BEGINNING THE SALE
AND MAKING THE PRESENTATION

Let us watch well our beginnings,
and results will manage themselves.
—ALEXANDER CLARK

Basically there are two kinds of sales calls: the initial call and the follow-up call. In the initial call the salesman has had no previous personal experience with the prospect. In the follow-up call the salesman has contacted the account before, so he knows something about what to expect.

THE INITIAL CALL

Most salesmen, as they gain experience, develop one or possibly several sales openings that seem to work out best for them when calling on a prospect for the first time. In other words, they use a more or less standardized opening, which they may alter and improve on as experience dictates.

On the initial call then, the salesman customarily uses the standardized approach that he either has perfected himself or has been taught by the company for which he works. Not infrequently, a standardized presentation is one that is memorized as prescribed by the sales staff of a company—the idea being that the presentation is so important that it is best not to leave it to the discretion of the salesman. Based on what he can find out about the prospect beforehand, the salesman adds whatever he feels may be especially appropriate for this particular ice-breaking session. Under some circumstances, and this occurs often in the industrial field, he may not even try to make a sale on the first visit. It is important to remember that the emphasis on the first call may be on building rapport, especially if it is a case in which the salesman's objective is to win a steady customer. Getting a foot in the door in itself is an achievement. Getting acquainted, familiarizing the buyer with the line, and perhaps obtaining only a small initial order to establish a relationship, may be as far as the salesman will attempt to go on a first visit.

Devising and Using Flexible Plans

Certainly, regardless of what his objective is on the first call, the salesman must plan beforehand what he is going to do and say once he gets in to see the prospect. It is poor practice to face a prospect without preparation. Proceeding with the sales presentation should not be left to the inspiration of the moment.

A salesman must not be a slave to a plan, however. Master salesmen develop great sensitivity and as a result know when to discard their planned approach and switch to something else if unusual circumstances dictate that another approach may be more effective. Veteran salesmen will often cite examples of how a great sale was made because they took advantage of a special circumstance. Seasoned salesmen know that alertness and flexibility pay off in sales work.

One example from the dozens that could be gathered at any sales convention will illustrate the advantages of flexibility. A young salesman for a large soap company had to make his first call on a wholesale grocery buyer who had a reputation for being very disagreeable. The young salesman intended to use the prepared approach that he usually used when making a first call. In the buyer's reception room, the young salesman found that there were four salesmen from other companies ahead of him. As is often the case in buyer reception rooms, the waiting salesmen were discussing the problem buyer.[1] All of them confirmed the fact that this particular buyer was most difficult to get along with. When the young salesman mentioned that he represented a large soap company, the other salesmen shook their heads. One of them pointed out that this buyer was especially rude to soap salesmen because the profit margins on soap were so low.

Being imaginative and resourceful, the young salesman decided not to use his prepared approach. When he finally got in to see the buyer, the buyer looked up at him and said, "Who are you?"

The young man said, "I'm the scaredest soap salesman in the United States!"

The startled buyer asked, "Why?"

---

[1] Some salesmen, perhaps wisely, have a policy of never discussing their business in reception rooms or with other salesmen. Salesmen are competitive by nature and will grasp at anything they feel could give them an advantage in the eyes of the person they are calling on. The occasional salesman is not above repeating something he has heard in the reception room to the buyer whom he is calling on. Furthermore, salesmen can be clannish. What a salesman says in a reception room or to another salesman can end up as a choice tidbit of information for the salesman's competitor. As has been emphasized, information is the lifeblood of salesmanship; hence, salesmen traffic in it to a point where it sometimes becomes scandalous. A general policy of being closemouthed is probably the most prudent course.

The salesman said, "Because I've heard that you dislike soap salesmen and that you are the hardest buyer in the state to get along with."

The buyer was so nonplussed and amused by the young man's bluntness and obvious sincerity that he went out of his way to prove that he was not as bad a character as he had been made out to be. The resourceful young salesman, by switching to an innovative approach when he saw that his conventional method was doomed to failure, was able to establish a friendly working relationship with a buyer who would otherwise have been difficult to manage.

THE FOLLOW-UP CALL

In the follow-up call the salesman has a great deal more to work with. He has already established a relationship of some kind with the person he calls on. Before making the follow-up call, he reviews and considers carefully the past history of previous calls, which he has recorded in some kind of filing system. He then sets up goals for what he wants to accomplish in this particular call. One goal may be to get information to add to the file he keeps on the buyer. Was he satisfied with the last order? Did the heavier weight metal the salesman had recommended last time do the job better, as the salesman predicted? Did the substitute merchandise for an out-of-stock model work out all right? What new production projects is the buyer's company undertaking? And so on.

Other goals might be to get the buyer to try other items in the salesman's line that have not been ordered before. The buyer may be splitting his business with other suppliers. The salesman, who may have been getting token orders, may attempt to become a full-fledged resource now that his company has had a chance to prove itself. A very common goal is to introduce buyers to new models and products.

Follow-up calls are inclined to be custom-tailored to take advantage of the specific circumstances created by past relationships. Initial calls are inclined to be standardized because there is no experience factor on which to fall back.

GETTING APPOINTMENTS

Making an Appointment Is Actual Selling

The salesman persuades. His first step in this process is to persuade the prospect to see him. Wherever possible, an effort should be made to see prospects and customers by appointment. Having an appointment usually means that the person to be called on will actually set time aside to listen to a sales presentation. "I have an appointment with Mr. Decision-Maker," used at the reception desk and mentioned to a secretary, is the magic phrase that saves time for the salesman and gets him past those people who otherwise stand as a shield between the salesman and the potential customer.

The salesman who succeeds in making an appointment already has a great advantage. The prospect has agreed to set aside time to listen to him.

Although it is never assured in the hectic business world, an appointment often means that the salesman will receive the prospect's undivided attention. There are a variety of ways in which to try for appointments.

The Letter Asking for an Appointment. Salesmen who must cover large territories often use letters to request appointments. For example, a fabrics salesman for a New England textile mill may cover the tristate area of Ohio, Indiana, and Kentucky. He might set up a trip to northern Ohio one week, southern Ohio the next, and so on. He would write to the people he plans to call on, explaining that he is coming from Rhode Island for the purpose of showing them his company's fall line of new fabrics and patterns. The letter itself, on stationery from an Eastern company and postmarked in Rhode Island, will probably get attention. The fact that the salesman is coming from so far away makes a request for a specific appointment reasonable. The fact also that a salesman in faraway New England writes and tells a buyer for a Cincinnati company that he has been selected to view the new fall line, is in a way flattering.

The salesman's letter will usually give the dates during which he will be in the buyer's vicinity. The salesman will make it as easy as possible for the buyer to agree to see him. For example, a phrase such as this might close the letter: "Please circle the time below that will be most convenient for you to see me. Return the letter in the stamped envelope enclosed." A letter asking for an appointment should give specific reasons why it will be advantageous for the prospect to see the salesman. General statements such as "I want to show you our line of generators," or "We have a line of lathes that will be of interest to you," are phrases that are seller- rather than buyer-oriented. Specific statements that are buyer- rather than seller-oriented are much more effective: "I want to show you a line of heavy-duty generators that I can prove will reduce maintenance costs in operations such as yours," or "Our new lathes will mean increased production efficiency for you because they incorporate for the first time anywhere an exclusive patented feature our company secured from Japan."

Carefully written letters requesting appointments usually include a phrase that facilitates the salesman's calling even if the letter is not answered. A phrase such as "I'll confirm our appointment with your secretary as soon as I arrive in Cincinnati," will give the salesman a chance to talk to the secretary about an appointment even if the letter has not been answered. When the salesman arrives in Cincinnati, he will telephone the secretary to say that he has called to confirm an appointment. The secretary will rightly assume that an appointment is in the process of being negotiated and may even make it without consulting the boss.

Telephone Appointments. The telephone has many advantages for getting appointments. It takes little time to use and since it requires no paper work it gets quicker results than a letter. Setting up an appointment by means of a letter usually takes at least a week, whereas a telephone call can secure an appointment in a matter of minutes. It is easy to ignore a letter but it is difficult for most people to say no when they are talking directly to someone. Also, by using the telephone the salesman can ascertain who it is he should visit. He may not actually get to talk to the right person on the phone, but he may receive some helpful information. The printing salesman, for example, can ask the person who answers the phone, "Is Mr. Blake responsible for buying printing for your company?" If the answer is yes, the next questions would be, "When are his office hours? May I make an appointment?"

One of the big problems a salesman has is finding the person in the company who makes the buying decisions for what he has to sell. If a letter is addressed to the wrong person, it probably ends up in the wastebasket. If a telephone call is made to the wrong person, the mistake is immediately detected and (most important) the salesman usually finds out who the right person is and has his call transferred accordingly. In fact, the telephone is undoubtedly the quickest and most reliable way to determine who is responsible for what in a company. Furthermore, the person's correct title, office location, and affiliations are readily determined.

As with anything in business, using the telephone for making appointments is not without its problems. The greatest problem is for the salesman to get to talk to the actual person he wishes to see. Most executives have secretaries whose job it is to shield them from persons who would infringe upon their time. If it is a regular buying office, a secretary often has authority to set up appointments for the boss. In most cases however, the secretary acts as a barrier and tries to discourage salesmen from speaking to the boss. The best way for the salesman to overcome this hurdle is to speak with confidence and authority. When asked who is calling, a nonhesitating "This is Jim Jones of the Claxton Corporation," will often discourage the secretary from acting as a roadblock.

One excellent way to hurdle the secretarial barrier is to use a long-distance telephone call. If the salesman is to call on a prospect in another town he can have a secretary in his own office make a call to the person he wants to talk to. The secretary will be instructed to say: "This is Mr. Suffrin's secretary calling long distance from Providence, Rhode Island. Is Mr. Buyer of Cincinnati there please?" When the buyer gets on the line (people seem unable to resist a long-distance telephone call), the secretary turns the call over to the salesman, who then talks to the buyer. This method of getting through to a buyer is most effective.

Once the salesman has his party on the line, it is probably best to come quickly to the point. The telephone is an intruder. It interrupts people right in the middle of what they are doing. The person whom the salesman has called is undoubtedly busy with something when he answers the phone. If the interruption is brief it may not be resented. Chances are that resentment at the intrusion will grow as the time that is taken lengthens.

The salesman should prepare remarks made on the telephone as carefully as those in a letter. Every word should count. His purpose should be stated clearly, and the advantages of the appointment, or the prospect's curiosity, should cause cooperation on the part of the person called. It is a mistake to go into a sales presentation on the telephone if the purpose of the call is to see the person face-to-face.

Confirming Letters, Folders, or Cards. In some cases, salesmen will send a letter, folder, or card with a written notation on it, confirming the appointment. There are several reasons for doing this. Some salesmen feel that a communication of this kind will probably end up in a company file where it may be referred to when something that the salesman sells is needed. In other words, a letter or card can lead to future orders. It also serves as a reminder that the salesman is coming and it encourages the buyer to prepare for his arrival. There are many cases where complicated inventories will be taken in preparation for a salesman's arrival, such as in the case of spare-parts stocks or stocks of merchandise in hardware or ready-to-wear departments.

PERSONAL-INVOLVEMENT EXERCISE NO. 7–1

SECURING SALES-RELATED INFORMATION OVER THE TELEPHONE. You have been reading about using the telephone to make appointments. You cannot really get the feel of using the telephone for sales purposes until you try it. This exercise will give you that opportunity.

In a Yellow Pages telephone directory select at random the telephone numbers of three companies. Assume that you are a salesperson for a printing concern that sells printed letterheads and envelopes. Assume further that you want to send a letter to the person in charge of buying stationery at each of the three companies you selected. Call the company and try to get the title, name, and address of the person to whom you would send your letter. (You will not actually send a letter; the purpose of this exercise is to introduce you to the telephoning phase of a salesman's work.) When you have completed your three calls, answer the following.

1. What have you learned as a result of this experience?
2. What do you feel are the advantages and disadvantages of using the telephone for getting information that the salesman needs?
3. What approach do you recommend for getting the best results over the telephone?

APPROACH METHODS

Fostering the Cooperation of Subordinates

There are usually one or more human hurdles that stand between the salesman and the company decision-maker he wants to call on. These people can be receptionists, secretaries, or administrative assistants, whose job it is to screen out those who will get to see the boss. None of these people will present a problem if the salesman has been lucky enough to be able to make an appointment beforehand, because when the salesman has an appointment with Mr. X he can use the magic phrase "I have an appointment to see Mr. X at three o'clock." This ploy causes all those who stand between the salesman and the boss to step aside (and perhaps even bow!). This is a big reason why salesmen should work hard to develop means for securing appointments whenever they can.

As we have mentioned earlier, modern selling is solution-oriented. For the salesman to provide a solution, someone in the company must define a problem. The boss himself may mention a problem. For example, he may mention to a printing salesman that his company intends to mail 10,000 folders to various customers. The salesman would think about this problem. In thinking about it, it might occur to him that typing printed labels to paste on the outside of each folder might be cheaper than mailing the folders in envelopes. Printed labels could mean an extra printing order for the salesman and a reduction in costs for the customer. Information as to whether the idea is feasible might easily come from the customer's assistant, who could also tell him such things as what form the mailing list for the folders is in, and the like. The salesman could get much of the information he needs to solve both his and the customer's problem from the secretary or the assistant. Furthermore, he might even get suggestions from the aide as to how to solve the problem in a way that would be even more satisfactory from the customer's point of view. The point to be aware of is that the boss, the people surrounding the boss, and the salesman all have a common aim: to see that the business operates as efficiently and as profitably as possible. If the salesman makes clear that his goal is the same as everyone else's in the company and that he stands ready to help them in their job, he has a very good chance to get people in the company to cooperate with his attempts to solve problems by involving the use of his products.

Of course, many salesmen are acutely aware of the importance of getting the boss's subordinates on their side. An assistant to an important decision-maker, for example, is approached by dozens of salespersons each week. All of them are bent on trying to ingratiate themselves with him or her. Many salesmen probably lose out by being too chummy before they really know the assistant well enough. They may use a breezy manner that is overly familiar or childish in their attempt to be noticed. A safe rule is to be courteous and sincere. Doing business is a serious matter. The people surrounding a busy decision-maker are selected for their intelligence and good judgment. The chances are that phoniness and insincerity are very transparent to them and that they will resent such behavior the minute they spot it. Therefore, sincere, mature, businesslike deportment is undoubtedly the best policy for assured success.

As has been mentioned, the building of a friendly relationship with a decision-maker's secretary or administrative assistant can be very rewarding. Passing the time of day with these people can result in their passing along helpful information. Never to be overlooked is the fact that *information is essential in making a sale*. A secretary can inform the salesman about what is going on. Assistants can be especially helpful in the matter of timing and on the status of decisions. A salesman who asks a secretary, "When will they go ahead with setting up production on the new models?" may be told, "They decided to come out a month earlier this year." By learning this, the salesman can adjust his plans accordingly and perhaps thereby get the edge on his competitor.

As one master salesman pointed out, the receptionist in a way sets the stage for the interview. If the salesman has created a pleasant relationship

with her, she will announce him to the boss smilingly and say, "Mr. Woodward is here to see you." If she's annoyed with the salesman she may glumly announce, "Here's that Mr. Woodward again!" First impressions and setting the stage properly are a series of little things the proper combination of which can add up to big sales.

MAKING A GOOD FIRST IMPRESSION

First impressions are terribly important in selling. The first impression determines how much attention and time the salesman will receive. If the first impression is not good, the salesman will find himself being shoved out of the office as quickly as possible.

Let us examine the process whereby people make first impressions. The very first impact is a visual impact. We see a person before we hear him speak. Therefore, whether we like it or not, impressions are made on the basis of a person's appearance.

Businessmen expect those with whom they do business to look and act like businessmen. Any deviation from the business stereotype may be noticed. If it is noticed (too loud a tie, unkempt hair, excessively flashy attire), there is a risk that it will be judged negatively. Good grooming and conservative dress are least likely to offend, and therefore are the most practical policy. The focus in selling should be on what is being sold, not on the person doing the selling.

Young people are often critical of "the establishment." They resent having to conform to so-called establishment rules. We must remember that the salesman is a businessman, not a reformer. He is in the business of accommodating himself to the world in such a way that he will function efficiently. When he is on his own time, he should express himself as he pleases. While he is working he should behave in ways relevant to the job at hand.

The salesman has the abilities of the chameleon, the delightful little lizard that changes color according to the color of its environment. A person able to adapt to the environment possesses a great skill. Immense personal satisfaction comes from this ability. The buyer wants to deal with people with whom he feels comfortable—the kinds of people he is used to. If the salesman who calls on him varies too much from the norm in dress, mannerisms, or speech, or is high-strung and uneasy, the buyer will feel uncomfortable and will want to end the interview quickly.

The Opening Statement

The first few minutes of an interview should be considered as a period of sizing up, settling down, and creating rapport. First, of course, comes the possible handshake and greeting. Whether or not one shakes hands depends on the prospect and circumstances. Handshakes, in a way, help set the tone for an interview. A limp handshake, a stone-crusher handshake, or the presentation of a sweaty palm can diminish a buyer's willingness to become involved with a salesman. The salesman whose hands do perspire should see to it that his hand is dry when he extends it (a handkerchief powdered with talcum can solve this problem). The grip should be firm, accompanied by a smile and a direct meeting of the eyes.

It is not wise to plunge immediately into business. Niceties should be exchanged, and they should be fairly imaginative, not mere comments about the weather. The best openings are topical, preferably some comment that is newsworthy and related to the particular company or industry that the buyer represents. Topical openings facilitate the switch from the niceties to the business at hand—making the sales presentation. Business pages of the local newspaper or the *Wall Street Journal* or any other periodical the salesman knows the buyer reads, provide many suitable subjects that are conversational lead-ins. The salesman keeps notes on what the buyer reads and briefs himself accordingly before each visit. Thus part of the preparation for the interview is to find a proper subject for opening the conversation. For example, a salesman calling on a component supplier for the automobile industry might lead into an interview with "Good morning, Mr. Corelli. I notice that General Motors is building a new plant in Marion, Ohio. Will your company get to supply them there, too?" Or a salesman calling on a drugstore might start by saying, "Hello, Mr. Paige. I see that Blue Cross has signed up the La Cross Company employees. Is that going to benefit your business in any way?" You will note that subjects of a positive nature are used for openings. Subjects that might have a negative connotation could spread gloom and set the stage unfavorably.

It has been suggested that the salesman avoid plunging into the sales presentation too quickly. A fair question to consider, then, is how long the salesman should talk about other things before he starts his presentation. A salesman must learn to sense this. It can be said generally that relatively little time should be spent on other-than-business matters. Buyers as a group are very busy. The salesman's time also has considerable value. Thus, since the time of both parties is at a premium, logic dictates that the salesman should get on with his business as quickly as possible. Within minutes after he is seated in a relaxed manner he should switch from his opening niceties and social inquiries and begin to make his sales presentation.

There is also the matter of smoking. If the salesman does smoke, he should definitely extinguish his cigarette or cigar in the reception area before he goes in to see the buyer. When he is in the buyer's presence he should not smoke unless he is invited to do so. Note that it is not a good policy to ask permission to smoke unless the buyer himself is smoking. Very few people refuse anyone permission to smoke after a courteous request to do so. Receiving permission to smoke from someone who is not smoking does not mean that he approves of smoking or that it does not disturb him. Nervous cigarette smoking can make a buyer nervous and easily cause him to press for a quick termination of the sales presentation.

CUSTOM-TAILORING THE SALES PRESENTATION TO FIT THE OCCASION

Objectives of the Presentation

The nature of the presentation depends on the goals of the salesman. It is true of course that the goal of any sales effort is to make an eventual sale. Salesmen do not expect or plan to come away from each sales interview with an order. Many sales calls are made for the purpose of cultivating a customer. Salesmen who sell component parts used in the assembly of tractors or appliances, for example, or who sell computer systems, may call on a prospect for weeks or even months before receiving an order. In some fields, it is not unreasonable for a salesman to spend a lot of time this way. After all, when he finally makes a sale for the rental of a computer system, or gets an order to supply parts that are used in the assembly of a customer's product, he probably has produced a regular customer who will provide steady business indefinitely.

When salesmen seek to establish regular customers their early objective in making calls may be to create visibility and awareness. A salesman of complicated products or services may not even attempt to make a complete presentation in one call. Each call may emphasize only one or two aspects of what the salesman has to offer. For example, several calls may be devoted to

covering different products in a company's line. Some companies may have dozens or even hundreds of products to sell. Other calls may be devoted to explaining such things as the research and development facilities of the company and the qualifications of its technical people—all of which are available to assist in solving customer problems. Still other calls may be devoted to explaining a company's research efforts, new products, and services related to the buyer's chief concerns. The theory is that the greater the buyer's awareness and knowledge of a salesman's company and products, the more the buyer's confidence will grow and the more apt he will be to view the salesman's company as an established source when it comes time to place orders.

In many cases, the salesman's objective is indeed to make a sale on the first call. A Fuller Brush salesman who goes from house to house, an Avon Products cosmetics representative, a clothing salesman, an automobile salesman, and so on, have immediate sales objectives. It probably can be said that the more immediate the sales objective, the more standardized the sales presentation. Salesmen who seek an immediate sale will call on larger numbers of people and do not have time to size up each prospect as carefully as a salesman who is seeking steady customers. When there is no time for extensive sizing up, the answer is the standardized sales presentation. That is, the salesman builds and uses one presentation that he feels will effectively present what he is selling to most people. The standardized presentation is the shotgun approach, in which a scatter shot is fired, with the hope of hitting at least something in the target range. The rifle approach uses custom-built ammunition and zeroes in on a single target, concentrating on hitting it and it alone.

Approaches in Making a Presentation

The subject of the approaches used in a sales presentation is widely discussed in sales literature. Some authors use extensive classifications of sales approaches, listing from ten to fifteen different kinds. They list such approaches as the shock approach (in which an insurance salesman opens an interview by showing the prospect a picture of what could happen to his family if he does not have enough insurance), the introductory approach (in which the salesman has secured a written introduction from someone the prospect knows), and the premium approach (in which the salesman gives the prospect a gift to oblige him to listen).

There is a danger in overclassifying and concentrating on the development of separate kinds of approaches. There may be too much focus on the approach and not enough focus on the prospect's problems. In other words, the means can become the end. The shock or dramatization element or the gift may get prime attention to the detriment of the product or service being sold. Unusual tactics can repel as easily as they can attract because they tamper with human emotions. Unusual approaches are always contrived and thus can introduce unnecessary elements of artificiality.

There is no denying that dramatic sales results have been achieved by using unorthodox methods. At this stage in your sales careers, however, it is best to rely on the safer and surer approaches. As the young salesman gains experience, he can experiment with unusual attention-getting, curiosity-arousing, problem-solving approaches that are natural for the particular situations he faces. The less contrived, the more sincere the approach, the better the chances for success.

SALES PRESENTATION CONSIDERATIONS

There are differences in the effectiveness of the various sales presentations. Certain salesmen are consistently top producers while others are consistently weak producers. There is no doubt that the sales presentation itself is as important as any other factor in distinguishing the good from the weak salesmen. What are the influences at work in the sales presentation? Analysis of these influences can provide significant insights.

Being Interesting and Enthusiastic

Being *interesting* is a matter of being *interested* in what you are doing. Prospects cannot be expected to become interested in something about which the salesman himself shows little enthusiasm. Enthusiasm is catching. It is also highly personal and not easily faked. A sales presentation that appears to be memorized—where the salesman stumbles on words that do not seem to be his own—or one that is presented in a rote way or as something that should be dispensed with as quickly as possible, fails to carry the magic ingredient of enthusiasm. Enthusiasm means that what the salesman says flows freely and naturally out of his convictions and deep interest in what he has to sell—not out of what the salesman has memorized.

Use of variety in the presentation holds the interest of the listener as does change of pace. Voice variations, questions, pauses, gestures, and eye contact all add variety. Many salesmen talk too fast and too much. Fast-talker types of salesmen are more or less a thing of the past. People today are too well educated and too inclined to be skeptical, because of Naderism and the consumer movement, to succumb to fast talk. The prospect should be given an opportunity to interject questions and reactions comfortably. Pausing before and after an important point first alerts the listener to the fact that something especially important is about to be said, and then gives him a chance to absorb what is said.

Involvement

No one likes to listen for too long a period. If a person is "talked at" for any length of time, his attention wanders. "Talking at" rather than "talking with" prospects loses many sales. "Talking at" is not communicating. Communications is a two-way flow. "Talking at" means that words are flowing only from the salesman to the prospect. The sales presentation must be designed so the prospect quickly becomes involved and feels that he is part of things. Asking questions is an excellent way to relax the prospect and to get him involved in the communication process.

Questioning the prospect about his company's operations is a good way for the salesman to determine what problems exist. For example, an office equipment salesman can ask, "How much incoming mail do you handle in an average workweek?" and then follow up with, "Are your peak weeks very much higher so that there are weeks when things pile up?" This line of questioning is directed toward a problem that a salesman handling mail-facilitating equipment is prepared to solve.

Psychologically, people are usually very much inclined to talk about their problems, for indeed they are looking for solutions. If a salesman can identify a problem area and demonstrate that he knows something about it, he has a good chance of getting the prospect's ear.

Another way of getting the prospect involved is to hand him samples that he can examine, and blueprints and layouts that he and the salesman can look at and talk about together. Physical acts such as holding a product model, helping unfold blueprints, and testing the way something works, produce a feeling of involvement and cause the salesman's comments to be natural and personal rather than stilted and artificial, as when a salesman simply sits across a desk and recites a list of memorized sales points.

Sensing the Sales Climate

The salesman making a presentation has to be able to sense how the prospect is reacting to what is going on. Trying to guess what is going on in another person's mind is an extremely difficult art. Some people are naturally more aware of how other people feel about things. However, whether or not one is inherently gifted in judging the reactions of others, one can at least learn something about it. The key to sensitivity about others lies in being observant.

When speaking to others there are often definite signs as to whether they are actually listening. A person who is listening is focusing his eyes on the speaker. The eyes follow the speaker's gestures, widen when something surprising is said, and so on. When the mind wanders, the eyes tend to wander and not to focus. If the buyer starts glancing at the objects on his desk instead of at the salesman or what he is doing, chances are his mind is wandering. People who are listening carefully tend to sit still. When they start shifting about in their seats, running their hands through their hair, tapping their feet—these are signs of impatience. When there are signs of the mind wandering or of impatience, a change of pace is called for. The salesman should shorten what he is talking about, switch to something else, ask questions, or get the prospect to comment on the progress of the presentation. Questions like "Would you like to look at pictures of this machine to see how it looks installed in factories similar to yours?" or "Which colors sell best in your store?" tend to recapture the wandering mind. They also provide the salesman with an indication of whether he is making any real progress toward making a sale.

The alert look in the buyer's eye and the knowing nod of the head in agreement at the right time tell the salesman that things are going well and that perhaps details about placing an order are ready to be discussed.

Thoroughness and Clarity

One of the difficulties a salesman has is determining the extent of the prospect's knowledge about what is being sold. It is very easy for a salesman to get overly technical about what he has to sell. Since the salesman handles the same product or service every day and repeats points about it so often, he may easily start assuming that others know more about it than they do. There is also, of course, the danger of offending or boring a person who does know something about a product with too much basic or repetitive information. If the salesman is unsure, it is better to err in the direction of oversimplifying. Being misunderstood endangers a sale more than does offending by oversimplification.

The astute salesman will interject questions from time to time to determine whether or not he is at the right level of sophistication in his presentation. "Do you know about the complicated way the absorption qualities of this material are measured?" is psychologically keyed for getting an accurate answer. When the salesman says the process is complicated, the prospect will not feel that he is asking to have something simple explained. If he knows about the process he will be flattered by the fact that he can say he understands it. Checking for understanding is always tricky because people do not like to admit ignorance.

In considering the thoroughness factor we mean that the salesman must be prepared to answer any and all questions that may arise. Whenever a question cannot be answered, the salesman should make a careful note of it and promise to answer as soon as possible. The salesman should be very conscientious about doing this, not only for the sake of the prospect but also for his own training and information. A question that comes up once can come up a second time. This is one way the salesman forces himself to keep up-to-date on what he is expected to know.

Taste in Language and Deportment

Salesmen should be concerned about the matter of taste. Some salesmen definitely limit their ability to sell by not developing good taste. Taste is the sense of knowing what is appropriate in a certain time, place, and context. Speech that is appropriate in a private situation may not be appropriate in an office or public restaurant.

True, society has become much more permissive. Four-letter words are used freely in much of our literature and on the stage and screen. Pornography seems to have few restrictions. But this should not cause a blindness to what is appropriate.

There are salesmen who feel they are expected to be cruder than other members of society. Some men feel that foul language enhances their manliness, that the dirty story is part of their stock-in-trade. The important thing is to know what is appropriate in time, place, and context. A salesman selling bulldozers to contractors would certainly be out of place using Oxford English and Victorian manners on a construction site.

It is very interesting to study master salesmen of various companies. It is quite noticeable that top producers have taste—they know what is right for different occasions. Poorer salesmen seem less flexible and less sensitive to knowing what deportment is called for under different circumstances.

Handling Interruptions

Interruptions are one of the salesman's biggest headaches. And like headaches, they are inevitable and unpredictable as to when they will occur. The telephone is the rudest of interrupters. Unfortunately, most people allow the unseen caller on the telephone, no matter how trivial his message, to have priority over the person with whom they are talking face-to-face. There are physical interruptions, too—a subordinate of a buyer will come in for an OK on some matter, or a secretary will request that an urgent letter be read and signed immediately. A screaming child will come bursting in to have a finger bandaged when a salesman is in the midst of showing carpet samples to a homeowner, and so on.

The salesman must size up the situation when he is interrupted and decide what to do. If he feels that the interview has been going well and that he has had the interest of the prospect, he can continue where he left off by reminding the prospect where they were at the time of the interruption—for example, "You will recall, Mr. Schmidt, that I was going over how the leasing of this machine is actually more profitable than buying one because of the tax savings." During the interruption the salesman should decide which selling point seemed to impress the prospect most. It is good strategy to review that selling point and then to continue on with the presentation at the place where it was interrupted.

If the interview has not been going particularly well, the salesman may wish to review the highlights of what has been covered so far, rephrasing these points so they do not appear to be obviously repetitive.

An interruption can be so serious that the buyer's attention is diverted to the point where he tries to terminate the interview as quickly as possible without really listening to anything further. When the salesman sees that the situation is hopeless, he should help by saying, "I can wind this up in just a minute or two." While he is doing this he can test by watching whether the buyer's attention comes back or not. If not, the best thing to do is to wind up quickly and to leave gracefully. The buyer may remember the salesman's willingness to cooperate by getting out quickly. Reappointments that are made after a salesman has had to cut short his presentation can be very productive. Sometimes a prospect will remember that the salesman had to make a trip back and as a result compensate him by being especially attentive at the time of the next call.

We can appropriately close this section by quoting Benjamin Disraeli, the British Prime Minister, who once made a statement that certainly applies to salesmanship: "What we anticipate seldom occurs; what we least expected generally happens." Certainly the unexpected is to be expected in salesmanship. The alert salesman can often capitalize on the unexpected instead of being overwhelmed by it.

PERSONAL-INVOLVEMENT EXERCISE NO. 7–2

WHAT IS YOUR POTENTIAL AS AN INTERVIEWER? Test yourself on the following true-false questions. If part of the statement is false, assume that the entire statement is false.

	True	*False*
1. Formulating questions in advance of the interview interferes with the spontaneity needed to sell convincingly.	___	___
2. Reviewing in your mind what you did right or wrong in an interview after it is over is probably a neurotic waste of time.	___	___
3. If the interview goes smoothly, there is no need for special information-getting techniques.	___	___
4. The best way for a salesman to get accurate information from a prospect is to ask him for it directly.	___	___
5. The good salesman listens well and avoids directing the conversation.	___	___
6. The best way to create rapport is to put yourself on an equal basis with the prospect.	___	___

	True	*False*
7. When a prospect is silent during an interview you can assume he is listening.	———	———
8. Asking pointed questions is one of the safest ways to let the prospect know that you are concerned about his problems.	———	———
9. Letting the prospect handle samples of the product or look at sketches or blueprints during the interview diverts his attention from the presentation and should be discouraged.	———	———
10. In an interview in which the salesman has come by appointment, if repeated interruptions occur, it is all right for the salesman to remind the prospect that he is there by appointment. Doing this can reduce interruptions.	———	———
11. In selling it is better to overstate than to understate.	———	———
12. When a customer reacts emotionally in a negative way, it is best to handle the situation directly and discuss it immediately.	———	———

SCORING: All of the statements, in the opinion of the author, for one reason or another are false. Score yourself minus one point for each "true" answer that you checked. A perfect score is 12.

COMPANY CHRONICLE

John Elsworth had a good working arrangement with the other salesmen in his office. He respected them and was proud of the fact that they all seemed to respect him. He liked the feeling that he was part of a team that was working together toward a common goal. Each member of the sales staff had a section of the city that was more or less his territory. Occasionally jurisdictional questions arose, such as one in which Elsworth became involved.

Elsworth had sold a home-improvement job (winterizing a porch) to a family in his territory. The homeowners had a daughter who had a home of her own. She was so impressed with her parents' porch remodeling that she wanted to have her porch winterized, too. She phoned Elsworth to tell him that she wanted her porch done like her parents'. The daughter's house was not in Elsworth's territory. There was a rather vague company policy that if a customer moved into another territory and called the salesman with whom she had previously done business, the old salesman could write up business in another salesman's territory.

Elsworth wrote up the order for the daughter's porch without mentioning it to Ned Shuster, the salesman whose territory the daughter's house was in. Elsworth knew Shuster fairly well. He had had coffee with him a couple of times and had shared a room with him once when they attended a sales meeting in another city.

Ellsworth was sitting at his desk doing some paper work on a Monday morning when Shuster came up to talk to him.

SHUSTER: Say, I've been looking over last week's consolidated call reports. I noticed that you wrote up an order for a Susan Atkins on 5810 West Addison Street. That's in my territory. What gives?

ELSWORTH: Oh yes, she called me to have her porch winterized.

SHUSTER: I can read call reports, and I recognize the phrase "porch winterized." That isn't what I want to know. I want to know what the hell you were doing selling in my territory.

ELSWORTH: Oh, she called me. I didn't call her.

SHUSTER: What's that got to do with it? You could have turned the call over to me.

ELSWORTH: You know there's a policy that you can sell one of your regular customers if she's in someone else's territory.

SHUSTER: The rule is that you can stay with a customer if the customer moves. The loan application of this customer says that these people have lived in their home for two years, and you've only been working here one year.

ELSWORTH: This woman is the daughter of one of my customers. I'm selling in the same family. In the home-remodeling business, the family is the customer, not a single person.

SHUSTER: Says who? That's your greedy interpretation, Elsworth. You bend the rules to suit yourself. I'm going to the sales manager about this. I'm going to bring this up at the next sales meeting, too. So everyone will know what a greedy snake-in-the-grass you are. That way the others will be warned so they can keep an eye on you.

STOP & THINK

1. What do you think of this situation? Analyze each man's case and discuss what is right and wrong.

2. What should Elsworth have done when the daughter phoned him?

3. What should Elsworth do at this point?

4. What is a good policy as far as working with fellow salesmen is concerned?

FIELD CHRONICLE

Elsworth was having lunch by himself on a Saturday. He was in a reflective mood so he started reviewing in his mind what had happened during the week. He thought about the difficult situations that had presented themselves while he was making sales presentations. He spent his lunch hour thinking about how he might have improved the way he handled a couple of situations.

A. Elsworth had almost finished making a twenty-minute presentation on the virtues of tiling a basement floor to a woman who was thinking about having her basement remodeled. Suddenly the woman's husband, who had been asleep upstairs, appeared.

HUSBAND: Why didn't you wake me up, Mildred? I'm interested in this tile installation, too. You can't put any old junk on a basement floor with all that dampness and expect it to hold up. The Blakes up the street had their tile warp.

WIFE: I had thought Mr. Elsworth and I could handle it ourselves, Elmer.

Elsworth was puzzled as to what to do. He couldn't decide whether to go over the whole presentation again, or what. He decided to give the husband a quick summary of the highlights of the presentation, and then go on and finish his presentation as planned. Here is what happened at the conclusion of the presentation.

ELSWORTH: (At the end of his presentation.) Well, I've shown you four different lines of tile. Which line do you like best, and which would you like to order?

HUSBAND: I think we can wait and decide later. Tiling a basement floor is a tricky business.

WIFE: I think this style (pointing) is the prettiest.

ELSWORTH: I can assure you that any of these tiles will hold up. After all, they are made especially for basements and our company guarantees them.

HUSBAND: Well, I always like to look around before I make up my mind.

WIFE: I don't think you'll find any prettier patterns of tile any place, Elmer.

HUSBAND: Beauty can be only skin deep. Maybe this is a company that makes things for looks, and the heck with the quality.

B. Elsworth was trying to sell a prospect a new sleeping room to be built in the family's attic. The sales presentation seemed to be going well until the prospect got on the subject of fire insurance.

PROSPECT: I just thought about the fire regulations.

ELSWORTH: Oh, our plans meet all of the specifications that the fire regulations require.

PROSPECT: But I don't know how much having an extra room up here is going to add to my insurance bill.

ELSWORTH: Our experience has been that it doesn't influence your insurance costs beyond having to pay slightly increased premiums for increased property valuation.

PROSPECT: They look for any excuse at all nowadays to cancel insurance.

ELSWORTH: I've never heard of a case where they cancel insurance because someone added a room to a house. Besides, the acoustical ceiling you'll be putting in is fireproof. So you'll be adding an insulation feature against fire. The insurance company will probably give you a medal for that. Certainly they won't cancel.

PROSPECT: Just the same, as a matter of courtesy and for my own peace of mind, I ought to discuss this with my insurance people.

ELSWORTH: I couldn't agree with you more. Be sure and point out to them that the room will be built by a company completely familiar with the city's underwriting codes and by bonded workmen. The electrical wiring even exceeds local building codes and meets federal recommendations which are even higher. Our company does not skimp on insulation. In fact, I'm sure our own insurance department will be glad to arrange coverage for you, if you're worried about your own.

PROSPECT: Well, I'll call you as soon as I go over this mess with my insurance people.

ELSWORTH: It's odd that you call this a mess. It's an improvement you'll be making which is far from a mess.

STOP & THINK

1. How do you interpret the prospect's behavior in each of the situations?

2. Analyze Elsworth's method of handling each situation. What was right about each of his actions and what would you have done differently?

3. Does Elsworth really know what's bothering these prospects? How could he try to find out?

DISCUSSION

Switching Jobs, a Sales Spurt, and a Sales Slump. Calvin Turner had been a successful salesman in a jewelry store for three years. He sold diamond rings, primarily to newly engaged couples. His boss felt that Turner was quite a showman because he made his sales presentations of wedding and engagement rings with a fine dramatic flair. An executive from a greeting card company who was in the store shopping one day observed Turner make a presentation and sell a young couple an expensive engagement and wedding ring set. He introduced himself and invited Turner to have lunch with him to talk about taking a job with his company selling a line of greeting cards to retail stores. He convinced Turner that if he applied himself selling greeting cards he could better his earnings by at least 30 percent. He also told Turner that greeting cards were more consistently easy to sell than diamonds.

Turner thought for some time about the opportunity to change jobs. He finally decided to switch jobs because of the higher earning possibilities and because of a feeling he had that salesmen could stagnate by selling the same product for too many years. He felt that switching companies and products would present challenges and would stimulate him.

He took over a territory that for years had belonged to a salesman who was now retired. The sales figures for the territory perked up immediately when Turner took over. The sales manager was especially impressed with the number of new accounts Turner was able to add. After the second year, the sales manager's pleasure changed to concern because sales in Turner's territory fell off, particularly with the larger and well-established accounts.

The sales manager decided to call on some of the larger accounts himself in an attempt to find out what the trouble was. Several of the old customers said they missed the former salesman because he had paid so much attention to details and had given them such good service. They explained that when they were out of stock on a fast-moving item, he would get additional stock. He would see that displays were kept up and watch inventories very carefully so that there was always a good selection of cards on hand from which the retail store's customers could serve themselves. Buyers said that Turner didn't seem to care about such things.

When the sales manager asked Turner to account for the sales slump he said the territory was a poor one because there were not enough new stores to sell to. The potential of the territory, according to Turner, was limited.

STOP & THINK

1. How do you account for the sales slump?
2. Do you agree with Turner that a salesman can get into a rut selling the same product and that it is a good idea to change jobs?
3. How can the sales manager help Turner?

To Use or Not to Use a Calling Card. Two salesmen, Frank Steigerwald and Tony Braun, who were old friends, had a discussion about calling cards. Steigerwald felt they were an important sales aid. Braun did not use them because he felt they had certain inherent disadvantages.

STEIGERWALD: I use calling cards wherever possible. It's most important to keep your name and the company's name in front of people you call on. The more they see it, the more likely they are to remember it.

BRAUN: When you give your card to a receptionist, she takes it into the boss. Then she comes out and says that he doesn't need whatever it is you're selling. It tips your hand too soon and reduces the number of people you can get in to see. If the boss doesn't know who I am or what I sell, he has to invite me in to find those things out. I don't want a card to tell him those things. I want to tell him that myself.

STEIGERWALD: If a man doesn't want to see you, you won't get in with or without a card. The card gets in to the man who won't see you. He may not throw it away. He's likely to put it into a resource file each time you call. Then when he gets a requisition for something you sell, he looks in his file to see who he's got there who sells the thing he's looking for. If he sees that there are four or five cards with your name on it, he figures you're really interested in his business and that you'll go out of your way to please him, if you've called that often. Many purchasing agents keep a record on each call a salesman makes. I've gotten orders from people I've never gotten in to see. I give that calling card of mine credit for some of those sales.

BRAUN: Well, I'm not against using calling cards. I just don't send them in ahead of me. You can be sure that I leave one after each sales presentation I make.

STOP & THINK

1. Whose argument is the sounder, Steigerwald's or Braun's? Analyze and evaluate each point that the men made.
2. When should a calling card be used? When not?
3. To be most effective, what should the calling card look like?

The Salesman as Whipping Boy. A buyer, who was a regular customer of salesman Joe Danzell, ran out of stock on an important item, causing his company financial embarrassment. Danzell had called the low-stock condition to the buyer's attention on two occasions. Each time, the buyer suggested to Danzell that he was trying to load him up (it seems that the buyer had been called on the carpet several times for excessive inventories).

One day Danzell got an urgent telephone call from the buyer. The buyer was obviously calling in the presence of his boss. He bawled Danzell out for failing to watch inventories, for not keeping promises, and for slow deliveries. Danzell was puzzled by all of this but said that he would get the needed merchandise out as soon as possible. He did his best to get the buyer off the hook.

The next time Danzell called on the buyer, he was received with the utmost courtesy. The buyer did not mention the unjust accusations that he had made over the telephone. He did give Danzell a substantial order that included some items he had been buying from a competitor of Danzell's.

STOP & THINK

1. How do you evaluate this particular situation? Was Danzell being treated unfairly?
2. What should Danzell do—drop the matter or discuss it with the buyer in some manner?
3. Is it plausible that a salesman should be expected to serve as a whipping boy on occasion? Is this unjust? Discuss.

CHAPTER REVIEW AND DISCUSSION QUESTIONS

1. What are the essential differences between the initial and the follow-up call? Why is one more standardized than the other?
2. Why is it prudent to be closemouthed in the reception room?
3. What are the different goals that may be set up for the follow-up call?
4. Explain the techniques involved in making an appointment by letter and by telephone.
5. Describe policies for fostering the cooperation of subordinates of persons being called on.
6. Why are first impressions important? Should a salesman be a conformist or can he enjoy the luxury of being an individualist? Is being a chameleon the same as being a hypocrite?
7. What are the dangers in using unorthodox approaches?
8. How can enthusiasm and customer involvement be generated?
9. What should a salesman's policies be in regard to simplification? How can a salesman determine whether he is at the right level of sophistication in his presentation?
10. Outline some policies for handling interruptions.

8

THE SELLING PROCESS: PART III
MECHANICS OF SELLING:
MEETING OBJECTIONS
AND SALES RESISTANCE

Chance fights on the side of the prudent.
—EURIPIDES

There was once a coffee shop near the campus of a large university. Early every morning dozens of half awake students would stop in for breakfast on their way to class. For years an exceptionally alert waitress served breakfast there. She would bounce up to a sleepy student with a cheery, "Good morning. What will you have?"

Ordinarily the student, with half an eye open, would mumble something about orange or grapefruit juice. Whereupon the pert waitress would smile and ask, "Big or large?"

It was incredible how many large juices this waitress sold each morning without most customers' even realizing that they were reacting to an artificial choice that in reality was no choice at all. She made her simple sales pitch for large juices with much good humor and finesse. Even those who realized what an absurd choice she was presenting ordered a large juice as a reward for her fine sales effort, and as a "thank you" for getting their day started with a smile.

People react to most sales presentations largely out of habit—just as the students made the choice between "big or large" without thinking. We make automatic responses to most things. If someone greets us and says, "How are you?" we automatically say, "Fine," regardless of our actual condition. And so it is when someone asks us to buy—it is our habit to say "no." The natural thing for a person to do is to object or say no even before knowing what it is that is being offered. Whenever a salesman approaches us, unless we have invited him, we react negatively without considering what he is saying. A salesman might want to present us with a goose that lays golden eggs. Every one of us would probably be very skeptical at best, think of and voice many objections, and be inclined to turn down his offer.

SALESMAN'S PROPER ATTITUDE TOWARD OBJECTIONS

It is important for us to know precisely what objections signify in the communications process. *If it were possible for us to record a hundred successful sales presentations we would find that in practically all of them the customer first reacted with one or more objections!* A salesman must realize that objections are the start of the sales communications process. If the salesman were to take beginning objections seriously, he would be needlessly discouraged. It is unjustifiable for a salesman to allow himself to become disheartened by objections because *an objection is no criterion at all for whether a sale will be made, since both the successful and the unsuccessful presentations start with objections.*

Veteran salesmen will agree that the most difficult prospect is the one who remains silent. Silence means that the salesman has nothing at all to go by. It is not until the prospect responds that the two-way communications process starts. The beginning salesman could wish for an unnatural first reaction—which would be for the prospect to agree with everything. This can and does happen. There are prospects who agree with everything that the salesman says. But here again, ask a veteran salesman what he thinks about the all-agreeing prospect, and he will say that this kind of person usually will not buy. The silent prospect and the all-agreeing prospect have one thing in common—neither one is communicating! Neither one is seriously considering the proposition. *Serious prospects raise objections because they are testing the sales proposition.*

The salesman must view early objections as the beginning of his investigation into whether or not he was a bona fide prospect. He must decide whether in the objection the prospect is really disqualifying himself ("I'm from Los Angeles visiting Chicago, therefore I don't want to subscribe to the *Chicago Tribune*"), or whether the prospect wants to justify his not taking the paper ("I don't miss anything by not subscribing to the *Chicago Tribune*"). If a prospect is really disqualifying himself, as in the first instance, the objection communicates this: it tells the salesman not to waste further time on this prospect. In the second instance, the objection communicates this: it tells the salesman to prove to this prospect that he *is* missing a lot by not taking the *Chicago Tribune*. These two examples illustrate how objections are really communications that tell the salesman what to do.

HOW TO INTERPRET AND HANDLE
REACTIONS TO THE SALES PRESENTATION

What Do People Really Mean?

There is a great difference between what people say and what people mean. We have repeated this statement from time to time on these pages because it is so important. The salesman must learn to recognize the true meaning behind the words the prospect uses.

When you were a child, you learned how to interpret the meaning of the particular "no" your parents used. You soon learned how to relate the "no" to the objection with which it was coupled. The objection is what told you whether the "no" was valid or not.

A "No, you can't go out tonight because you should study," gave you a signal that you should remind your mother that you had improved two grades last week and therefore should be rewarded with some time off tonight. A "No, you can't have another dollar on your allowance because you hardly did any work around the house this week" by your father caused you to point out that you cut the lawn two days earlier than usual because it grew so fast because of the rain. You wanted to be sure the grass looked nice for your father's visitors, so you made the supreme sacrifice of cutting it early, and so forth, and so forth. In both cases, you gave the answers that you felt would reverse the "no." In each case you identified what your parents really wanted, assurance on points that they did not express in so many words but that they nevertheless signaled in their objection. Your mother wanted assurance that you were improving your grades in school; your father wanted evidence that you were more than earning your allowance. You felt that if you could convince them accordingly, you would have a good chance to get them to remove their objection and agree to what you wanted.

A "no" with an objection can communicate with equal accuracy in sales situations. It is up to the salesman to identify what the prospect is signaling by means of the objection. For example, if a shopper looking at Venetian blinds says, "Venetian blinds are too expensive," he possibly means that he would like to know how the cost of regular window shades compares with that of Venetian blinds. A salesperson might point out that Venetian blinds have a life of twelve years, while window shades have an average life of three years. Since blinds cost only three times as much as good shades, blinds are cheaper, and keep their appearance longer. The salesperson knows the prospect is interested in venetian blinds, or else he would not have stopped to look at them. Thus, the price objection in all probability is valid as the reason for not buying. Through the objection, the salesperson definitely knows what to focus on in order to make the sale, something he would not know if there had been no objection or an "I'm just looking" (the silent type). Truly, objections help the salesperson. Therefore, they should not be feared nor be a cause of discouragement.

Verifying the Objection

People are anything but precise in their objections. The salesman must be careful to pinpoint what the objection is because it will usually be expressed in general terms. A man looking at raincoats may say, "I don't like this kind of finish." The salesman who went ahead on the assumption that the man was comparing a material with a sheen to it with one with a dull finish might needlessly spend time talking about how high fashion raincoats this year are made of materials with a sheen rather than with a dull finish. Questioning the shopper may have revealed that "finish" to this man simply meant the waterproofing of the material.

Questions are most helpful in pinning down objections. They also help to get the prospect involved with the product or service. For example, an objection to a car might be: "I don't like the way Chevrolets handle." This objection is terribly vague and could mean many things. It could mean that the car is difficult to park. It could mean that it feels clumsy. It could be questioning acceleration, and so on. At any rate, the objection certainly should signal the salesman to take the prospect out on a demonstration ride so that all aspects of handling can be tested out by the prospect himself. If the prospect drives the car himself, presumably he will check the elements that he feels relate to handling. The observant salesman can thus provide specifics on the particular items the prospect tests. If he tests acceleration, the salesman can provide comparative statistics. If he tests parking the car, the salesman can focus on the virtues of power steering and provide wheel-base statistics.

Indeed, *many times the prospect does not know how to express his objection.* The salesman who helps him express himself gains his appreciation and respect. A person buying a car may say, "I don't like a car this big because I can't see where I'm going when I drive." The salesman who says, "That's all a matter of seat adjustment. Let me show you just what you can do with this front seat," may easily have hit on the point that will make the sale of a large car.

An objection should be treated with respect. Certainly, the salesman must listen carefully while the objection is being expressed. It is really important that the salesman fully understand the objection so that he will know what to focus on to overcome it. No objection is trivial unless the salesman makes it so—at the risk of losing the sale.

One way an objection can be acknowledged (the prospect wants to know that the objection registered with the salesman) is to repeat it. In repetition it can be restated less harshly. A prospect's "I don't like this flimsy construction" can be reworded as, "You don't care for this new, sturdy, lightweight alloy that makes it easier to lift?"

Verifying objections is a digging process whereby the salesman defines the issues so he will know which are the most important ones to focus on in order to make the sale.

Timing the Response to Objections

There is an understandably debatable question: When should objections be answered? Our feeling is that the salesman should consider each objection and how it is made, and then decide when it would be best to answer it. The student will understand the matter of timing better if he reviews the various schools of thought on this subject.

One school of thought argues that objections should be more or less ignored. Answering objections when they are brought up interrupts the sales presentation and can seriously upset the continuity of thought, thereby ruining the effect of the carefully staged presentation. Immediate handling of objections can cause detours into unimportant side issues. Also an objection may be only an excuse to stop the presentation before listening to it in its entirety. By avoiding answering objections until the presentation is finished, the salesman tests the seriousness of the objection. Those objections about which the prospect feels strongly will be repeated. When they are, the salesman knows that the repeated objection must be handled, and there is no time wasted in discussing unimportant matters. Those objections that are not repeated can safely be forgotten.

Another school of thought recommends that when an objection is judged to be serious, the salesman should acknowledge it and answer it right away. The feeling here is that once the prospect has raised a serious objection, his mind will be closed to anything further that is said. The way to get the prospect's mind off his objection is to face and settle it to his satisfaction.

The objection should be acknowledged. If it is felt to be a secondary objection, an "Oh, yes," or "Let's hold that for a minute, it may be answered by what I'll be saying," can handle it. If the objection seems to be serious, the reply "That's an interesting point. I'll go into that for you in just a bit" can be used as a promise that the salesman must keep.

There are some kinds of objections that are definitely not taken up immediately. First, and most important, there is no reason why one should stop for an early price objection. The prospect, of course, does not know what he is paying for until the sales presentation is completed, so there is no real basis for his saying prematurely that something costs too much. It is logical not to place a value on something until one knows what it is, so it is quite all right for a salesman to say, "Yes, Mr. Barrett, the price does seem high, but only until you fully understand what you are getting for your money."

Another objection that the salesman should quickly acknowledge and then ignore is the one that anticipates something that lies ahead in the sales presentation. This kind of objection can be interpreted as encouragement for the salesman, because the prospect is interested enough in the presentation to be thinking ahead. For example, a salesman selling garage doors with an automatic opener may be explaining the construction of the doors and discussing the location of the automatic opening device. The prospect at this point might say, "Those automatic door openers give any clever thief access to your garage." The salesman can handle this by saying, "Wait until I go into that later. You'll be pleased to see how theft-proof our door openers really are."

The Status Halo

The ingenious salesman looks about for means of giving as much status as possible to his proposition. Status psychology is an additive that can often make a contribution by toning down or preventing objections. To start with the more obvious, the halo phenomenon works in situations dealing with the consumer. The *Good Housekeeping* Seal of Approval, endorsements by *Parents' Magazine,* and "advertised-in-*Time*" tie-ins illustrate this. Salesmen use the device when they attempt to extend the halo of prestige organizations: "Du Pont just installed this office device (if you're smart, so will you!)."

Advertisers and salesmen have long exploited status. Book salesmen tell professors that prestige universities have adopted textbooks on their lists; movie stars or other well-known personalities are mentioned as users of a product; and so forth. The astute salesman harnesses factors of this kind and puts them to work defusing objections.

Avoiding Objections by Anticipating Them

Experience shows that people react in predictable ways. In fact, one of the bases in the apprehension of criminals is the detective's ability to predict criminal behavior. Sherlock Holmes pointed this out when he said, "People as individuals are unpredictable enigmas. In the aggregate they become mathematical certainties." This same principle serves the salesman.

As his experience in dealing with people accumulates, the alert salesman begins to see predictable behavior patterns emerging. Thus, as he makes his sales presentation, he is able to anticipate objections. When he sees an objection coming, he provides the information and logic beforehand, making it unnecessary for the prospect to voice the objection. The prospect then either says or thinks to himself, "I was just going to mention that," which creates a state of mind that is much less negative than if he had actually been allowed to voice the objection.

There are many objections that are virtually automatic in any business. The sequence of the sales presentation should anticipate the automatic objections. For example, anyone selling resale items to the retail grocery industry knows that the shelf-space objection is sure to be raised. Competition among products for shelf space in the self-service grocery store is extremely tough. It would be utter folly for a salesman not to have a strong case ready to forestall this objection. The salesman must convincingly demonstrate that his product justifies using the shelf space that would be required if the buyer decided to add the product.

Avoiding Overreaction

There is an unfortunate yet forgivably human tendency to overreact to objections. A salesman who overreacts is on the defensive. It is natural for people to conclude, when they have put someone on the defensive, that they have struck a sore point and that their objection may indeed be valid. A relaxed attitude and a slowing down instead of a speeding up of speech tempo are called for lest the salesman create the impression of high-pressuring to overcome an objection. High-pressuring when a prospect has a real objection will lose the sale. The prospect who has a real objection must be given time to think so he can compromise the objection to his own satisfaction.

Also, it is probably best to avoid overcomplicated, overlengthy answers to objections unless the prospect indicates in some way that he expects a detailed, technical explanation.

Often a simple, forthright handling of an objection is best. Here is a case in point. A truly shrewd saleswoman, totally unschooled in modern techniques, brilliantly sold her product in a farmers' market in the following manner. Questioned by a prospect as to whether her maple syrup was good, she said, "Stick your finger out." The prospect complied, whereupon she poured syrup on it. The startled customer (your author) gasped as he looked at his dripping finger. "Now lick it," directed this master saleswoman. After a slurp of that finger, a pleased prospect became a jolly customer for a quart of fine maple syrup. Surely a less direct or more complicated and technical explanation about maple syrup would not have made the sale as effectively or as efficiently.

PERSONAL-INVOLVEMENT EXERCISE NO. 8–1

WHICH ALTERNATIVE IS BEST? Choose the best alternative for handling the objection. Also, to stimulate your creative ability, you may think up an alternative that you formulate yourself.

Objection	*Possible Answers*
1. On the last order, the buyer did not get the service he thought he deserved.	a.—— Explain that errors will occur and beg him to give you another chance.
	b.—— Tell him that you will do your best to find out what caused it and will straighten it out to the best of your ability.
	c.—— Explain that he has placed many orders with you and that this is the first complaint that he has had.
	d. Other
2. The prospect claims he had once been refused credit by your firm when his firm was just getting started.	a.—— Tell him that his credit rating is now excellent and that your company will be glad to extend him credit up to his limit.
	b.—— Apologize and say the credit department goofed.

Objection	*Possible Answers*
	c.—— Apologize and tell him that you'll call it to the credit department's attention. Explain how risky it is to extend credit to new firms and that in his case they must have been overly cautious.
	d. Other
3. The prospect is in an argumentative mood.	a.—— Excuse yourself and say that you'll be back on a day when he feels better.
	b.—— Let the buyer talk himself out without your arguing back.
	c.—— Try to explain the points he is arguing about without losing your own temper.
	d. Other
4. You are unable to answer several technical questions, so the buyer objects to you as a salesman.	a.—— Say you're sorry but you just haven't had experience. Explain that everyone has to begin somewhere, and that you'll do your best to get the facts to him quickly.
	b.—— Tell him that his questions were extremely technical for a beginning salesman, but you'll try to find the answers for him quickly.
	c.—— Ask him to give you another appointment to give you a chance to do some homework.
	d. Other
5. The buyer caught you making a false claim for your product.	a.—— Admit the mistake and assure him it was not deliberate.
	b.—— Say that you got carried away in your enthusiasm for your product.
	c.—— Tell him that he misunderstood you.
	d. Other
6. The buyer says you contradicted yourself —that you promised him a better deal last	a.—— Tell him that he is trying to put something over on you.
	b.—— Tell him he can't be serious in what he says and try to laugh it off.

Objection	Possible Answers
trip. (You know this is not true.)	c.——— Show him the records of your last call in which there is no contradiction of what you said today. Say that you may have made a mistake last time, that the deal you are explaining today is the right one.
	d. Other
7. The prospect says you are too pushy.	a.——— Explain that you aren't—that he is just interpreting it that way.
	b.——— Explain that you are so enthusiastic that you just get carried away.
	c.——— Apologize and ask that he please not interpret your manner in that way.
	d. Other
8. You tactlessly criticized one of the products of the buyer's company without realizing it. He calls this to your attention.	a.——— Apologize and tell him that sometimes you don't know when to keep your big mouth shut.
	b.——— Just try to laugh it off.
	c.——— Tell him that you didn't mean it.
	d. Other
9. The prospect belittles everything you say.	a.——— Ignore his attempts to get under your skin and be all the more relaxed and pleasant.
	b.——— Suggest that he be fair and treat all human beings with respect.
	c.——— Defend yourself whenever he belittles you.
	d. Other
10. The buyer calls you on the carpet for being too chummy with people in his outer office.	a.——— Tell him you'll stick strictly to business from now on.
	b.——— Tell him you don't understand what he means.
	c.——— Explain that it is your nature to be friendly but if he objects you'll be glad to be less so in his office.
	d. Other

The most reasonable answers are considered to be: 1. *b.* 2. *c.* 3. *b.* 4. *a.* 5. *a.* 6. *c.* 7. *c.* 8. *a.* 9. *a.* 10. *c.* How you rate: Excellent: 1 wrong. Good: 2–3 wrong. Fair: 4–6 wrong. Poor: 7 or more wrong.

COMMON OBJECTIONS

Objections are easily listed because they are so stereotyped. There are not really very many that the salesman runs into, considering how varied they could be if prospects really applied themselves to expressing objections! This means that *a prospect has not really thought about his objection until he mentions it!* Thus, the experienced salesman has the upper hand because he has heard all of the objections before. He can always respond from a prepared position. He can answer a stereotyped, unimaginatively phrased objection with a fresh, innovative reply. For example—Retailer: "Business is awful." Salesman: "There's nothing like perking it up with a few new fresh things to sell that I can supply you with."

It is an excellent idea for any salesman to list the objections he runs into in his particular business. Whenever he runs into a new one, which will be seldom, he should add it to his list. The list should be studied regularly. After each objection on the list, the best answers that the salesman can think of should also be listed. The list should be continually studied and improved. Some salesmen keep their objections with answers on cards. These are easy to shuffle when studying them and also simple to add to or alter when better answers are devised. Having objections on one side of the card and answers on the other facilitates memorization. Eventually the salesman will become so adept that he will always have a good, thoughtful, and refreshing answer for every stereotyped objection. The objection as voiced by the prospect suffers from the start because it is ordinary, while the answer devised by the salesman is extraordinary. It certainly increases the salesman's self-confidence when he realizes that he has the upper hand because he is prepared with something fresh, while all the prospect has to offer is something routine in the line of objections!

The salesman must not allow himself to get into a rut with the answers he uses for objections. He should review his list regularly to see how his responses can be freshened up. Responses are best when they relate to something current and timely. For example—Retailer: "I'm not interested." Salesman: "You will be interested, Mr. Stacey, when you see how beautifully this new line of merchandise of ours will tie in with your store's annual fall back-to-school sale that you are planning for next month." Responses should not be allowed to become completely automatic. Before a salesman calls on an account he should review his list of possible objections and ask himself which ones are most likely to come up. He should then think about the best responses to use and if possible tailor-make a response that suits the particular account, as in the example just quoted that relates to a store's planned merchandise promotion. In the example cited the salesman had recorded that the store had an annual back-to-school promotion. He was thus able to make his response timely and to relate it to one of the buyer's problems—finding merchandise to feature for the special sale.

It is useful and stimulating for a salesman occasionally to talk shop with other salesmen about objections and how best to meet them. By asking another salesman about what works best for him, new twists can be added to improve one's own responses. And after an objection is handled, the salesman should study and consider what happened. Alterations in responses should regularly be incorporated on the basis of what did and did not work in the past.

A salesman should always handle an objection with respect. Certainly he should listen carefully and not cut off the prospect's discussion of it. Because a salesman has heard most objections before, he can easily make the mistake of cutting the speaker off before the objection is fully stated. The salesman knows what is coming, he feels, so he does not need to wait for the finish! Being cut off is offensive to most people and is immediately interpreted as a high-pressure tactic—something a salesman should carefully avoid.

Following is a listing and review of some of the most common objections. The suggested ways to handle them are by no means exhaustive. The discussions will serve as a starting point for anyone interested in developing a list of responses of his own to use for the objections that may come up in his particular sales field.

1. *I Want to Think It Over.* This is not a real objection. It is a cover-up for a hidden objection. It definitely means that the prospect has not been completely sold. It is either an attempt to delay the buying decision or a method of getting rid of the salesman. This ploy is expressed in a variety of ways such as "I'll let you know on your next round," "I think I'll wait a while," "I'll let you know when I make up my mind," or "I'm not in the market right now."

What must be done when the prospect uses a delaying tactic is to find the real objection. Usually a direct question can be asked such as, "There must be a reason why you are willing to deprive yourself of the benefits of this product. Won't you please tell me why you want to put off making up your mind?" or "If you were fully convinced about buying, you wouldn't wait. Won't you please tell me why you are hesitating?"

If the prospect won't reply with anything definite, the salesman can try to guess what the objection is in this manner: "I had a woman in the other day who wanted to wait. When I told her about our money-back guarantee which I had forgotten to stress, she was completely satisfied that she couldn't go wrong. So she placed her order immediately and was able to enjoy the use of her new movie projector right away." Delaying means that there is uncertainty in the prospect's mind. Stressing a money-back guarantee or the product's service policy is an appropriate sales point under such circumstances.

2. *I Don't Care to Deal with Your Firm.* There are various criticisms that involve the prospect's opinion of the salesman's company. The IBM salesman hears charges that his firm is dangerous because it is too large. The salesman for a small company listens to charges that it is unwise to deal with a small outfit. Heads of important companies are often in the news and may be controversial. Thus a salesman for the Hughes Tool Company prob-

ably has learned how to react to derogatory comments about Howard Hughes.

If the objection to the salesman's company is not specific, the salesman must find out exactly what the prospect does not like about the company so he can deal with it. Charges against companies are often based on false information or on unfounded rumors. Once the salesman establishes what the negative opinion is based on, the company's side of the story is usually explained easily. A salesman should welcome an opportunity to correct negative ideas of this nature.

Interestingly, objections to companies are often voiced to test salesmen. A buyer may indeed be wondering about a company, which incidentally is often very important to resale and industrial buyers. So as a matter of good buying procedure, a purchasing agent will test a salesman's loyalty to his company. If a salesman is clearly loyal to his company, the buyer reasons, this means that it is a good company to work for. If it is a good company to work for, it can be assumed that it is also a good company to buy from.

A fundamental rule is that a salesman must be completely loyal to his company if he is really to succeed in selling the company's products. People quickly lose respect for those who criticize their employers. And rightly so, for if they cannot respect their company, they should be working for one they can respect. Furthermore, how can anyone be expected to buy from a company if the salesman himself is not completely sold on it? Disloyalty is equated with distrust. It would be hard for a buyer to trust someone when he detects disloyalty in that person's character.

3. *I'm Satisfied with My Present Supplier.* Actually the buyers who are loyal and devoted to their present suppliers should be considered as prime targets for any salesman. Attaining them is well worth the extra effort and thought. Look at it this way: if they are hard to shake loose from their present suppliers, they will be equally hard for your competitors to lure away from you once they become your customers.

The aim for the salesman with this kind of prospect should be to take the initial step. He should select one of the most attractive products in his line that is exclusive with his company and push hard to sell it. His best odds will be if he can find something in services or products that the other supplier does not have. He can then imply, "You don't have a supplier for this, therefore you can't say that you are satisfied with your present source." A clue to weaning away an account lies in your study of the competing supplier. He has weaknesses. If they can be pointed out to the buyer he becomes less certain about his wisdom in being so loyal.

Other approaches are:

"No supplier has a monopoly on good products or ideas, Mr. Buyer. You owe it to yourself and to your company to check out all sources in this day and age of such rapid change. There is only one way to keep up with developments and that is by making comparisons."

"Satisfaction is fine. I congratulate you in finding it. But don't make the mistake of having the basis for your happiness tied to only one source. Give your supplier a reason for keeping on his toes. You believe in competition,

Mr. Buyer. Competition is the spice of life. If your present supplier knows that he's got competition, he'll work even harder to please you and so will I!"

An effective way to upset the status quo with a supplier is to introduce a little fear. Very frankly, oftentimes when buyers say they are satisfied with their present suppliers, they are really being too lazy to consider alternate sources. It is easier for a buyer to stick with an old supplier. Dealing with a new supplier introduces uncertainties. The thing to do is to introduce a degree of uncertainty about the old supplier that counterbalances the uncertainty that comes from dealing with someone new. Salesmen can easily find actual, convincing examples in their industry of how a company lost position or even went bankrupt because it did not change with the times. By subtly (in no case overtly) accusing the buyer of deliberately overlooking opportunities or avoiding comparisons, the salesman can often move him off dead center.

4. *Let Me Take the Goods on Consignment.* This is a case that occurs in the resale field. Retailers and wholesalers sometimes ask that goods be shipped but be paid for only if they are sold. If the product does not sell they have the right to return it, paying only for what was sold. In such a case the salesman should realize that he has the goods only partially sold. The salesman is obviously on the right track because what the buyer is doing at this point is dickering for the best possible terms. The salesman can point out that it is against his company's policy to sell on consignment. Such a request from a buyer indicates that his company is short on working capital. The salesman should then center on how the customer can pay for the goods and consider whether his own credit department can provide some means for easing the burden of paying. The salesman might well take time to explain why his company has a policy for not selling on consignment.

"It has been our experience that people who buy on consignment are not really interested in the goods. Consequently they take little interest in seeing that they are sold. Consignment selling would raise our costs. The reason I can offer you such good prices is because we don't sell on consignment."

5. *I Can Make Do with What I Have.* This objection is one in which the need is not recognized as being strong enough. Most consumers have to make a sacrifice in order to buy. Money spent for one product or service deprives them of being able to purchase other things. Often, when prospects are wondering whether their old dishwasher, television set, or automobile will last another year, they are thinking of other things for which they want to use their money. It would be difficult and pointless for a salesman to try to find out what these other things are. He can, however, focus on the product that should be replaced and on the new model.

One of the best approaches is to emphasize the risks and possible expenses that could occur in trying to make the old product do. Possible repair bills, inconvenience, and loss of prestige all can undermine the determination not to trade in the old product for the new model.

Most people are aware that old appliances and automobiles will have to be replaced. They are conditioned to accept this. The only question that remains to be resolved is *when* the item will be replaced. Either fear of the consequences of keeping the old model, or the monetary advantage in buying now, can be a prime mover for making the decision to replace an old product. Carefully pointing out all the advantages that the new models have over the old is, of course, terribly important. Dramatizing the new features often can easily sway the prospect to wave good-bye to his old product.

6. *I'm Not Interested.* This is probably the most difficult objection of all to overcome because the salesman has absolutely nothing at all to go on. His chances of guessing what might arouse a prospect's interest are pretty slim unless he gets some clue from the prospect. A novel approach to overcoming this objection is to find out what the prospect *is* interested in. Once the prospect's main interest or interests are established, the salesman can try to relate his product or service to these interests.

For example, in Objection 5, *I can make do with what I have,* which we have just discussed, probing by the salesman might come up with the fact that the prospect is concerned about ecology, a growing reason why people resist buying. In their view, needless consumption is socially undesirable because production causes pollution and the unnecessary exhaustion of natural resources. There is such a thing, however, as consumption for ecological improvement.

Fortunately, the same techniques that you are learning to use to sell goods and services for self-indulgence purposes can and should be used to sell people on the idea of consuming in ways that will benefit society. These ideas are discussed more fully in Chapter 10, the concluding chapter of this book. As industry becomes more aware of the consequences of polluting, many old products should, for social reasons, be replaced with products that are socially more desirable. Thus, when a prospect says "I'm not interested," he may mean that he is not interested in indulging himself by consuming more for self-gratification. His interest could easily be aroused, however, when the salesman has an ecologically superior product to sell. A referral such as this one could easily cause him to take notice: "This new model car goes beyond the government's minimum antipollution requirements. Your present car pollutes 25 percent more than this new one. If you buy this model and the safety and additional durability features that are options for this car, instead of additional conspicuous-consumption gadgets such as wheel covers and extra chrome, you will be contributing to society by putting an automobile on the road that is ecologically more sound than your present one."

Many people are not interested in consuming more because they feel that it is socially pointless and even boring. This is why large segments of society put less and less value on conspicuous consumption. The hippie movement contributed to the development of this social ethic. The salesman who concentrates on consumption for the social welfare will be in the forefront of the movement to preserve and improve society. This is one of the biggest selling jobs that lies ahead!

Classifying Objections and Planning for Them

It is not necessary to list all possible objections because most of them are merely variations based on just a few factors—need (well stocked now, not interested); price (cheaper elsewhere, not worth the money); source (don't like your company, buy from friend); salesman (don't like, wrong religion); time (talk over with partner, too busy); space (no room, buy locally); and business policy (reciprocity arrangement, can't take on another line).

Which objections the salesman runs into most often depend on what the salesman is selling and to whom. The economic situation also influences which objections the salesman will hear most often.

Objections may not be objections at all. The expressing of an objection should be considered as the key to determining whether or not the person called on is qualified as a prospect. When a person says that he has no money or has no use for a product, the salesman should immediately raise this question: Is the person a prospect? Time has value and it must not be needlessly wasted on those who do not qualify as bona fide prospects.

Handling objections is a matter of thinking ahead of time about what might happen during the sales presentation. The salesman should be prepared for all eventualities, just as the professional baseball player is. If there are no men on base, the fielder plans ahead of time what to do if the ball comes to him. If there is a man on base, another set of options applies. The fielder plans ahead by resizing up the situation each time it changes. The professional player does not wait until the ball comes to him to decide where to throw it. He thinks about the options open to him before the ball is hit. And so it is with the salesman. He thinks about what might occur and is ready to respond accordingly.

Following is a list of objections that illustrate variations on a few themes, many of which you are already familiar with. Select products and services and practice how you would answer the objections if you were selling what you have selected to sell.

"I don't have time. I have to be out at the airport in an hour."

"Your company pollutes the air."

"My wife's brother is in your business and we buy from him."

"My neighbor bought one of those and he says it's terrible."

"I bought something from your company once and I couldn't get any service when I needed repairs."

"The boss told me to buy from X."

"I buy locally. Why should I patronize a company that's 300 miles away?"

"We've got a reciprocity agreement. They buy our product and we buy theirs."

"We're handling three brands of that product already. We just can't spare the shelf space for a fourth."

"I'll have to talk it over with my wife first."

"*Consumer Reports* magazine gave your product a poor rating."

"I'm not interested."

"I've got other things to do with my money."
"Your competitor's prices are lower."
"Our present supplier is just great."

QUESTIONS OF PRICE

The matter of price follows our discussion of objections because we do not consider price to be an objection. Price is a debating device, not an objection. One debates whether one can afford it, one debates whether it can be bought cheaper, and so forth. If a salesman has done a good selling job, price will play a minor role or no role at all. The prospect who has been sold properly will not make too much of an issue of price. Of course, he may try to make an issue of it and even attempt to get a better price. But he often does this as a matter of course rather than out of conviction because he feels that every buyer should try to get the lowest price possible.

Where the salesman resorts to price cutting in order to make a sale he is admitting that he has failed as a salesman. He has been forced, as it were, to use the emergency exit. Cutting prices is not salesmanship.

Price no longer plays as important a role in salesmanship as it once did. In the days of high-pressure selling, salesmen were often given flexibility on prices. With the growth of the problem-solving sales approach, prices tend to be firmly fixed by the company. Since the salesman has no discretion over setting prices he is no longer expected to reduce them. This does not prevent people from complaining to him that his company's prices are too high or from telling him that someone else is selling cheaper.

Whether the price obstacle is handled successfully depends a lot on how much the salesman knows. First, the salesman must know his product and company thoroughly. Products and companies are not alike. Even if the prospect says he can get the same thing someplace else, the product will not necessarily be the same; certainly the companies are not. The salesman must raise questions to help the prospect check out exactly what the price of the competitor includes. Most prospects will appreciate this, for they will feel that they are getting a professional analysis of a complicated matter. The salesman who knows his competitor will know his weaknesses. He will also be able to point out several ways in which his own product or company differs. He will emphasize these differences and those in packaging, services, exclusives, and benefits in such a way that he will explain away any real or imagined price advantage that comes from dealing with a competitor.

The story is told about the shrewd John D. Rockefeller, Sr., who amassed one of America's largest fortunes. A salesman made an impressive sales presentation. After it was over, Rockefeller said, "I was impressed with all the reasons why I *should* buy your product. I know that in order to make such a fine presentation you had to study your proposition thoroughly. Now tell me all the reasons why I *should not* make this purchase. Then I'll decide on balance whether I want to buy." The salesman thoroughly and honestly complied with Rockefeller's wish. The story has it that the salesman made his sale!

The method of quoting prices can be enormously important. The "It pays for itself" method is one of the soundest. The salesman who figures out costs so the prospect can clearly see and understand them in terms of savings is on the right track. So much for down payment, so much allowed for trade-in, so much for reduction of possible repair bills and upkeep on an older model, should paint a price picture that shows the prospect that he will save money in making the investment.

Oddly enough, customers who buy big-ticket items at retail often are not interested in total cost. Talk to any automobile salesman to verify this. He will invariably tell you that it is the size of the monthly payment that swings a deal rather than the total cost. Thus, quoting prices as so much per month or price per day removes the sting and breaks the problem down so that the prospect can grasp it in terms of his pay check and fixed expenses. Apparently all he wants to know is whether or not he can handle the price.

TECHNIQUES FOR DEALING WITH OBJECTIONS

Whether techniques for overcoming objections will be effective depends on the skill and attitudes of the salesman who is using them. A fine selling technique used by someone who is inadequate is like a pro's golf club in the hands of a duffer. To succeed, sales techniques must ride in on a magic carpet held up by the poise, tact, attitude, sincerity, and relaxed manner of the salesman. The magic carpet sags when ill winds are set in motion by arguing, contradicting, overclaiming, high-pressuring, or criticizing competitors.

An attitude of welcoming objections is an honest and correct attitude. After all, the prospect has a right to express his reservations and to get honest and thoughtful responses to what is disturbing him. The ideals of the various consumer movements should not be violated by salesmen.

Prospects are quick to recognize sincere and honest effort—when they recognize these qualities in a salesman, the odds are that the techniques for dealing with objections will produce results. The key to how to be effective with the prospect is expressed in this famous old marketing couplet that bears repeating:

> If you want to sell Jane Smith what Jane Smith buys,
> You must see Jane Smith through Jane Smith's eyes.

The salesman must carefully listen to objections and show that he understands them; he must acknowledge objections and not ignore them; he must respect objections and not belittle them.

Restating the Objection

When the salesman restates the objection he can accomplish a number of things. First of all, he can put the objection into his own words and, in the process of doing so, soften the language and shift the emphasis. In the following example, the objection is rephrased so it ends up as a very effective compliment of the salesman's products. "You sell to every Tom, Dick, and Harry in town" can be reworded as, "You mean you're surprised that others are anxious to handle an outstanding line of merchandise?"

When the salesman repeats a dogmatic statement with a shift in emphasis, it often sounds overly harsh or unreasonable to the person who made it. Interestingly, at that point the prospect himself may rephrase the charge he made in order to tone it down. Let's follow a sequence of remarks of this kind:

PROSPECT: All things are made so poorly nowadays, you're a lot better off using what you've got.

SALESMAN: *All* things are made poorly these days?

PROSPECT: Well, it seems like most of them are.

Once a salesman gets a prospect to reword his objection in more reasonable terms, the process of overcoming the objection has already begun. Whenever a salesman takes time to repeat an objection, he is on solid ground. By rephrasing it he can be sure he correctly understands it so that he can deal with it. The prospect is also satisfied that the objection has not been ignored—a circumstance that can alienate him. Restating the objection is a first step in resolving it.

Assuming the Role of Adviser

The problem-solving approach to selling suggests that the salesman's attitude should be that of an adviser and counselor. An objection then becomes a means of helping the prospect explore whether a wise choice is being made. The objection presents an opportunity for showing the prospect that the problem can be solved. By buying what the salesman suggests, the prospect will get credit from his superiors for being a good buyer (Problem: to get recognition from his boss); he is finding merchandise that will resell so his department will make a profit (Problem: to make money for his company); and so on. The way objections are answered must relate to the problem that is being solved. Unless the salesman has in mind what the problem is he cannot answer objections in a way that is relevant to the prospect. Nor can he be a true adviser because advisers deal with other people's problems.

Lead-ins such as those that follow are problem-solving–oriented. They set the stage so that the prospect will consider the salesman as an ally and not as an adversary:

"The point you raise is a sensible matter to look into."

"If I were you, I'd want to have that matter clarified, too."

"Let's take time and look into this important point you have raised."

"I'd want an answer to that question, too, if I were spending my money for something like this."

Agree, and Then Build on the Disagreement

This method, widely recommended in most textbooks on salesmanship, is usually referred to as the "Yes, but" method. Actually, there is more to this psychology than "Yes, but," which, if used superficially, is simply a device for politely shoving aside the prospect's objection. The idea is to agree with the objection and thereby take the edge off it. The prospect is taken by surprise because he expected the salesman to disagree. The salesman goes along with the objection only to the point beyond which it would weaken his position.

Using this technique requires skill. The critical point is switching to the rebuttal after the "Yes, but." If what follows is appropriate and not a contradiction, refuting the objection can be most convincing. For example, a salesman selling an electric typewriter to a person who has always used a manually operated machine will run into this: "I think electric typewriters are overrated. They are clumsy and awkward to use. You can get just as much done on a manual and it costs only a fraction of what an electric costs." The salesman answers: "You're so right, I felt exactly as you do. I used a manual machine for years and wouldn't even try an electric until I had to because I started selling them. Now I can't stand using a manual, believe it or not! Ask anyone who has used an electric for six months or more—he wouldn't switch back if you paid him."

This technique is especially useful in such cases as the electric typewriter example. It is customary to get resistance from users of satisfactory old models who are asked to switch over to something new. People resist change. Therefore, it is always wise to agree that the old product or system has its virtues. The salesman should acknowledge and even praise the old before launching out into new territory. When the prospect knows that the salesman appreciates and understands old values and virtues he mellows and becomes willing to listen to and evaluate the new because he feels he is talking to someone who understands how he feels. To continue the example of the electric typewriter—salesman: "Those old machines really took a beating, didn't they?" (It's wise to get the prospect to agree with different points). "Well, do you know that these electric machines can take even more punishment because they have fewer moving parts?" Acknowledging virtues of the old, identifying them, and relating them to the new in an expanded manner are very potent ways to reduce sales resistance.

Price objections can also succumb to the "Yes, but" treatment. Prospect: "These typewriters are more than I can afford." Salesman: "Yes, I know that some of them may be. We have a number of price ranges. That's why I want you to consider what you'd be getting at each price level. Then you can decide which price you can afford in terms of what you'll be receiving."

Admit That the Objection Is Valid

There will be times when an objection is perfectly valid. In such cases the only thing to do is to admit it. As any student knows, when a student asks a teacher a question that he cannot answer, the teacher who says "I don't know" does not lose the class's respect. It is the teacher who tries to bluff an answer who loses the respect of everyone. And so it is with selling. Everything about what the salesman is selling cannot be superior. And as with the teacher who admits to an occasional "I don't know," the salesman who admits to an occasional weakness gains the respect of the questioner. For example, the prospect who says that gasoline consumption is excessive in the car the salesman is trying to sell can be handled in this manner—salesman: "I know the mileage that you get on this model is not as good as what you would get on other makes. But that's the way it is with most things in life—you can't have everything. If you want acceleration, you have to make some concessions on economy. You can have one or the other, either that extra power and safety factor on the highway when you're passing someone, or more mileage for your gasoline dollar."

The real estate agent selling a house continually runs into valid objections because there is no house that does not have some disadvantages. Thus the prospect who says, "I like this house, but it would take me too long to get downtown to work," is answered in this way by the salesman: "This same house would cost you $2,000 more if it were five miles closer to town. I'll admit it's a little far out. Would you like me to show you one closer in where the air isn't so fresh and the price is higher and the lot is smaller?"

Some Concluding Thoughts About Objections

At the start of this chapter the statement was made that an objection is really an aid to selling because it starts a serious dialogue between the salesman and the prospect. When a sales presentation is made it is entirely a one-sided communication until the prospect starts questioning and making objections. Therefore, the salesman who has a proper attitude and is in command of techniques for handling objections is well prepared to turn in a good sales performance.

There are times when false objections will be made. It is the nature of some people to bait salesmen deliberately to see how they react or how well they can take it. In a way, this can be viewed as a chance for the salesman to prove himself. If he handles himself right he can win the admiration of the person who set the trap.

In the case of the false accusation the salesman must deny it pointblank, but without malice or belligerency. If this is done right, the salesman will have gained a psychological advantage because the prospect will be convinced that he was wrong and may want to make up for it by cooperating with the salesman.

PERSONAL-INVOLVEMENT EXERCISE NO. 8–2

In order to become adept at handling objections, the salesman must be able to identify them quickly. Furthermore, he must have a proper answer at his fingertips for each kind of objection. The following exercise will introduce you to this identification process. The quicker you can accurately size up an objection, the better you will be able to cope with it.

In the following chart there are three lists. The first is a list of objections that are typical of those in the real world. The second is a list of responses that could be used to answer objections. The third list contains various kinds of strategies for meeting objections. Read the objection in List 1. Then search through List 2 for the response that best answers the objection. Place the number of the best response in front of the objection you are matching it with. Search List 3 for the strategy that is best for handling the objection. Place the number of the proper strategy in front of the objection to which it relates.

COMPANY CHRONICLE

Elsworth usually got into the office early on Monday mornings because he liked to get his accumulated desk work out of the way at the beginning of the week. He had learned that families were more receptive to listening to him toward the end of the week so he preferred to be out selling then. He had no fixed hours when he had to be in his office; however, he usually limited the time that he spent there to those hours when it was difficult to call on prospects. Elsworth felt that the great flexibility of the work and the control that he had over his time were two of the great advantages of being a salesman. It was not a 9-to-5 job, and while he put in as many hours as the man who worked in an office, he liked to feel that he was free to work when he wanted.

When he first started selling, one of the things that surprised him was how much office work there was for a salesman to do. Reports had to be filled out, telephone calls had to be made, correspondence had to be answered. Also, there was a lot of leg work to do in checking the progress of customers' orders, billings, and so forth. He began to notice that his office work supported his field work and often when it was well done, it made him more efficient in the field.

One Monday morning he had an extraordinary amount of internal leg work to do. Let's follow him around and see what it involved. His first stop

		List 1 OBJECTION	List 2 RESPONSE	List 3 STRATEGY
2	3			
		I Want to Think it Over		
—	—	1. "I've thought it over and have decided not to buy."	1. "You're not buying from me, you're buying from my company. Here is my employee's identification card. This is a copy of my company's Dun & Bradstreet rating."	1. Get focus away from the salesman onto the product.
		Inferior Product		
—	—	2. "I don't think it will wear well."	2. "In what ways do you feel your situation is different from other people's?"	2. Find out why the prospect feels his situation is different.
		Satisfied with Present Arrangement		
—	—	3. "I'm perfectly satisfied with our present supplier."	3. "Oh, come on now, everyone goofs once in a while. Does everything go right in your own company all the time, or do you sometimes have to break in new people who make mistakes, too? One thing a goof-up does is that we work hard to see that it doesn't happen again."	3. Review the wisdom of continuing present arrangements so the prospect will compare what they have with what you have to offer.

2	3	List 1 OBJECTION	List 2 RESPONSE	List 3 STRATEGY
		I'd Like to Talk It Over First		
——	——	4. "I want to talk it over with my partner."	4. "There is a special sales advantage that the brochure doesn't cover. Let me go over it quickly. It will only take a few minutes."	4. Verify what others think about your company.
		Objections to the Company		
——	——	5. "How do I know that your company will stand behind their products?"	5. "How long has it been since you reviewed what other suppliers in the field are doing? Let me review what we can do for you. If we can't really do more for you, we'll forget it. You owe it to yourself to know what's going on among suppliers."	5. Give the advantages of considering things now.
		Unsatisfactory Service		
——	——	6. "If I do give you an order, you'll louse it up again."	6. "Your ability to manage this large, well-kept house tells me that you	6. Find out the reasons for saying "no."

7. Identify the prospect's reason for concluding that the product is inferior and explain why the inferiority is not real.

8. Give assurance that future service will be good.

know how to make sound decisions. Renting this water tank, which indisputably saves you money over your present system, is a way to save money that your partner will be delighted about."

7. "I respect your decision. Would you please tell me what made you make the decision you made?"

8. "This material looks like it won't wear because it is so lightweight. We wanted to avoid bulkiness because it makes the garment uncomfortable to wear. Actually our testing lab has proved that the lightweight material outlasts the heavier material we used last year."

I'll Give You a Call

—— 7. "Just leave one of your folders. I'll look it over and give you a call."

Objections to the Salesman

—— 8. "You're a pest. I just wouldn't care to do business with you."

List 1 OBJECTION	List 2 RESPONSE	List 3 STRATEGY
I Don't Buy from Strangers 9. "I don't buy from anyone I don't know."	9. "You're a businessman, Mr. Jones. I'm sure there are a lot of people you do business with who you don't like. You do business with them because they have something that it is to your advantage to buy. That's all I ask. Judge my product, not me."	9. Present evidence that verifies your own and your company's legitimacy.
Our Business Is Different 10. "The situation here is different."	10. "Let me show you this newspaper article about our company that appeared last week."	10. Convince the prospect that an independent decision will be respected.

2   3

was on the fourth floor at the advertising department, to talk to Miss Lehman, who worked in newspaper advertising.

ELSWORTH: Good morning, Miss Lehman. May I have copies of the series of ads you ran last week on basement remodelings? I want to push those this week and those ads will make a nice talking point.

MISS LEHMAN: Did you order them last week as you should have?

ELSWORTH: Well, no. I just got the idea for using them when I was planning my week.

MISS LEHMAN: How do you expect us to have what you need if you don't give us a chance to order what you need? You know how things are done here.

ELSWORTH: I'm sure you can spare a couple of tear sheets from last week's newspapers. You gave some to Judy Perkins, our departmental secretary, last week when we didn't order ahead. I'm not asking you for the world, you know.

MISS LEHMAN: You always expect us to bail you out when you goof up.

                                               ❊ ❊ ❊

Elsworth's next stop was on the third floor at the accounting department, where he talked to Mr. Rosenberg at the accounts receivable desk.

ELSWORTH: Good morning. One of my customers, Mrs. J. D. Bach, called and said that she sent in a check two weeks ago and got a bill today stating that her account was overdue.

ROSENBERG: What's her account number?

ELSWORTH: Golly, I forgot to ask her for it.

ROSENBERG: Great. I suppose since you've only worked here for over a year, it's a little too much to expect you to know that customers have accounts.

ELSWORTH: All right, wise guy. Bill Clements in our department forgot an account number last week and you looked it up for him without the sarcasm.

                                               ❊ ❊ ❊

Elsworth's next stop was on the first floor at the billing department. Here he talked to Lydia Grey.

ELSWORTH: Good morning. One of my customers says he was billed for Style 650 carpeting when he ordered Style 415. There's a 35¢-a-yard difference in price so he wants his bill adjusted.

MISS GREY: All right. Just give me the bill and I'll take care of it. Beautiful day, isn't it?

Miss Grey was a great socializer and took her time. She made Elsworth wait forty minutes during which time he noticed her passing the time of day with several people. When she finally came back, Elsworth was rather hot under the collar.

MISS GREY: Here you are. Everything's all set.

ELSWORTH: Do you realize you've made me wait here for forty minutes to do a job that should have taken ten minutes?

o   o   o

Elsworth's next stop was on the seventh floor at the credit department where he talked to Mr. Smythe.

ELSWORTH: Good morning. I want to find out why you're only approving Mrs. J. S. L. Holland's credit for $500. I could sell her a job for $800.

SMYTHE: We figure she'd be overextending herself.

ELSWORTH: Eight hundred dollars isn't all that much more. Besides, she's a good credit risk.

SMYTHE: It wouldn't be fair to her and it would be a risk for the company.

ELSWORTH: Well, it isn't fair to me when I've already sold her for $800. You raised the credit limit on one of Roy Snyder's accounts last week. Why can't you do the same for me?

SMYTHE: Look, I told you what the situation is and that's that. Rules are rules.

o   o   o

By the time Elsworth left the credit department, it was time for lunch. He ate with an older salesman who was a friend of his. He was so discouraged by his experiences of the morning that he told his friend all about it. His friend made a remark that started him thinking. He said, "Look, inside contacts within the company are as important to a salesman as outside contacts. I think you forget that you have to sell yourself to people inside the company, too, if you're going to get them to cooperate. You're being a good salesman when you call on prospects—try being one when you talk to company people, too."

STOP & THINK

1. What did Elsworth's friend mean by "sell yourself to people inside the company, too?"

2. Analyze each of the incidents. How should Elsworth have handled each situation?

3. In general, what do you think of the all-business attitude that Elsworth seems to display when dealing with people in his company?

4. Why do people working for large companies and government agencies find ways to bend the rules a bit in some cases and not in others?

FIELD CHRONICLE

Elsworth made a call on a married couple in their early 30s. They wanted to put a recreation room in their basement. Here are excerpts from what happened.

ELSWORTH: This bar set is both good looking and very practical. It's sixty inches wide and comes with four comfortable bar stools.

HUSBAND: I don't see putting all that money into expensive stools like that. I've never seen anyone sit any length of time at a basement bar.

WIFE: But they are beautiful. Maybe people don't sit on stools because they're so uncomfortable.

ELSWORTH: You can have cheaper stools if you want them.

☆ ☆ ☆

ELSWORTH: This floor covering looks like carpeting, yet it can withstand the dampness you sometimes find in basements. It has plasticized backing that really sticks to the floor so you'll never have any bulging.

HUSBAND: I prefer tile. If anything happens to a tile you can replace it; if you burn a hole in a carpet, you've had it. Besides, isn't tile cheaper?

ELSWORTH: Yes, tile won't cost you as much.

WIFE: But carpeting looks so luxurious. Tile is cold-looking, which is one of the problems in making people feel comfortable about being in a basement.

ELSWORTH: You can have either tile or carpeting. Let me show you the fine assortment we have in both and then you can decide which you prefer.

☆ ☆ ☆

ELSWORTH: This fireplace is real and can be installed in your basement very easily because you've got a flue running right down that wall.

HUSBAND: People never use fireplaces. Imitation ones are cheaper and you don't have all that mess. Besides, wood costs a lot of money and for what?

WIFE: But imitation looks so artificial. There's nothing like watching a real fireplace burn with real wood in it. You used to be romantic before we were married, George!

HUSBAND: You can watch the one upstairs burn.

ELSWORTH: Your wife has a feeling for atmosphere. Why don't you go along with her and order a real fireplace?

STOP & THINK

Elsworth, as you see, sided with the husband in the first case, remained neutral in the second case, and sided with the wife in the last instance.

1. How should a salesman handle a husband and wife situation?

2. What would you have done in each of these cases?

3. Should the salesman always remain neutral in cases like this? Why or why not?

DISCUSSION

Objections That Are Peculiar to a Specific Kind of Business. As a beginner, Phil Ruprecht sold space in business publications quite successfully. He started his career at a time when business conditions were rather bad. Later, when business improved he expected his sales to improve also. He was surprised when he ran into a new objection caused by business prosperity. Many of his clients were inclined to want to reduce advertising expenditures because they felt that they did not need the stimulation of advertising when business was good. They argued that they could save the cost of advertising now and reinstate it when business was again on the downgrade.

STOP & THINK

1. How would you answer this objection if you were Ruprecht?

2. Think of other objections that relate only to a specific business. In each case how would you handle the objection?

3. What kind of objections relate to economic conditions? Discuss how they are best handled.

How You Say It Is as Important as What You Say. Some people antagonize other people without being aware of it. Let us consider this matter. Voice intonations, mannerisms, emphasis, facial expression—all communicate meaning to the questioner. The remarks that prefix the answer to the objection have much to do with setting the stage for how the answer will be received. Below are some situations that help you test some of these things.

Say the following aloud in front of a mirror, first with a smile and then with a scowl.

"You surely can't believe that this model is inferior."

What are the differences in meaning that are conveyed by the change in facial expression?

Say the following aloud, stressing the word that is italicized.

"This *is* the best regardless of what you may have been told."

"This is the best regardless of what *you* may have been told."

What are the differences in meaning that are conveyed in the change of stress?

Say the following statement aloud using a different prefix as listed each time.

Statement: ". . . but what you say just doesn't apply to my product."

     a. "That's what you may think . . ."
     b. "That could easily seem to be the case . . ."
     c. "It's interesting that you should say that . . ."

STOP & THINK

1. How does each situation set the stage? Which is the most effective? Which is the least? Why?

2. What advice can you give for formulating phrases that lead in to answers to objections?

Sometimes the Salesman Has to Sell Himself Instead of His Company. A sales manager for the Ajax Corporation was talking to two of his salesmen. Salesman A had one half of the city as his territory, and Salesman B had the other half of the city as his territory. The two salesmen and the sales manager were discussing an industrial concern in A's territory. The sales manager mentioned that an unfortunate situation had occurred ten years ago and no one in the company had sold a thing to this attractive account since then. No Ajax salesman could even get to first base with the purchasing agent. Salesman A mentioned that neither he nor the two salesmen who had had the account before him could budge the purchasing agent. Salesman B spoke up: "Let me have the account even if it is not in my territory. If I succeed in getting an order, I get to keep the account. If not, I'll give the account back to Salesman A." The other two men agreed to let him try. "I'll even take the two of you out to dinner on the day you get your first order," said the sales manager.

The salesman went to call on the purchasing agent. When he told him who he was, the P.A. said, "I swore I'd never again buy from a low-down company like Ajax. You're wasting your time." The salesman replied, "The people who upset you ten years ago probably aren't even with our company anymore. I make a living as a salesman. I try to be as honest and efficient as possible just as the salesmen who work for your company try to be. I assure you I wouldn't be working for Ajax if your feelings about it were true. I'm going to call on you every other week until you give me a chance to prove to you that I'm a respectable man working for a company I believe in."

The salesman held his promise. He called on the P.A. every two weeks, doing something thoughtful for him on each visit. One time he provided him with a folder that contained clippings that related to his work. Another time he presented him with a checklist that would simplify one of his buying chores, and so on.

After the salesman had called for six months, the P.A. finally said on one visit, "You win. I've bought what you stand for. Your company can still go to hell. But with a salesman like you, it can't be all bad. Here's an order for 100 units of your model XL700. I've denied my company that superior product long enough."

STOP & THINK

1. Generally, should a salesman sell himself or his company? Discuss the pros and cons of each alternative.

2. What did the salesman in the example sell? His product? Himself? His company?

3. Wouldn't the salesman have been better off going into the history of the bad relationship? As it was, he didn't even know what it was all about. Discuss the pros and cons of finding out what it was.

4. What other approaches could have been used? How about one which would have shortened the time it took to get the first order?

CHAPTER REVIEW AND DISCUSSION QUESTIONS

1. Why are we inclined to say "no" when a salesman approaches us before we even know what it is that he has to offer?
2. How should a salesman consider objections—should he fear them or welcome them? Why?
3. What do the silent and the all-agreeing prospect have in common? How can a salesman handle these types in order to determine whether or not he has a bona fide prospect?
4. When a prospect is vague with an objection, why should a salesman be interested in helping him be specific?
5. When should objections be answered?
6. How does avoiding an objection by anticipating it work?
7. Why should the salesman be careful not to overreact to an objection?
8. Discuss some of the most common objections and how they should be handled.
9. Explain how the customer who is against the needless consumption of products can be persuaded to buy for ecological purposes.
10. What factors are involved in handling price objections?
11. What attitudes toward objections should the salesman attempt to convey to the person objecting?
12. Describe and discuss the techniques for handling objections. How can the problem-solving element be introduced?

9

THE SELLING PROCESS: PART IV
CLOSING AND FOLLOW-UP

*Stopping at third base adds
no more score than striking out.*
—THOMAS A. EDISON

"Nothing happens until a sale is made." This phrase, frequently heard emanating from sales circles, is a perfect, succinct way to tell nonsales people that selling is the heart of any business. This classical phrase is great for outsiders. For insiders—the sales staff itself—a pithier, more relevant phrase is used: "Nothing happens until the close is made!" *For the close is the heart of the sale.*

Close is the term used in the sales field to designate the point in the selling process at which the prospect agrees either to buy or not to buy. It is the point to which the salesman builds up. It is the point at which success or failure of the sale is determined.

Throughout this book we have discussed, dissected, analyzed, studied, and provided practice exercises and involvement opportunities for learning the art of salesmanship. Your instructor probably has given you examinations to determine the degree to which you are learning the subject. Significantly, however, there is only one real test and measure for determining whether one has mastered the art of selling—and that is closing the sale. Until the sale is closed everything that precedes it is without value.

Closing in sales is like what the Spaniards call the moment of truth in bullfighting. The bullfight is a great and colorful spectacle. It is an ancient sport and art form practiced by highly skilled matadors. The entire drama builds up to the exciting climax, the moment of truth—the point at which the matador proves his mastery over the bull. The making of a sale is a similar contest, the climax of which also has a moment of truth—the close, or signing on the dotted line!

THE ATTITUDE OF THE SALESMAN
TOWARD CLOSING

It has been found that salesmen who are not good closers are afraid of closing. The fear comes from a deepseated human trait—the fear of having someone say "no." It takes more courage than many people have to face up to the moment of truth. Young men are afraid to ask a young lady they admire for a date because they are afraid of the "no," which is said to be the coldest word in the English language! Young ladies are afraid to invite a young man they admire to go to a club picnic for fear that they may be turned down. Fear of rejection lies deep in the human psyche.

Analyzing the basis for this fear and developing an attitude toward it help immeasurably to overcome it. One excellent way to view the close is to adopt the attitude of the matador who undoubtedly is very fearful, too. His attitude can probably be expressed as follows: "The moment of truth is the test of the man. It is the moment at which I prove that I am master of the situation. I look forward to this moment with excitement and anticipation. It is the moment I have worked and trained for. It is the moment at which I prove to myself that I am a man."

The salesman who incorporates such an attitude into his personality will not be fearful, for he will drive for the close with the courage and determination that is required.

THE CLOSING PROCESS

Since the close is the climax of the sale it is the point at which the salesman is inclined to be most anxious and nervous. He knows that it is the ultimate test of his sales ability and the step that determines the size of his income. In addition there is that innate fear that we have already described that is present in most people—the fear of being turned down and of having our egos bruised.

Because the close is so overwhelmingly important, it is inclined to build up internal tensions and pressures in the salesman. This is unfortunate, for closing is precisely the time at which a nonpressure, low-profile atmosphere should prevail. A favorable buying decision requires the building of an understanding between two people and a meeting of the minds. When the stage for closing is set so there is no tension and where the atmosphere is relaxed, the buyer will feel that he has made his own decision to buy and that it has not been made for him. High pressure can easily lose the sale. Even if high-pressure methods succeed, the achievement can be short-lived for order cancellations and customer dissatisfactions often result. The salesman must learn to sublimate his natural tensions so he does not jeopardize the close by projecting external pressure onto the buyer.

Timing the Close

Few prospects ask to buy. Thus, they need help from the salesman. The master salesman makes it so easy for the prospect to buy that it is unnecessary for him to ask! In a good close all that is needed from the prospect is a nod of the head, an "uh-huh," an "OK," or at most an actual "yes." In other words, all that is sought from the prospect is a verbal or nod-of-the-head signal that he has agreed. This can come at any time during the interview.

Selling actually is not the orderly and tidy step-by-step process that many textbooks would lead one to believe. The drama of a sale is not like the drama on the stage where the curtain goes up for each act, where the series of scenes builds up to a climax with the curtain ringing down at the end, and where the principals come out to take their bows at the finale. The sale can climax at any time. The principals can take their bows and leave even in the middle of the first act!

Closing represents a decision that has to be made in the prospect's mind. The salesman can never know how rapidly the prospect is approaching the favorable decision or how close he is to it. So during the presentation the salesman must check from time to time to see whether the prospect has reached his decision.

In the early days of selling it was thought that there was one psychological moment for the close. Salesmen were taught to look for and seize the closing opportunity at this one magic moment. Modern psychology has disproved this theory. The best approach is now considered to be one in which the salesman seeks to close early in the interview, continuing to work for an agreement to buy throughout the presentation. The right time is whenever the prospect seems to be ready to agree to buy. The signals that he gives indicating agreement are discussed in the next section. Since there are many right times to close it is not fatal if the salesman misses one or two opportunities. The sound sales presentation is not a wisp of smoke that is blown away just because someone breathed too hard. Sound selling means that a prospect has made a rational buying decision on which he is fully prepared to follow through. Actually *once the prospect has made the decision to buy he is relieved and he wants to close.* We can all see this characteristic in ourselves when we make a decision. Aren't we glad that we have finally made up our mind and aren't we then anxious to get on with things?

There is another good reason why the salesman should try for a close as the sales presentation proceeds. Once the prospect has made up his mind to buy, if the salesman does not recognize this, he can talk himself out of the sale. Sustained sales effort after the prospect has made up his mind is oversell. This is often viewed as high-pressuring. When the feeling that he is being high-pressured creeps in, the prospect will start questioning the wisdom of his decision and possibly reverse it.

There is still another reason why the salesman must periodically probe for a close. Actually he has no way of knowing how presold the prospect is. A woman buying a stereo set may have been looking at stereo sets and considering them for weeks. She may come into the store and ask for clarification on one or two points and be ready to buy immediately without any further discussion at all. A buyer for a retail store may have decided long before the umbrella salesman arrives that he wants to feature umbrellas to tie in with a planned raincoat sale. Thus, at the very outset the salesman must check to see if it is time to close.

Some Observations About the So-Called Positive Attitude

Many textbooks on salesmanship make it a point to discuss the importance of and recommend the so-called "positive attitude" in their treatments of closing the sale. They focus on the positive attitude at this point because they know that many salesmen are afraid to try for a close. Encouraging a positive attitude helps salespersons overcome their fears, or so the theory runs. Therefore, in a variety of ways the point is made that a very definite positive attitude is highly desirable in order to improve chances for closing. The same discussions also point out that a negative attitude sells nothing.

While we believe that a positive attitude is certainly desirable, an over-display of positivism at any time, especially at the time of closing, can imperil the chances for making a sale. True positivism is a state of mind. It is not something that is exhibited to people by means of excessive smiling, artificial enthusiasm and joviality, or exaggerated optimism. We can safely assume that most people are sensitive. Those who are in positions of authority for making buying decisions are even more sensitive than the average person because they talk to and observe so many salesmen. They can spot the phony. Forced positivism is quickly identified for what it is. If it is unduly exhibited at the time of closing it can ruin the sale. For when the prospect is deciding, one of the questions he consciously or unconsciously asks himself is: Am I being high-pressured? If the answer is "yes" he may well ask for time to think things over, which at best will delay the sale, and at the worst cause it to be lost entirely.

When a prospect makes a decision to buy, he wants to feel that he has made a sensible and balanced decision. He wants to feel that he has taken all factors into consideration and that he has made a decision that he can live with.

The salesman who facilitates the balanced-judgment feeling at the close will be ahead of the salesman who steps up the positivism tempo while trying to close the sale. Leading salesmen tend to end sales in the roles of counselors and advisers, creating an atmosphere of relaxed confidence.

Recognizing the Signals for Closing

From the time they are born, people react to the stimuli they come into contact with. We all go through life responding favorably to what we like and unfavorably to what we dislike. It is only to a degree that we learn to control our external reactions. There is no way in which we can control our emotions internally. It is this fact that makes use of the lie detector possible. Our internal reactions are so acute and sensitive that telling a lie versus telling the truth registers on the graph of a lie detector.

The skilled salesman can also learn to read the signals that indicate that the prospect may be ready to close. Practicing one's skill in this subtle art is one of the most fascinating aspects of selling. Veteran salesmen often claim that they have developed a sixth sense for picking up signals to close. The prospect's shifting in his chair, a lighting of his pipe, a shuffling of his feet may be a signal to the salesman who knows him that he is ready to buy. If a lie dectector can pick up impulses that distinguish a truth from a nontruth, there is no reason to doubt that the sensitive salesman can learn to read under-the-surface signals of those he calls on.

Some of the signals that a salesman should try to read are obvious, others are quite evasive. Signals can be divided into two categories—those that are overt, and those that are disguised. The overt signals are usually verbal; however, they can also include action. Let us consider examples in each category that signal the salesman that it may be time to try for a close.

OVERT SIGNALS

(*A woman considering a new television*)
"What kind of time-payment arrangements are available on this TV?"

(*A young couple looking at sets of silverware*)
"Do you have this pattern in stock?"

(*A man considering a new car*)
"What kind of delivery date could I get if I ordered this model with a V-8 engine?"

(*A purchasing agent considering the purchase of some lift trucks*)
"Does your company keep an inventory of spare parts in the city?"

(*A buyer of canned goods for a wholesale grocer*)
"Open up a couple of cans so I can taste them."

(*A buyer for a manufacturer*)
"Let me take your stapling machine and see what the clerks in the office think about it."

DISGUISED SIGNALS

A buyer who has been relaxed tenses up and leans forward to watch a demonstration more closely.

A prospect who is listening to a presentation for three types of insurance leafs back to look at a folder on one of the plans that has been discussed.

A prospect's eyes light up when he hears how much his trade-in is worth.

A man nods his head and smiles when he hears that he can buy the floor model of a power mower at a slight discount.

A farmer looking at a tractor looks pleased and sits up straight and proud after he climbs into the driver's seat.

Of course, any signal, either overt or disguised, that is detected does not indicate conclusively that the prospect is ready to buy. The salesman should view the signal as an opportunity to try for a close. He alone must judge whether the signal is strong enough and indicative enough to merit trying for a close. As a rule, a salesman should try to close on almost every signal he gets. There is no limit on how many tries he can make. The unforgivable mistake is not to try to close, a mistake all too many salesmen make.

PERSONAL-INVOLVEMENT
EXERCISE NO. 9–1

HOW WELL DO YOU READ CLOSING SIGNALS? Following are twenty remarks on which you can test your skill at reading whether the salesman should try to close. If you feel that a remark is a signal and that the salesman should try for a close, choose "Yes." If he should wait, choose "No." If you are not sure, choose "Maybe."

	Yes	No	Maybe
1. The buyer to whom the salesman is talking goes over and opens the window.	——	——	——
2. A man is listening to a salesman selling a termite-eradication job for his house and asks, "How far down in the ground do you go to place the poison?"	——	——	——
3. A young woman considering buying a bicycle says, "Can I take it for a ride around the block?"	——	——	——
4. A woman looking at wigs asks, "May I try this one on?"	——	——	——
5. A husband listening to a presentation on swimming pools says, "Don't the kids get tired of a pool after a while?"	——	——	——
6. A woman looking at oil paintings takes one over to the window to look at it in the daylight.	——	——	——
7. A purchasing agent for a large bakery pours some syrup on a piece of paper to test its viscosity.	——	——	——
8. A buyer for a jewelry store asks, "How much of an advertising allowance will you give me if I buy this style?"	——	——	——
9. A purchasing agent starts clicking his ball point pen.	——	——	——
10. A woman listening to a travel agent describe an ocean cruise asks, "How much time is there on the stopover in Venice?"	——	——	——
11. A woman looking at watches for a graduation present says, "What kind of a guarantee comes with this make?"	——	——	——
12. The telephone rings, and the buyer calls to his secretary, "Tell them I'll call back later."	——	——	——
13. A man looking at tires asks, "Is there a trade-in allowance for my old tires?"	——	——	——

	Yes	No	Maybe
14. A retail buyer looking at housewares samples asks, "I think this style will sell better than that one."	____	____	____
15. An industrial purchasing agent asks, "May I see the engineering drawings on these valves?"	____	____	____
16. A woman looking at mattresses says, "Did you say that this is the one with the coil inner springs?"	____	____	____
17. An office manager considering a set of cookbooks for his wife says, "My secretary looked at them and didn't think much of them."	____	____	____
18. A shoe buyer for a retail chain asks, "How much lead time do you need to get deliveries?"	____	____	____
19. A purchasing agent for a hospital says, "I like the idea of buying disposables, but I don't like the idea of increasing the amount of waste that accumulates."	____	____	____
20. A couple looking at a house agree, "The kids could use this room as a rumpus room and keep their mess out of the rest of the house."	____	____	____

Compare your scores with those of the experts. There are no "right" answers. However, there is value in your comparing your results with those of experienced people working in the sales area. This test was taken by seventeen salesmen or sales managers. Their choices were as follows.

	Yes	No	Maybe			Yes	No	Maybe
1.	3	12	2		11.	17		
2.	6	6	5		12.	7	8	2
3.	12	5			13.	16		1
4.	8	6	3		14.	16		1
5.	5	11	1		15.	7	4	6
6.	11		6		16.	11	2	4
7.	8	3	6		17.	4	11	2
8.	16		1		18.	15		2
9.	4	8	5		19.	8	4	5
10.	13	1	3		20.	16		1

Comments were received from sales managers who replied to the involvement exercises. One sales manager selected "Yes" for all twenty situations, adding this comment: "Always Be Closing!" Howard W. Bacon, vice president, marketing, Michigan Blue Cross/Blue Shield made this comment, which is worth pondering: "When a buyer admits a willingness to involvement, he is to a large degree committing himself to a purchase. Except for number 12, I believe a professional salesman could most likely close all of these buyers."

CLOSING TECHNIQUES

There are a substantial number of definite techniques for closing the sale. Anyone studying salesmanship should become familiar with them. Those that seem to suit the product or service that you are thinking of selling and your own particular personality should be remembered and tested. Any salesman should have a considerable number of closes at his disposal. Thus when it comes time to close he can use the one that seems best for the circumstance. If the first fails, another that is felt to be appropriate can be used and so on until, it is hoped, one eventually hits its mark. Most salesmen will, of course, develop one or two methods for closing that work especially well for them and will be inclined to use them most often. As you review the following closes, please remember that no list is all-inclusive nor can any of them be used in any particular situation without first being adapted. The ideas behind each close listed have been widely tested and hence are sound. It is up to you to adapt them so they become appropriate to your particular use.

It has been said that the road to success is always under construction. The same may be said about the roads that lead to the close. They should always be under construction, too. They should be constantly improved and worked over, with plenty of attractive detour possibilities.

Long-Range Versus Short-Range Sales

The closing techniques that are discussed here relate to selling situations that typically are expected to have a short-range payoff. That is, the sales pitch is made and the order is sought immediately as part of the sales presentation. Not all selling is of this nature. There are many industries that offer excellent selling jobs where the payoff is long-range. In the medical equipment field, for example, a salesman may work as long as a year to sell a piece of complicated diagnostic machinery to a hospital. When the sale is finally closed it may be for a piece of equipment that costs from $10,000 to $15,000. Signals for closing such sales relate to long-range selling. In the wholesale grocery field buying committees are commonly encountered. In industrial selling the salesman frequently runs into value analysis (see page 135). Whenever selling is long-range because of the highly technical nature and expense of the product, or because of a buying committee or a value analysis, the salesman's efforts in closing consists primarily of furnishing information and in checking up on progress of the deliberations that are taking place among decision-making executives. Where the salesman checks carefully on progress, he can determine what is delaying things. Often it may be the lack of a particular bit of information. The alert salesman selling long-range products will facilitate matters considerably when he anticipates what information will typically be required.

Both long-range and short-range selling require an eventual meeting of minds between the salesman and the buyer. Figure 9–1 illustrates the steps and interactions that take place between buyer and seller in the process of closing the sale.

Following is a list of the more common closes used in selling and discussions that explain the psychology behind each of them.

Building a Series of Affirmative Acceptances by Questioning. The idea behind this method for closing is to put the prospect in a positive frame of mind by using a series of questions that are sure to be answered in the affirmative. The prospect is first asked relatively minor questions that the salesman feels certain will elicit a positive response. The first minor questions are followed by a sequence of questions (all calculated to produce a positive response) that the prospect continues to answer in the affirmative as he ascends steps that lead to his total commitment. This process starts out best after the prospect is asked to make a choice as illustrated in this example.

SALESMAN: (*To a woman considering a custom-made drapery installation.*) Mrs. Evans, do you prefer heavier materials that do not require a lining, or do you prefer the lighter weights that require a lining?

PROSPECT: Oh, I think draperies with linings always hang better.

SALESMAN: Oh good, because the most attractive patterns are in the lighter

Figure 9–1

THE TWIN PYRAMIDS OF SELLING INTERACTION

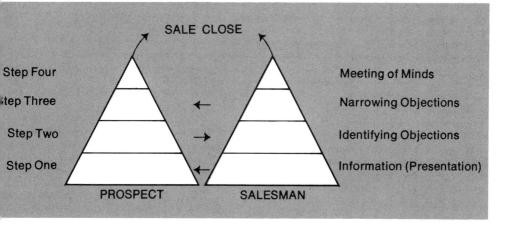

PROSPECT:

SALESMAN:

materials. This orange print you've got your eye on is a real beauty and it's a lighter material that fits well with a sateen lining. It's really a beautiful, bright color, isn't it?

PROSPECT: Yes. I must admit it is nice.

SALESMAN: You said you need full-length draperies that go right down to the floor, didn't you?

PROSPECT: Yes.

Note: Observe how the salesman gets the prospect to confirm information that she has previously told him.

SALESMAN: And you indicated that there is one picture window and two side windows in your living room?

PROSPECT: Yes, that's right.

SALESMAN: Then let's decide on which fabric you want. Will it be convenient for you to have the man come out to take the measurements next week?

PROSPECT: Yes, if he comes before Friday.

SALESMAN: *Right:*
I'll arrange it for the beginning of the week then. Now which of these patterns that we've been looking at do you like best?
Wrong:
Now which of these patterns we have been looking at have you decided on?

Note: Observe how in the "right" question, the salesman assumes that the decision to buy has been made. In the "wrong" question, the salesman unnecessarily brings up the matter of the decision. This is an example of where a slight difference in wording can make a big difference in the outcome.

People find it difficult to uncommit themselves once they have been making a series of confirmations and have been involving themselves in a series of choices. In the example, the woman has made a series of easy decisions that make the final decision virtually automatic and certainly painless.

When asking a question, the salesman must be careful to phrase it so it will not get a definite "no." Some "no's" are quite final, others are conditional so the salesman can ignore them, or get around them.

Wrong:
SALESMAN: Do you want the men to come out to measure your windows for draperies?

PROSPECT: No. I want to think it over first.

Right:
SALESMAN: Would it be convenient for you to have a man come out to measure your windows for draperies next week?

PROSPECT: No. I want to think it over first.

SALESMAN: I can schedule an appointment after the first then. That will give you over a week to think about it. You can always cancel your appointment.

Assuming That the Prospect Will Buy. The assumptive close is facilitated in a variety of ways as illustrated in the following examples:

"I assume you are going to want white sidewalls on your new car."

"Will you want the deluxe rather than the economy model if I can get them to throw in the carrying case for free?"

"I suspect that you'll want us to ship via rail. Am I right?"

"I can see why the blue fabric has caught your eye. I'll call the tailor to check the fit."

"Will you want this or that set of attachments to go with your new sewing machine?"

"Will you handle the financing, or shall I see what I can arrange?"

"We'll have delivery on that as early as Thursday."

Assuming that the prospect will buy should be a natural part of the sales presentation. Assumptions are made about many things in life. It is assumed that one will introduce one's companion when one encounters another friend on the street. It is assumed that a mother will be responsible for the conduct of her child. Certainly it is not unreasonably presumptive for a salesman to assume that a prospect is buying.

Assumptive selling is more certain to succeed when it is done gradually. Words and phrases that imply that the prospect will buy are slipped in throughout the presentation. "You'll enjoy these twin speakers." "You can add a tape recorder to your outfit next year." "You can set your dial in this position when you watch the hockey games." "When you make your January payment, we can arrange refinancing."

Asking for the Order Directly. Asking for the order directly is closely related to the assumptive close because even when the order is requested directly it is usually tempered so it does not sound overly blunt or rude. "Are you going to buy?" besides being blunt would sound both odd and unnatural.

Actually, if the presentation is going smoothly and the prospect is receptive, the direct approach has merit. It is certainly the most honest, natural, and forthright approach. The use of devious approaches is just that—devious. Deviousness can trigger suspicion. When this happens, the prospect can easily balk at buying.

Asking for an order directly can be done naturally and pleasantly. Certainly it is the most efficient method since it wastes no time. It is businesslike and it creates the atmosphere that the salesman is there to sell and that the prospect is there to buy. Note how perfectly natural the examples are:

"Can I put you down for a dozen of Style 100?"

"Since we've covered everything, may I write up the order?"

"May I assume that you'll want this style?"

"Can I go ahead and figure out what the freight charges will be?"

"Is it all right for me to go ahead and take an inventory of your present stock and write up an order that will take care of you through the season?"

The direct approach also is inclined to get direct responses. Such a response, of course, can be negative and quite blunt. But at least the salesman knows precisely where he stands. Once directness has been established, an advantage may accrue—the prospect may for the first time tell the salesman

exactly what his objection is instead of trying to hide it for the sake of delicacy. This serves to instruct the salesman as to where he must focus the resumption of his sales presentation and also tells him what to stress.

Summarizing the Selling Points. This method reviews the sales presentation in terms of what would be logical from the buyer's point of view. Emphasis is placed on those points to which the prospect reacted most favorably and also on the objections he raised in order to show again that they are not important when considering the overall picture. Let us look at an example of how a salesman's summary might proceed.

Step 1. "Let me review what this product is prepared to do for you in terms of the amount of money it will save."

Step 2. "We now know beyond a doubt that this machine will save you money. When we relate those savings to the cost of the machine that certainly makes the price right."

Step 3. "We've considered the matter of service. Clearly, that depends on the company that stands behind the product. I've told you about my company's service policies, facilities, and well-trained personnel."

Step 4. "You know that the best time to order is now, before our busy season starts next month. You'll get your best deliveries and financing terms this month."

Step 5. "So now I think I've covered everything that you could possibly question. All that remains is for me to write up the order. May I go ahead and write it up?"

It is very important that the summary be made in a relaxed and pleasant manner; otherwise, the prospect may get the feeling that he is being bombarded in a hard-sell fashion. This tends to overwhelm a prospect and give him the feeling that he is being high-pressured. A summary must assure the prospect that the salesman is viewing the buying decision from his point of view.

Comparing Advantages with Disadvantages. This method is an appeal to the person's logic and relates closely to the summarizing method just described. This method is also called the balance-sheet method, a reference to double-entry bookkeeping in which traditionally the credits (assets) appear on one side of the ledger and the debits (liabilities) appear on the other. Balance-sheet references and terminology are excellent to use when customers are business-oriented. Thus, industrial and resale merchandise salesmen frequently use them with good effect. Use of balance-sheet terminology would be disastrous in most instances when dealing with the general public.

A salesman, especially one who deals with nonprofessional buyers, must be very careful about the terminology and references he uses. He must constantly remind himself that *most people simply are not business-oriented.* A salesman, of course, is a businessman. He works for a business and is probably by nature and inclination business-oriented. He has been trained perhaps by taking business courses in school. The people he works with in his company all use the vocabulary of the businessman. They assume that people they talk to have a business background. It would never occur to them to define terms like assets, liabilities, supply and demand, markup, and so on when talking to someone. Yet these terms are not comprehensible to most people who make up a cross-section of the population.

It is all too easy for a salesman to take the language spoken inside the company he works for and use it when talking to people he calls on. In most cases this is a serious mistake, because the terms and references of a company that specializes are inclined to be too technical for general consumption. The salesman must learn to wear two hats—one that is appropriate for talking to colleagues at work, the other that is appropriate for those he calls on. He must carefully train himself to use nonbusiness English when talking to nonbusinessmen. Thus, when closing a sale with people who are business-oriented, balance-sheet or double-entry bookkeeping references can be used. When closing with those who are nonbusiness-oriented, it is best to talk in terms of advantages and disadvantages.

The logic of weighing the positive side of a sales proposition and comparing it with the negative side appeals to many people (assuming reasonable intelligence on their part). Salesmen who use the method skillfully by putting it in terminology that relates to a person's background find that it can be a powerful and effective closing method. The method works well because it parallels what is going on in many people's minds when they are trying to decide whether or not to buy. They are also weighing the pros and cons. So the salesman using this method is helping them with their own thought process. In closing, if the salesman helps them in this weighing process, he can increase the odds that the decision will be made in favor of buying.

In discussing closing by comparing advantages and disadvantages, Howard W. Bacon, vice president, Marketing, Michigan Blue Cross/Blue Shield, pointed out that in order to use this method effectively, the salesman has to understand fully the prospect's needs. Bacon had these observations to make about the importance of determining needs:

> I would like to emphasize "need selling," and offer an example presented by one of my sales managers.
>
> He and his wife decided to build a porch on the back of the house, and they inquired for bids from modernization companies. One of the salesmen proceeded to tell them he hadn't seen a wooden porch in years, and they were rather antiquated. Their response to him was, "My wife and I are weird that way." Still not catching on, the salesman continued to tell them that maintenance was terribly high on a wooden porch. Their reply to that was, "We have ten children, and that would keep them busy and out of trouble."
>
> The point I am trying to make, is that he never took the time to inquire about their needs, which was due to one of their children being handicapped. The construction of a wooden porch would allow her to leave and enter the house on her own. Needless to say, they didn't buy a porch from him.
>
> Some buyers are not aware of their real needs, and therefore, there must be a period of questioning in order to determine those needs. He may, at times, think that he knows his need, but indeed it is not his real need. Often, a buyer will not want to expose his real need for a variety of reasons, and this is where a professional salesman becomes a consultant as well as a salesman. The greatest pitfall that a salesman can encounter is that of assuming a buyer's needs. The salesman will almost inevitably be off target.

Closing on a Side Issue. The psychology of decision-making is both complex and extremely subtle. There are many people who cannot bring themselves to make a major decision to buy. Interestingly and significantly there are also salesmen who find it difficult to ask anyone to make a major buying decision. Studies show that more sales are lost because the salesman fails to ask the prospect to buy than for any other reason. Psychologically, it is sometimes helpful for both the prospect and the salesman to focus on a decision of reduced magnitude. So instead of asking the prospect to buy, he is asked to make a decision on a side issue. This sometimes makes it easier for the salesman to ask and also makes it easier for a prospect to respond. Thus a prospect who cannot be made to say "I'll take it," can be made to respond with a "yes" to "Do you want this with automatic controls?" or "Shall I ship this via air freight?"

This is a variation on the "assuming that the prospect will buy" method. Either-or choices are presented in the form of a question about a relatively simple detail such as "Will you be paying cash or charging this purchase?" or "Will you want a carrying case for this equipment?" In using this method, the salesman turns the decision from one of "if" to one of "which."

Narrowing the Choice. Even the most simple purchase requires an array of choices. In buying a soft drink, decisions must be made. Where to buy it? In a bottle or in a can? A single bottle or a six-pack? What brand? What flavor—cola, lemon? and so on. People make choices about buying every day so it is a process to which they are accustomed. *Once a salesman sets the choice-making process in motion, he sets the buying-decision process into motion.* That is why the salesman should get the prospect involved in making choices as quickly as possible.

Encouraging the making of choices not only sets the buying process into motion, but also gets the prospect involved. Involvement leads to creating interest, for presumably we become interested when we are participating. Furthermore, when the prospect declares himself by making choices he is in essence telling the salesman about his preferences. "Do you need a heavyweight or a lightweight saw?" "Will you use the truck primarily for hauling on the farm or for driving into town?" "Will your son be using this pen for school or for work?" Answers to questions such as these enable the salesperson to narrow choices so that only the merchandise that is most suitable receives major attention for the close.

The preselecting process is a matter of narrowing the options and is done by the salesman through questions of choice. It eases the closing because fewer choices remain to be made at the time of closing. Closing is complicated if there are too many choices. A man buying ties may have considered ten of them. The smart salesperson will remove those that received little interest and have only two or three left for the closing.

The Scarcity Close. This particular close trades on two human traits. First, no one likes to be excluded from something that is desirable or attractive (rejection). Second, no one wants to miss an opportunity (desire for gain). This close is sometimes referred to as the SRO or "Standing Room Only" close. How well it works depends largely on what the salesman sells. In some instances it is virtually meaningless; in others, it is a major closing device. It is especially effective in real estate, or in any other field where one-of-a-kind things are sold or where there is a limited supply, as in the case of used cars and trucks, antiques, and works of art.

In real estate, the salesman can honestly and with real reason say, "There are only three of these lots left. Other salesmen are showing them too, so they could be gone by tomorrow." The buyer who is purchasing a lot for investment purposes stands to lose a chance to make a profit; the buyer who is purchasing a lot to build on may be excluding himself from building in a desirable neighborhood. Indeed, the used-car salesman, the antique dealer, and the art seller never know how long something will be available. Salesmen of such products work hard and with considerable effect to get closing commitments by using the SRO pressure method. The commitment from the potential buyer is eased by asking for a small down payment to hold the property in question—which in most instances is a declaration to buy.

Special Inducements. This is a method that actually has little to recommend it except when it is part of a planned company sales-promotion program. It is mentioned only because it is sometimes used by a company for special purposes, such as new-product introduction or for acquiring first-time orders from new accounts. Inducements are in the nature of double stamps for merchandise that is bought on Thursdays; special discounts for slack-season orders; 25¢-a-case off on initial orders; one case free with twelve case orders this month only; and so on.

Where the special inducement relates to an overall company sales-promotion program, it can be a big help to a salesman to increase his number of closes. A salesman must be very careful about making a special offer to one customer if he is not prepared to make similar offers to all his customers. Technically, it is against the law to give special prices or inducements to any one customer. Furthermore, special inducements for only certain customers is the beginning of bribery. In addition, it is bad business because a customer who accepts special inducements comes to expect special considerations in the form of rebates, allowances, and gifts.

Where the salesman has a company-planned special offer, he can use it wherever he feels it will produce most long-range benefits. Sometimes a salesman can come up with a little special gimmick from time to time that produces results. For example, for a while one salesman said to customers who hesitated, "Sign the order and you can keep the pen as a souvenir." It worked successfully until the novelty wore off. Gimmicks offer a change of pace and for that reason sometimes can be justified.

Using an Objection to Close. Sometimes a salesman saves an objection that he knows he can overcome as a ploy for closing. He works to satisfy all the customer's objections *except the one he is sure he can demolish.* Usually the prospect will come back to the objection that the salesman leaves unanswered. Finally the salesman acknowledges the objection and prepares to answer it. Just before he answers (assume he is selling automobiles) he says, "Now are you satisfied on all counts except that you would like to have this exact car in Nile green?" If the prospect says "yes," he proceeds. "Then do I understand that you will buy if I can get the color you want?" If the prospect again says "yes," the salesman has closed, provided of course that he has the Nile green car. This method has merit in that it saves time. The salesman has the prospect committed when he produces what the prospect says he wants. Too often prospects will express a wish for something that the salesman does not have in stock. When the salesman goes to the trouble to get what the prospect says he is interested in, he may still have the problem of closing unless he has already induced the prospect to make a commitment. The experienced salesman will use this technique in order to spare himself frustrations that come from inability to pin people down.

The single-objection closing technique is used with effect in the case of a price objection. If the buyer does not *promise* that he will buy if given a special low price, he may still balk when that price is offered, in hope that he can get the price dropped even more. To handle this the salesman says, "Well, I'll see what I can do. Now if I can get $10 more for your trade-in, will you accept the deal?" In this manner the salesman is assured that he has closed a sale once the new terms are made available.

Pressing for a "Yes" or a "No" to Avoid a "Maybe." Most of us undoubtedly have received one of those oversized mailings originated by *Reader's Digest* and copied by many others (it is said that copying is the highest and most honest compliment that can be paid to a person or idea). The request to subscribe and thereby enter a contest asks the recipient to answer "yes" or "no" by inserting the appropriate token in a slot in the reply card. Each mailing, of course, has both a "yes" and a "no" token attached for this purpose.

On the surface, this might seem like a waste of money—to ask those who do not want what is offered to return a reply card just to say "no." But there is good reason. To every direct mail offer, a large group initially answers "maybe" to themselves after they read the offer. From some of these, an order eventually may develop. But the majority just put off the decision and then soon forget all about it. By asking recipients to make a decision right away, some of the "maybes" are converted into orders before the offer is set aside and then forgotten.

The most important lesson to be learned from this *Digest* mailing technique is the importance of pressing for a specific decision. The salesman cannot be timid when it comes to asking for a response of "yes" or "no." Human nature, leaning as it does toward procrastination and inaction, means indeed that "the bold shall inherit the orders!"

PERSONAL-INVOLVEMENT EXERCISE NO. 9–2

IDENTIFYING CLOSING METHODS. On the left-hand side below is a list of the eleven closing methods that have been described in this chapter. Anyone studying salesmanship should become familiar with these methods. A first step in learning to use them is to be able to identify them. On the right side is a list of examples for each closing method. Place the number of the example in the space in front of the name of the closing methods at the left.

——— Building a series of affirmative acceptances by questioning.

——— Assuming that the prospect will buy.

——— Asking for the order directly.

1. "Since you don't like this trimming, if I can get the tailor to change it, will you buy the dress?"

2. "Are these buttons all right or shall I see whether the tailor has another set?"

3. "Will you want summer-weight material or will you want something a little heavier?"

—— Summarizing the selling
points.

—— Comparing advantages
with disadvantages.

—— Closing on a side issue.

—— Narrowing the choice.

—— The scarcity close.

—— Special inducements.

—— Using an objection to
close.

—— Pressing for a "yes" or a
"no" to avoid a "maybe."

4. "There's a lot of interest in
this house. Other salesmen
are showing it, too."

5. "Will you want this shipped
out this week?"

6. "Let me go over what we
have covered."

7. "May I write up an order
for 3 dozen of these?"

8. "You don't get as good gas
mileage but you do have
the power when you need
it."

9. "I think I can get them to
pay the freight if you place
the order now."

10. SALESMAN: Isn't the blue
beautiful?
PROSPECT: Yes.
SALESMAN: You can wear
blue very well.
PROSPECT: Yes.
SALESMAN: Why don't you
step into the
fitting room
and try it
on.

11. "Can I write up the order
now before Monday's
price increase?"

DEPARTURE ROUTINES

There are a few matters after the close that require consideration and attention. Being a salesman is more than just making the sale. Winding things up properly requires thought and attention, too. A salesman has several objectives in mind when terminating the transaction. He wants to 1) get on to his next call as quickly as possible to conserve both his time and that of the customer; 2) set the stage and create goodwill for repeat business and future calls; 3) assure himself that he has complete information and all the necessary forms filled out in order to serve the customer that he has just sold; and 4) get leads for additional business.

A departure that is made gracefully and with a flair is an important adjunct to the selling process. Skilled actors and entertainers always pay particular attention to getting off the stage and out of the limelight, for they know that a good exit contributes in an important way to how people evaluate the entire experience. "Leave 'em laughing, and they'll say they loved the whole show" is an ancient byword of theater lore. We can paraphrase this so it applies to salesmanship. "Leave 'em happy and with a feeling of goodwill and they'll be your loyal supporters in the future."

Winding Up After the Sale Is Made

Care must be taken to prevent the customer from questioning his decision to order. There are psychological factors that can set up reservations in the customer's mind if the salesman is not careful.

Subtleties in Showing Appreciation. If we place ourselves in the shoes of the customer who has just placed an order, how would we view the winding-up process? Undoubtedly, we would expect some sign of appreciation from the salesman acknowledging that an order has been placed. Indeed, the salesman must indicate that he appreciates receiving an order; however, he must be very careful not to be unduly grateful or else the customer will wonder whether he has been taken advantage of. When a salesman over-reacts to being given an order, the buyer starts to raise such questions in his mind as these: "Has the salesman gotten a better price than he expected?" "Has he sold something that is hard to get rid of?" "Have I been a 'push-over'?" "Have I considered the purchase carefully enough?" Or what is even worse, the customer may think: "Maybe I should look around more. I can still cancel the order."

By all means, the salesman should act with restraint when he receives an order. After all, a proper sale is a mutually beneficial arrangement in which both parties stand to gain, so there is no need to overreact to a point where the customer starts to question the transaction. It is easy for a salesman to overreact on receiving an order because he has been under tension wondering whether his efforts would get results. The order relieves tensions, and the salesman is inclined to overreact. A restrained, matter-of-fact behavior is called for at the time the order is given. That the order is appreciated should be made clear: "We do appreciate your business. We'll show our appreciation by doing our best to keep you as a satisfied customer." A statement such as this is about the most that should be said in appreciation.

Departure Assurances. If we further explore the customer's frame of mind after he has committed himself to buy, we find that at this particular phase, he is primarily interested in assurances. One assurance that he appreciates is that the salesman recognizes that he is a busy person and anxious to get back to what he was doing before he was interrupted. Since the salesman is also busy and interested in calling on his next account, the time factor is one of the best that can be used to exit gracefully. "Well, you've certainly been more than generous with your time, Mr. Blake. I'll wind this up quickly and be on my way." The salesman is careful to avoid leaving abruptly or giving the appearance that he is anxious to rush off. A relaxed, let-me-get-on-with-my-business manner serves the salesman well at this point. If the customer wants the salesman to linger and chat a while, the salesman must decide if doing so will serve a beneficial purpose.

The customer also wants assurance that he has made a wise purchase, that he will not have servicing problems, that the company he has bought from is reliable, and that he will be happy with this purchase. The following statements are samples of how such assurance can be passed along gracefully:

"Next winter you'll be pleased with the cleanliness of your new furnace and with the reduced fuel bills, Mrs. Sanders."

"If there are any problems at all, call me before 10 A.M. any morning and I'll take care of whatever comes up right away."

"My company stands behind its products. I'm happy that you've given me a chance to prove that to you."

"The nice thing about your stereo set is that it will give you satisfaction not only when you first turn it on but literally for the rest of your life. I had a hard time getting a man to replace one of our sets that was over twenty-five years old!"

Cultivating for Future Calls. In the case of resale and industrial goods selling, the salesperson must make sure that he is welcome to make future calls. In retailing, it is a matter of encouraging the customer to come back. We all have experienced annoyance when a retail salesclerk treats us with indifference after the money has been collected. We get our change without a smile or a "Thank you, please call again." All of us tend to remember the indifferent treatment and are disinclined to make further purchases whenever it is displayed.

There is another kind of indifference that can creep in after the sale is terminated. There are salesmen who change their deportment so much that they give the impression that they are people with dual personalities. It is not unusual for people who observe many salesmen to notice this phenomenon. There are salesmen who exhibit charm and do their utmost to create goodwill when they make appointments and when they call on prospects. Once they have completed a sale they leave without nodding good-bye to those they greeted effusively on the way in. This definitely gives the impression that the salesman is gracious only when he feels that those he greets can be of help to him. It is just as important to take time on the way out to cultivate goodwill as it is to do so on the way in. People are quite right to conclude that a salesman is a manipulator when he ignores them on the way out. Secretaries and assistants continue to wield influence. Since they expect the salesman to go out of his way to be cordial when he wants to get in to see the boss, they accept special treatment then as a matter of course. They are not so accustomed to having a salesman shower attention on them on his way out. Where this is done, the chances are that it will be remembered.

Soliciting for Sales Leads. Where it is felt after a sale that enough goodwill has been established and when circumstances seem to justify it, a graceful probe can sometimes yield further leads. The salesman must be very sure of his ground. If he is uncertain as to where he stands with his customer after a sale, it is best not to risk asking for leads. An insurance salesman winding up a sale of a life insurance policy can say to a young father, "It is certainly best to buy insurance at your age when your family responsibilities are growing and your premiums are lower than they will ever be. Most young people who are assuming family responsibilities don't realize that it is best to buy insurance at your age. You might be doing a young friend or relative a favor by calling this to their attention. If there is anyone you know who should be considering insurance, I'd like to have the opportunity to call on them."

A salesman could casually say the following to an office manager: "I have just two more of these excellent discontinued models with the 25 percent discount like the one that you just bought. Do you know of an office manager at another company who would appreciate knowing about this savings on equipment?" One office manager will indeed know another office manager because they usually belong to a common professional association. One young father will know other young fathers because they are the kind of people he socializes with.

Pushiness and overanxiousness to sell should be avoided. Chances for further call-back business can be jeopardized if the client gets the impression that the salesman is overeager. Where soliciting for further leads is done in a natural way in a low-key manner, it can often secure highly productive leads. The salesman has a great assist when he can call on someone and say that a friend suggested the call. If the customer has been sold well, he indeed will feel that he is doing a friend a favor by calling a similar purchase opportunity to his attention.

Winding Up If No Sale Is Made. Indeed, in most cases, the salesman leaves without having made a sale. This is the nature of selling. Depending on what is being sold, and the skill of the salesman, the ratio of sales to nonsales is anywhere from one in three to one in fifty. A nonsale does not necessarily mean a lost sale. In some fields, such as computers and manufactured components or space sales in a trade publication, it would be unusual to make a sale on the first call. In sales of complicated equipment sold to hospitals, airlines, and manufacturing plants, it can often take a year or more to consummate a sale that comes about as a result of fifteen to twenty calls. It often requires several people or departments to approve such a purchase order.

Whenever a salesman leaves when no sale is made he must do so just as gracefully as when he has made a sale. There is nothing gained by showing disappointment or impatience. Such displays merely make it more difficult to reestablish the next contact with the prospect.

A courteous and proper thing to do is to thank the prospect for his time. This is proper because whether he has bought or not, he did give the salesman his time and this should be acknowledged. All a salesman has to do if he finds it difficult to thank nonbuyers for their time is to think of all those who would not even see him! In winding up a nonsale situation, the salesman should, where a possibility for a later sale still exists, keep the door open for a friendly call-back.

The After-Sale Analysis and Record Keeping. No salesman can remember all the important facts without writing them down. In fact, one of the most valuable assets that a successful salesman has is the records that he keeps on the people he calls on. A good set of records requires a lot of time because records that are not kept up-to-date soon lose their value.

The best time for a salesman to make his customer files current is immediately after each call when details are fresh in mind. Five minutes of scribbling in the salesman's car after a call can be equal to thirty minutes of effort during the call-back. In the case of a nonsale, the salesman should decide whether or not the person is worth calling on again. If the prospect for making a sale is remote this fact should be noted. If the sale is a possibility, the salesman should decide when and how the follow-up contact should be made. In cases where sales have been made and where a call-back is recommended, details on what happened on the current turn-down call—prices quoted, promises that were made, what merchandise was shown, and so on —must be recorded. Any additional information, such as the name of the new secretary, company plans, personality traits of the buyer, should be noted. Actions should also be planned for and followed through. The salesman might decide to send the buyer a letter to provide further information; he may want to call on one of the buyer's competitors to see whether he can get some information he knows is of interest to the buyer.

A valuable thing for a salesman to do is to make a self-analysis of how he handled the call. He should plan his call-back on the basis of this self-evaluation. The notes he makes on what he did right and wrong will enable him to plan the call-back in terms of a new approach. Otherwise he might use the same tactics that have just failed the next time he calls on the customer.

FOLLOW-UP AND CALL-BACKS

Follow-up refers to the activities the salesman undertakes to keep customers happy after he sells them something. A call-back refers to the act of going back to see the customer again. A call-back may be part of the follow-up to assure that the customer is kept happy.

Follow-up is best viewed as an investment of the salesman's time to keep customers satisfied so they will remain or become loyal customers. The reason that follow-up should be viewed as an investment harks back to a point that has been made repeatedly in this book. A salesman's time is his major asset. How he uses it relates directly to his earnings; therefore, he cannot afford to squander it.

Follow-up and call-backs should be undertaken chiefly on a long-term-return-on-investment basis except where no future sale possibility may exist, but there is a moral obligation to follow up on a promise.

The Salesman Represents the Customer to the Company

We take for granted that the salesman represents the company that employs him. A salesperson at the J. C. Penney Co. represents that company in the eyes of a shopper. The Firestone salesman represents that company when he calls on a trucking company. What is not widely realized is that Penney salespeople and Firestone salespeople represent their customers to their company. The great source of feedback to the company from customers comes via the sales force because the salesman is any company's prime customer contact. It is at the follow-up point that the salesman determines whether his company is backing him up by delivering promptly, by providing merchandise as it was represented, by servicing as promised, and so on. In other words, in following up on orders the salesman determines how his own company is performing. If his company falls short of expectations, the salesman takes action to see that promises are kept. He will check on deliveries, he will find merchandise in his territory to give to customers who were shorted on a shipment, he will call to the service department to see why there are delays, and so forth. A good salesman will work conscientiously to see that his own company does what is expected of it—in this way he performs a very important service in society. For without their own salesmen's suggestions and prodding, most companies would be much less efficient in meeting customer requirements.

Follow-up and call-backs should always be combined with selling. If not combined with getting a further order, they should at least sell goodwill that will lead to future orders.

How does a salesman decide when to give a customer extra attention? This is a difficult thing to decide. In general, however, it can be said that *customers should be given follow-up attention when they will appreciate it most.* Below are examples of when follow-up attention is justifiable. Follow-up, of course, relates very much to what the salesman sells. Complicated items like computers and expensive items like transportation equipment would demand relatively large amounts of follow-up attention. Routine, low-cost items would merit little if any follow-up.

Whenever the salesman's company is failing to keep its promises, follow-up is most essential. Failure to meet a delivery date, shipment of substandard merchandise, and mix-ups in billings demand prompt, personal attention from the salesman. Even if someone else in his company is handling the problem, the salesman should be there to interpret the customer's point of view to his company.

In the case of selling to retail sores, stock inventories, point-of-purchase displays, shelf conditions, and so on, are matters that a manufacturer's salesman will want to keep under surveillance. Retail buyers usually appreciate assistance with keeping their stocks in order.

When personnel has to be trained to operate new equipment, the salesman's presence can build goodwill immeasurably.

When the salesman's fixtures, machinery, or equipment is being installed, his presence is highly visible, effective, and appreciated.

When there is a special event of importance to the customer, the salesman's presence is also appreciated. The opening of a new factory, the dedication of a shopping center, a special promotion, and so on, all require everyone's attention if the event is to succeed. If the salesman does not see to it that what he has sold is at the grand opening and functioning properly, he can create an enormous amount of ill will for himself and the company that he represents. At special events, top management eyes are watching. Whoever fails to show up and cooperate is sure to find himself in most serious trouble. If the computers are not operating when a new branch bank is opened, you may be sure that everyone from the chairman of the board of the bank on down will know about it. The salesman of the offending company is a most likely candidate to receive the brunt of any and all complaints under such circumstances.

Salesmen who understand how to keep customers happy with conscientious follow-up attention are always among those who most successful. There is nothing more effective than good follow-up for building a loyal customer following.

COMPANY CHRONICLE

It has been pointed out that the public is very aware that a salesman represents the company that he works for. What the public and even nonselling business people often do not realize, however, is the extent to which the *salesman represents the public to business*. This chronicle shows how extensively the salesman is involved in representing the public to his company and to other business decision-makers. It is said that the salesman is the

eyes and ears of business. Here we demonstrate this vital point, showing just how essential the salesman's function is in society.

We accompany Elsworth through a series of incidents that take place in the field and show how he communicates them back to his company and others. We show how Elsworth sets forces into motion that result in improved consumer products and service by influencing not only retailers, transportation agencies, and other facilitators but also manufacturers.

TUESDAY EVENING

Elsworth is selling a woman the installation of a new kitchen.

ELSWORTH: Now that you've picked the cabinets and paneling that you want in your new kitchen, we can select the floor tiling. I have here our selection of tiles.

WOMAN: Oh, I saw a beautiful kitchen floor advertised in a magazine the other day. It was in a burnt-orange and black color. It was one of the richest looking colors I've ever seen. Do you have anything like that?

ELSWORTH: I'm not sure I do. Do you remember what magazine that ad was in?

WOMAN: I think it was in *Better Homes and Gardens.*

ELSWORTH: Which issue would that have been?

WOMAN: I looked at it just last week. It must have been the April issue.

ELSWORTH: Do you remember what company advertised it? Or even better, do you still have that magazine?

WOMAN: Oh, I'm afraid not. I never keep magazines more than a few days. But if I remember correctly, it was the Armstrong Cork Company that ran that ad. It was a full page, so you won't have any trouble finding it.

ELSWORTH: Thank you very much. A woman yesterday mentioned the same ad and last week another customer described that color tile to me, so he must have seen that ad, too.

WOMAN: Well, it certainly made a striking-looking kitchen.

ELSWORTH: Here's a suggestion I can make that comes close to it. It's this brown and yellow speckled tile.

WOMAN: Yellow isn't as warm-looking as orange.

ELSWORTH: If you put up curtains with orange in them, you'd produce the same effect.

WOMAN: Maybe I could, that's an idea. I'd still like a chance to consider the tile I've been talking to you about.

WEDNESDAY MORNING

Elsworth phones Mrs. Findlay, the home furnishings buyer at the department store through which he is billing the woman's kitchen installation job.

ELSWORTH: Good morning, Mrs. Findlay. This is Elsworth of B.C. Industries calling. How are you this morning?

MRS. FINDLAY: Just fine, thank you. I've noticed that you're doing a good job for us. I thought I saw your name on four good-sized orders last week.

ELSWORTH: Oh, thank you. I have had a bit of luck lately.

MRS. FINDLAY: A salesman makes his own luck.

ELSWORTH: Well, maybe that's so. I know that you could help improve my luck for me in floor tiling.

MRS. FINDLAY: How's that?

ELSWORTH: Well, I picked up a copy of the April issue of *Better Homes and Gardens* last night after I left the home of a customer who referred to it. Actually she was the third party in less than a week who referred to a certain ad run by Armstrong Cork that showed an attractive orange tile.

MRS. FINDLAY: We don't handle the Armstrong Cork line, but if orange tile is getting that kind of reaction from just one ad, I'd better get after our suppliers to make up a similar color. We want to keep our salesmen and our customers happy. We've got to respond to what people want or we'll be left behind. Thanks for the information.

✿ ✿ ✿

It was Friday morning. Elsworth was at his desk. He had resolved to try to bring order out of the paper work chaos that was piled high. The phone kept ringing, preventing him from doing much about his good resolutions. Let's tune in on a few of the calls.

CALL 1

ELSWORTH: John Elsworth.

CUSTOMER: This is Mr. Zaponi. I tried to roll down that awning your people installed last week and the mechanism jammed. Those bolts on the crankcase came loose, so the shaft vibrates and the gears don't mesh. You ought to find some way to get that to hold better.

ELSWORTH: Let's see, that awning assembly was made by the Red Sail Awning Company, wasn't it?

CUSTOMER: Yes, can you get someone out to fix it?

ELSWORTH: Let me call you back as soon as I find out what the situation is in our service department. In the meanwhile, I'll tell the Red Sail Awning people about those bolts that came loose. They shouldn't come loose in a week. They ought to redesign that assembly so that can't happen. The need for service can be reduced by designing things so they hold up. Thank you for calling this to my attention.

CALL 2

ELSWORTH: John Elsworth.

CUSTOMER: This is Mrs. Sampson. Those men who came out to put up that fence last week left right in the middle of the job. They said they ran out of those posts they were using. According to them, the company that makes them is on strike. They were only seven posts short.

ELSWORTH: Yes, those posts come from our Indianapolis factory and it is still on strike. Let me see whether I can scrounge around and come up with enough posts to let them get your job finished.

CALL 3

ELSWORTH: John Elsworth.

CUSTOMER: This is Mrs. Kidd. I got that equipment for my new playroom. Three of the crates that the things came in were damaged. One of them is so badly packed, I think some of the parts fell out. That equipment is awfully heavy to be packed in such flimsy cardboard.

ELSWORTH: Were those cartons shipped from Grand Rapids?

CUSTOMER: Yes. That isn't so far. I'd hate to think what those crates would look like if they were shipped across the country.

ELSWORTH: Let me see what I can do to pick up that damaged crate and replace it. In the meanwhile I'll call that company up and tell them to get on the shipping company to handle things more carefully or look into using shipping containers that stand up better.

STOP & THINK

1. When Elsworth went to lunch with a friend that day he reported the following: "I wanted to straighten out the mess on my desk this morning. I didn't accomplish a thing because the phone kept ringing all morning."
Do you agree with Elsworth when he says he did not accomplish anything? What did he accomplish?
2. Would businesses be inclined to respond more to complaints that come through salesmen or directly from customers? Discuss.
3. What follow-up, if any, should Elsworth undertake on these calls?

FIELD CHRONICLE

A distasteful side of selling is customer complaints. They are often quite time-consuming and aggravating for everyone concerned. Elsworth was sitting at his desk in his office one morning when the following incident took place.

ELSWORTH: (*Answering the phone.*) John Elsworth.

CUSTOMER: Say, I want you to get over here right away and look at this mess in my basement that is supposed to be a home improvement job. The only thing that job improved was the size of your commission.

ELSWORTH: Let's see, you're Mr. Anderson on Dale Avenue, aren't you?

CUSTOMER: That's right. But not the same Mr. Anderson you knew. I'm just furious.

ELSWORTH: I'm sorry to hear that. What's your gripe?

CUSTOMER: Gripe? Who wouldn't have a gripe if he'd been gypped for $1,400?

ELSWORTH: Now, now, Mr. Anderson. No one is gypping anybody. Just tell me what it's all about. I can't do a thing unless I know what you're hollering about.

CUSTOMER: I've got plenty to holler about. All that paneling is coming off the basement wall. That's what. Furthermore, it's staining and warping something awful. You're supposed to be a salesman! You'll sell anything just to make a buck whether it's the right thing or not. That paneling obviously isn't made for use in basements.

ELSWORTH: Say listen here. I know as much about what I'm doing as anyone. That paneling is certainly suitable for basements. Sounds like you've got a crack in your basement wall that's letting water come in. You can't blame me for faulty construction of your house.

CUSTOMER: We've never had any water in that basement. Anyway, those are things you're supposed to check out. Any salesman who knows what he's doing should know about those things.

ELSWORTH: Wait a minute. I do know what I'm doing and I did check it out. I recommended the paneling that I thought would do the job.

CUSTOMER: Well, if you want paneling to do a job of peeling off and cracking, it's doing the job all right.

ELSWORTH: There's no need to get sarcastic. I'll be over and take a look at it. When can I get to see you?

CUSTOMER: You get over here tonight any time after six.

ELSWORTH: I've got my evening all scheduled. I can't make it until tomorrow night. How about seven tomorrow night?

THE NEXT EVENING

ELSWORTH: Good evening, Mr. Anderson. Well, let's go down and look at the basement.

CUSTOMER: You bet we'll go down and look at that basement.

ELSWORTH: (*In the basement looking at the paneling.*) Well, the paneling is certainly not staying on this east wall. But it's OK on the other two walls.

CUSTOMER: I've never seen such a mess. That stuff is made so thin that it just doesn't have enough body to stand up the way it should.

ELSWORTH: How come it stands up just fine on the other two walls? You've got a leak in the concrete on this east wall. You'll have to have that fixed before anything will hold on that wall.

CUSTOMER: There's never been a drop of water come off that wall. Anyway, you're supposed to check those things out before you sell anybody anything.

ELSWORTH: I did check it out. It looked all right to me. You didn't say anything about a leak. Surely you must have seen something. If you didn't see any leak yourself, how do you expect someone else who is here for ten minutes to see it?

CUSTOMER: You're going to have to fix anything that's wrong with that wall. That's what I paid for. A paneled wall that would hold up in a basement.

ELSWORTH: Now listen, Mr. Anderson. You know very well we're not responsible for the basic condition of your home.

CUSTOMER: Well, my lawyer will see about that.

ELSWORTH: You get that leaky wall fixed, and we'll put new paneling on it when you're ready. Period.

CUSTOMER: You get someone to fix that wall. That's your job. Period.

ELSWORTH: When you get your wall fixed, give me a call and we'll put some new paneling on it. Good-bye.

STOP & THINK

1. Overall, what do you think of Elsworth's handling of this complaint?

2. Review the incident on a step-by-step basis. Explain whatever you would have done differently and why.

3. In general, what are some of the policies you would recommend for handling angry customers?

4. How important is the handling of complaints in a sales job? What are the consequences of handling a complaint well? What are the consequences of mishandling?

DISCUSSION

What to Do When a Customer Is in a Bad Mood. It was Monday morning. You are a salesman calling on supermarkets. You got started early and had good luck with the first two store managers you called on. You were pleased with how well the week was getting started since the two men you had the luck with were not men you usually got along with so well. You weren't concerned about your third call because you always got along very well with Tom Blatt, the forty-year-old chain store manager whom you've been calling on every three weeks for about a year and a half.

You weren't prepared for the reception you got. You found Blatt in his back room, mad as all get out. He greeted you with, "You salesmen are all a pain in the neck." It was evident that he wasn't ready to listen to the presentation you wanted to make so you asked him what was bothering him. He told you about a run-in he just had with someone he called a friend of yours, a salesman you knew who worked for a large soap company.

Blatt's story about the soap salesman went like this: "That friend of yours, Joe Blow, is as phony as a three-dollar bill. He's always giving me a line of sweet talk about some deal or other. He overloads me every chance he gets because he figures I'm an easy touch. I'm getting a reputation as a soft touch. You guys are all alike, always out for yourselves."

WHAT WOULD YOU DO?
Select one of the following alternatives.

a. You listen to the story, then make your product presentation as best you can. You decide to keep away from talking about Blatt's relationships with other salesmen.

b. You try to talk to him about salesmen, saying that they're not all alike. You then make your product presentation.

c. You just ask him if there is anything you can do for him, and then you go on your way. You feel you shouldn't talk to a man when he's all upset.

d. You make your product presentation and tell Blatt you'd like to talk to him about salesmen on a future visit.

How Does a Salesman Handle Emergencies That Interrupt His Plans? You are a salesman calling on supermarkets. You planned your day with special care because you've got a sales presentation to make that takes more time than usual. Just before you leave the house in the morning, your boss calls. He says that you'll have to make special calls right away on three Red & White stores in your district. It seems that labels are coming off the cans in a shipment that went to the Red & White stores. Your boss promised the Red & White buyer who was furious that all the cans in his stores would be checked out that morning. It will take you about two or three hours to check out the Red & White merchandise. What do you do with your carefully made plans?

WHAT WOULD YOU DO?
Select one of the following alternatives.

a. Make all of your calls anyway, even if it takes you a couple of hours overtime.

b. After you finish the Red & White stores, start your day as you originally planned it. Work as many calls as you can until your normal quitting time and forget about those you can't get to.

c. The day is shot. Start out all over again as planned tomorrow morning.

d. Take the time needed to replan in terms of the importance of the calls. Put the least important calls at the end of your plan so they will be the ones not called on in case you run out of time.

Win An Argument And Lose A Customer? [1] Dale Thurston called on the buyer of his best local chain supermarket account. He had called on this buyer only twice before. He sold him 100 cases of laundry bleach with "3¢ off" printed on the selling-price labels, which the buyer planned to feature in a store display and in advertising.

The understanding was that if the 3¢-off label wasn't available at all or in the proper quantity, Thurston would reimburse the buyer for the price difference. Thurston made the agreement because he knew that sufficient quantities were available in his supplier's warehouse for shipment.

---

[1] Supplied by Dale Thurston, Paul Inman Associates, Inc., Franklin, Michigan.

One week later, Thurston dropped in at the store to see whether the 3¢-off-label bleach had come in. He looked at the floor display and found it consisted entirely of 3¢-off-label bleach. He didn't bother to check the stock in the back room. He left because the buyer was out.

The following week Thurston again called on the store. The buyer presented him with a bill for $18 to cover the 3¢-off-label merchandise that he said had not come in. Thurston told the buyer that he had seen the 3¢-off-label display the week before, so the merchandise must have come in. The buyer said this wasn't so.

WHAT WOULD YOU DO?
Select one of the following alternatives.

a. Thurston continued the discussion to try to convince the buyer he was wrong.
b. Thurston paid the bill and mentioned to the buyer that he may have made a mistake.
c. Thurston asked the buyer to check his invoices to prove once and for all who was right.

CHAPTER REVIEW AND DISCUSSION QUESTIONS

1. Why are salesmen afraid to close? What can they do to allay their fears?
2. What is the "right time" for making the close?
3. What are the reasons for probing for a close from the beginning of the presentation up to the end, or until the sale is made?
4. Describe signals that indicate that a prospect may be ready to close.
5. What is the difference between short-range and long-range closing? How do the techniques used differ?
6. What are the eleven different closes and how are they used most effectively?
7. Why is the salesman apt to be too technical in the language he uses unless he deliberately guards against it?
8. What are the salesman's goals after the close is completed?
9. Psychologically, what does the customer look for after the close?
10. Is it advisable to ask for sales leads after the sale has been made? Explain.
11. What are the most effective policies for follow-up calls?

10

THE PERSONAL ASPECTS OF SELLING: OPPORTUNITIES AND RESPONSIBILITIES

You'll make a living between 9 and 5;
You'll make a success between 6 and midnight.
—ANON.

"Life is what you make it" is a phrase familiar to most of us. If this statement was not first made by a salesman, it should have been. It clearly describes the essence and the challenge of selling. There are probably few other career fields in which success or failure is more directly in the individual's own hands. Because the salesman is required to be largely self-sufficient in his work and because he must be so dependent upon his own resources, his personal attitudes are of overriding importance. Personal attitudes of the salesman affect each of five important areas that surround selling: self-management; personal ethics and regulation of selling; ethics related to customers; ethics related to the company; and the bases for buying —what motivates people to buy?

SELF-MANAGEMENT

What is the purpose of self-management? It is to make everything you do yield the best possible returns. In other words, it is personal efficiency. Personal efficiency is not a matter of happy accident. People who manage themselves efficiently view their talents and their time as assets just as they view money as an asset. They conserve and invest their time and talents as they would money. There is a wide range of techniques that good self managers have learned and which those who are not skilled in self-management can learn.

The Use of Time

There is probably only one area in which all human beings are completely equal. We refer to the allocation of time. Each individual has precisely the same amount of time. Each person has exactly twenty-four hours in each day. No more. No less. Yet what an enormous difference in the ways people utilize their time! Some are very productive, others are not.

Larger companies have many salesmen. All of them are carefully selected on the basis of mental alertness, intelligence, appearance, education, and so on. In any company they all are exposed essentially to the same training programs and work with identical sales aids and materials. Yet there is a wide range in how productive they are. Why? Salesmen who are on top often produce ten or twenty times the sales volume of those on the bottom. Why? Many analyses have been made to determine reasons for the differences in sales productivity. Invariably, those factors that head the list of what contributes most to sales success have to do with the management of time. Top salesmen manage their time effectively. Poor ones do not. We have often heard the all-too-true statement: "If you want to get something done, get a busy man to do it." We say this because we know that the busy man knows how to manage his time! People recognize his ability to manage time and reward him by keeping him busy with profitable and worthwhile projects. Think about it. Opportunities gravitate to people who know how to use their time effectively.

Temptation, the Salesman's Nemesis

Working efficiently, or managing time productively, is the magic ingredient that contributes much to success. This is true in any career field, of course. However, we probably stress the factor of time management more in the sales field simply because *it is so easy for a salesman not to work!* He has little supervision. No one but the salesman himself ever really knows how he spends his time. Interestingly, his skill in being a likable person can be self-defeating. To be successful, the salesman develops an attractive personality, which means that he is sought out by anyone who wants a companion for playing hooky! Furthermore, people think that a salesman's time is his own. They feel, rightly or wrongly, that it is flexible, so if they want someone with whom to idle away the time, their salesman friend is the one to whom they turn.

Self-discipline is very crucial in selling. There are so many traps that a salesman can fall into because of the nature of his work. The salesman can easily fritter away time by playing golf instead of making calls; piddling unnecessarily with the details surrounding selling; being overly gregarious because of the pleasures of socializing; drinking too much; interjecting too many coffee breaks; and prolonging luncheons and dinners. These are just a few of the many ways in which he can dissipate time that should be used for selling.

Using Time Efficiently Is a Matter of Attitude

As has been pointed out, the man who is a good manager of time views it as a valuable asset. He seeks *to invest time, rather than spend it.*

Strangely, most people have a false impression of how they use their time. Most people think that they are really more efficient in their use of time than they actually are. Studies that analyze students who get high grades, and compare them with those who get low grades, show that just as with salesmen, better students tend to do a better job of managing their time.

PERSONAL-INVOLVEMENT EXERCISE NO. 10–1

There is value for you in making a study of how you use your time. Here are suggestions on how this may be done. First, write out a forecast of how you think you will allocate your time for the coming week—so much time for studying, sleeping, socializing, walking, driving, working, eating, grooming, and so on. Then for each day of the same week, keep a detailed diary on how much time you actually spend on each activity in your forecast. When the week is over compare your forecast with what you actually did. If you are typical of most people, there will be a considerable discrepancy between what you think you do with your time and what you actually did with it. By occasionally keeping a weekly diary of how you actually spend your time you will be able to make improvements in how you use your time. It will also help you develop a constructive attitude toward time that will cause you to use it more effectively.

Sales managers sometimes insist that their salesmen do a weekly analysis of how they spend their time so improvements can be made.

The Variables in Time Usage

A peculiarity of the salesman's time is the different value of his hours. Some hours have greater potential than others. In order to plan effectively the salesman must be acutely aware of this. Most salesmen have a rather narrow range of hours during which they can call on prospects. Industrial buyers often will not see anyone before 10 A.M. or after 4 P.M. In house-to-house selling there may be little point in calling on young mothers before the children go to school, and so on. Salesmen who are good users of time will reserve the best hours for calling on prospects and will do less important things such as paper work, handling of complaints, and sales reports during hours that are less effective for calling on prospects. The idea is to do less important things during less valuable time. This humorous remark made by a salesman, "I'm so busy, I'm not getting any work done," indicates that he is aware of the fact that he is spending a lot of time on nonessentials.

There is evidence that better salesmen have an awareness of long-range versus short-range investment of time and that they plan in these terms. The salesman who uses his time only for *short-range* purposes (planning only for his regular calls for the week, filling out sales reports, reading company brochures, and the like) is inclined to place a limit on his success. Long-range investment of time should also be provided for. This includes such things as the following: reading general business newspapers, magazines, and books to broaden one's knowledge; calling on new prospects for new business in addition to calling on old accounts; attending trade association meetings; taking classes; and socializing with people from whom one can learn and gain contacts.

Efficiency Techniques in Using Time

Reading Skills. It is clear that the salesman who analyzes how he spends his time should ask himself how he can do the things he spends time on more effectively. Salesmen spend a considerable amount of time reading. The average person reads about 250 words per minute. Reading efficiency courses can more than double reading speeds. Increasing reading speed is an example of how the use of time can be improved.

Succinct Explanations. Another matter to consider is whether the salesman is communicating as efficiently as possible. One person can say something effectively in twenty words while it may take another person 200 words to say the same thing and with less effectiveness. The criticism behind the quip "You ask him what time it is, and he will tell you how to make a watch," often applies to salesmen. They often become so enamored of what they are selling that they waste time by discussing things in too much detail.

Interruptions and the Work Steps. Good managers of time know that time is used most efficiently in larger blocks. A sales report that took fifty minutes to write because it was written in ten intervals of five minutes each as a result of interruptions such as telephone calls, coffee breaks, and sharpening of pencils, could have been written in less time and more effectively if it had been done in one uninterrupted sitting. It is an accepted fact that there are people who are accident-prone. A casual observance of people at work shows that there must be many people who are interruption-prone. One boy will manage to get an entire lawn cut without a single interruption; another will take endless breaks for drinks of pop, inspection of the mower, discussion of the project, and so on. A salesman interested in improving his use of time should consider his interruption-proneness and try to remedy the situation.

Every piece of work consists of four work steps. Let us analyze the traditional work steps in terms of doing a weekly sales report.

Work Step 1. The "Get Ready." As we sit at our desk, we must find the forms used to do the report—probably they must be taken out of a briefcase, file cabinet, or desk drawer. Writing implements must be found and possibly be fussed with. The reference notes we have gathered in the field must be assembled and reviewed.

Work Step 2. The Actual "Doing." The reference notes must be copied onto the report forms; summaries and totals must be made; and so forth.

Work Step 3. The "Cleaning Up." The notes must be sorted for filing or placed in the wastebasket, hands may be washed, and the desk straightened up.

Work Step 4. The "Disposing" of the Finished Work. The finished report must be placed in a mailing envelope and be mailed. The carbon copies must be filed.

All work projects involve these four steps. A review of them should make it apparent that projects done in one sitting without interruption are bound to result in a more efficient use of time. Work done without interrupting the four-step sequence is done most efficiently.

Knowing When to Give Up. Another point related to time is the matter of knowing when to give up on something. Salesmen often pride themselves on refusing to take "no" for an answer. Determination about selling and persistence are fine traits in a salesman; however, like most things, they can be overdone. A salesman planning his time, just like a gambler, must always think in terms of the odds. As at the racetrack, the odds change. The salesman should regularly reassess his odds for making a sale. He may have invested a great deal of time trying to sell one prospect. It is often a poor investment of time to continue spending time on a difficult prospect. Knowing when to give up is an efficiency measure that is worth developing.

WRITING AND TIME-USE EFFICIENCY

"Write it down" is a brief phrase that conveys a depth of meaning. It is not possible for any busy person, whether he is a salesman or a student, to remember everything that needs to be done; to recall what was said in conferences, classes, and interviews; to keep in mind appointments; and to know by heart the answers to all questions that come up.

A salesman should be an inveterate note-taker. He calls on so many different people that he cannot possibly keep straight in his mind what went on in each call. If he does not keep careful notes, he will not only forget essential details, but what is worse, he will confuse accounts. Notes from the past provide guidelines for today's actions. Not only do they assist in deciding what to do in current actions but they also help assure proper follow-through. The most common cause for follow-through failures is forgetting what was promised.

While proper note-taking and efficient filing for speedy information retrieval have obvious advantages, a less obvious benefit that derives from easy and certain recollection is the great peace of mind that it provides. The salesman should guard against personal tensions. Trusting to memory results in overloading the mind and in burdening the memory with trivialities. Stress as well as inefficiency is sure to result from overtaxing the memory. Psychiatrists state that trying to remember too many things is one of the major sources of stress. The trick is to keep the memory free for information that is truly essential. One should train oneself to forget trivia and to make notes on information that has value.

Since we are considering in this section the matter of saving time, giving advice to take notes and to file data (even at the cost of maintaining a complex filing system) may seem to be contradictory. Discretion should, of course, be used in note-taking and in information assembly, too. Taking notes in and of itself is no virtue. The person who saves and records everything may also be dissipating his time.

Notes help to make the mind more precise. Interestingly, writing down information focuses mental concentration twice—at the time a note is written, the writer is forced to review what has transpired; and at the time notes are consulted the mind again focuses on the information that has been assembled. The salesman usually makes notes in his car, right after his sales interview, on what transpired in the interview. When he makes such notes he can often see omissions in what was covered, and if information *is* missing he may be able to get it with an immediate telephone follow-up call while the situation is still fresh in the minds of both people concerned.

Note-taking is of special importance when the telephone is used. Information should be jotted down as the conversation proceeds and written out and expanded when the call is completed. It may sometimes be advisable to send the highlights of understandings reached on the telephone to the cus-

tomer involved to be sure to avoid misunderstandings that so easily can arise when doing business by telephone. In every oral dealing of importance, whether it is face-to-face or by telephone, a safe rule is to confirm immediately by letter what has been agreed on. When things are in writing there is little room for misunderstanding.

The Mechanics of Written Records

An excellent device is to keep lists of things to be done. Such lists, sometimes headed "To Do's" or "Action List" may be kept in a notebook or on a daily desk calendar. Desk calendars, with a sheet for each day, are intended for keeping lists of appointments and other matters that are to be accomplished. One advantage of keeping lists of "To Do's," other than that of remembering what is to be done, is that they save one from deceiving oneself. In keeping a desk calendar, things are crossed off the list as they are completed. Things that are not completed remain, and must be transferred to the next day's list. The daily listkeeper soon becomes aware of self-deception when he finds himself regularly transferring difficult or undesirable things to do onto the next day's calendar list. We all tend to put off doing those things that we consider unpleasant.

When making up the day's list of "To Do's," priorities should be assigned to certain things. Things that must be done that day, and things that can be done if there is time, should be sorted out and listed accordingly. Again, care must be taken so time is not used only for immediate and short-range projects. Larger projects can be broken into smaller segments to assure their eventual accomplishment.

The keeping of files does much to increase efficiency. An alphabetical file of 3" x 5" cards, which may be kept in the salesman's car or in a desk drawer, is excellent for keeping reference cards on customers and prospects (see Figure 6–4, page 114). Their names, addresses, and telephone numbers are kept at the top of the card. Their credit rating and history is kept on the body of the card. The salesman will often pull the cards for people he intends to call on during any one day or for a week. A day's cards are placed in route order, carefully arranged for maximum driving efficiency. Much driving time can be wasted backtracking or crisscrossing if a street map is not carefully considered before planning calls.

A sense of routing is a valuable means of efficiency for salesmen to cultivate. *Routing* refers to *prearranging and directing the order and execution of sending things to or visiting destinations.* Efficient routing of the day's calls does much to conserve time. It is of value to know that the local newspaper office can often provide route lists for calling on shopping centers, supermarkets, gasoline stations, and so on. Such lists are provided by newspapers as a service to advertisers so their salesmen can cover with maximum efficiency the retail and wholesale outlets in a city that is strange to them. It is used in this manner: the salesman calling on supermarkets finds the first market on the list. After that all he has to do is to ask the supermarket manager where the next store on the list is. The manager he is talking to surely knows the location of the store, for it is his nearest competitor! With a newspaper route list, the salesman who has never been in a town before can cover it as quickly as a resident salesman.

As has already been mentioned, a salesman usually makes notes on calls right after the call is completed. Care must be taken to write such notes so that they will make sense when they are reread, perhaps weeks or even months after they were made. Some sales managers, with good reason, insist that notes on accounts be written so they are comprehensible to anyone. Such files may be considered to be the property of the company rather than of the salesman. Thus if a salesman becomes ill, quits, or is transferred to another territory, another salesman can make use of account reference cards without too much difficulty.

File cards are excellent for anticipating needs. It has been said that they organize foresight. And foresight is one of the most valuable attributes that a salesman can develop. A successful sales executive in the financial field has pointed out that if there are proper notes about various facets of a developing selling situation, half the battle for eventually making the sale is over. A good set of file cards is so valuable that some salesmen take the precaution of keeping duplicate sets in separate locations in case of loss or theft.

It is a good idea to make notes of items that come to your attention from your reading. Ideas and information from books, newspapers, and magazines should be put into usable form so they can be filed and referred to when needed or passed on to others who may be interested.

Many salesmen keep a clip board in their car for holding cards and notes for the current day's calls. Clip boards are easy to refer to and to write on. Notes and memoranda should always be dated. It is an inconvenience and an irritation when needed dates are not there.

Many successful men keep pads next to their beds or in their cars to record ideas and thoughts that come up during the night or while driving. The subconscious mind is always working, especially when the mind is not functioning on the conscious level. Since ideas lead to sales, care should be taken to provide for recording the often valuable outpourings of the subconscious mind.

PERSONAL ETHICS AND REGULATION OF SELLING

A prime requisite for the salesman is to win and hold the respect and confidence of others. In addition, and perhaps even more important, it is essential that he maintain his respect for himself. Selling, like any activity that is blindly directed toward amassing a fortune of material wealth alone, can become a social menace and can cause mental anguish. For example, the man who high-pressures a family of low intelligence to go into debt beyond their means is using sales techniques without consideration of social consequences. Peace of mind and respect from others are possible only when the salesman is honest and in possession of a strong moral sense.

Plutarch, who lived in the first century A.D., wrote something about Phocion, the Athenian statesman who was elected forty-five times as one of the ten chief officers of the state. It provides a model for salesmen. For it testifies that character by far outweighs any other factor in influencing people. Said Plutarch: "Appreciation of him was due not so much to his eloquence as to the influence of his character, since not only a word, but even a nod from a person who is esteemed is of more force than a thousand arguments or studied sentences from others." The point is that character outweighs technique.

Selling Skills Are Amoral

Good self-management habits and a mastery of selling techniques can do much to advance a salesman's career. However, any self-management program or use of sales ability is handicapped if it is practiced by persons without sound character and strong inner moral convictions. Moral deficiencies erode any methods or procedures used in dealing with free human beings. Unfortunately, the nature of the salesman's work makes him especially vulnerable to moral corruption. He faces all too many temptations that can lead him into taking advantage of people by lying, cheating, manipulating, contriving, or bribing.

The techniques and methods that are learned in the study of salesmanship are potent! They are very powerful and they can be dangerous to the public welfare if they are used to further goals of questionable social value. *Philosophers through the ages have cautioned that power corrupts. Sales power is no exception.* Some of the nation's greatest swindlers were unquestionably masters in the use of sales techniques. They used sales power for corrupt purposes.

It is not surprising that the techniques of persuasion, which are the basis of salesmanship, have been adeptly employed by the world's most spectacular swindlers. A sampling of quotations from biographical sketches of notorious swindlers illustrates how effective they were as persuaders. A story is told of Richard Whitney, the Wall Street swindler of millions of dollars who served over three years in Sing Sing. After his case went to court, on his day of judgment, he reminded some accountants—who were talking about wine bottles—of the proper nomenclature for champagne-bottle sizes. "Gentlemen," he said with the flair for showmanship and the commanding voice that had enabled him to swindle so convincingly, "they're not two-quart and six-quart bottles. They're magnums and jeroboams." [1]

A biographical sketch of George Musica, who, using the alias of F. Donald Coster, is sometimes referred to as his decade's greatest swindler, indicates that he also had a masterful flair for salesmanship. The following quotation describes his selling encounter with a group of bankers. "With his slightly old-fashioned clothes, his earnest, punctilious manner and his Price, Waterhouse audit, Coster captured the Bridgeport bankers. Not only did they lend him $80,000 of the bank's money but added $27,500 of their own to buy 275 shares in his company." A concluding quotation from the same

[1] Harold Mehling, *The Scandalous Scamps.* New York: Henry Holt & Company, 1959, p. 2.

biography states, "In his Fairfield home, on the morning of December 16, 1938, Musica stood before a mirror with a pistol . . . . even in suicide, he wanted to die a tidy man."[2] The description of his death indicates that Musica insisted on setting the stage for his suicide with the same dramatic eye that set the stage for so many of the swindles that brought about the final dramatic act.

The clever salesman has the ability to use the great power of controlling and influencing people. Unfortunately, the skills of the salesman can be put to use for moral and immoral purposes with equal ease. It is necessary to caution those who study salesmanship that they must use their newly acquired skills with care. *Selling skills themselves are amoral—it is the users of the techniques who are either moral or immoral.*

Government Regulation of Salesmen

Society is quite aware of the weaknesses to which the salesman may fall prey. In order to protect the public from the abuses of unethical salesmen, the various states sometimes go so far as to regulate salesmen in certain fields. The state of Michigan, as one among many examples, regulates salesmen in the real estate and the home-improvement fields by requiring them to pass examinations and to be licensed. State laws dealing with the regulation of salesmen are recommended as informative reading. In Appendixes A and B of this book, there are sections of the laws of the state of Michigan pertaining to salesmen (see pages 271 to 276).

State laws vary greatly in how they regulate and license salesmen. It is therefore advisable, before entering the sales field in any state, to check with a local office of the state's labor department regarding state licensing requirements for salesmen. Better Business Bureaus are also good sources of information regarding licensing requirements for salesmen.

The range of legal problems that a salesman can become involved in is difficult to comprehend because it is so varied and extensive. A comprehensive index of legal cases related to marketing and the law appear in Appendix C of this book (see pages 277 to 278). It is strongly recommended that the student read over this index for familiarization purposes.

The Ethical Dimension

Ethics are the principles of conduct that govern an individual or a profession. They deal with deciding what is good or bad, or right or wrong, and with moral duty and obligation.

Ethics are not a matter of law alone. To consider only what is legally right and wrong is to view morality much too narrowly. Viewing ethics only in terms of the law encourages a "do whatever you can get away with without being caught" attitude on the part of the salesman. A salesman who manipulates a customer into signing a contract knowing full well that the cus-

[2] Alexander Klein, *The Grand Deception*. New York: J. B. Lippincott Company, 1955, p. 368.

tomer does not understand its provisions nor the consequences of what he is signing is legally right and ethically wrong.

What is and what is not ethical is most difficult to define, for nowhere is it or can it be written out as in the case of the law. Ethics vary in different societies. Bribery, which is considered unethical in the United States, is accepted as a way of life in many societies. Citizens from such societies have emigrated to the United States undoubtedly carrying some of these mores with them. To make a fair profit is acceptable and has a desirable connotation as being part of the American way of life. However, to make an excessive, or unfair, profit is frowned upon and may be considered unethical. Yet what is excessive profit? What is considered a fair profit by one American may be considered unfair by another. In communistic societies, all profits are considered to be immoral and unethical.

Ideally, ethics should be a matter of the salesman's feeling in his heart and mind that he is not taking unfair advantage of any situation or person. As it works out, the ideal policy is also the best long range business policy. "Honesty is the best policy" persists as the best foundation on which to conduct business.

ETHICS RELATED TO CUSTOMERS

A customer can buy most things from alternative sources. Often the only reason he buys where he does is because of the salesman. The integrity of the salesman ranks very high in the value scale of most customers. Repeat orders, word-of-mouth recommendations from one customer to another, and the customer's extending the welcome mat—all are advantages that accrue to the salesman as a result of a proven record of conscientious and reliable service and the building of customer respect. Loyalty is integrity's reward.

Sharing Confidences

In a way, the salesman who gains the respect of a customer also creates a situation that can lead to difficulties. Customers begin to talk freely and frankly to a salesman they trust. In doing this they share confidences that the salesman must be careful not to disclose. The professional salesman is just like any other professional man. The lawyer or physician is expected not to reveal private matters of his clients and patients to others. The same rule applies to the salesman and his customers. The salesman has a professional responsibility to be discreet about the business of those who confide in him. He often calls on accounts that compete with one another and who are anxious to know about each other's secrets. Also, the salesman is probably tempted to be more gossipy than those in other professions because he may shortsightedly feel that revealing inside information might ingratiate him with a buyer and thus lead to a sale. What the salesman should realize is that the person to whom he is giving the inside information loses respect for him and labels him a blabbermouth. When this happens, the salesman closes the door to communication with this customer. The more the salesman knows about his customer and his problems, the better selling job he can do. If by gossiping he causes the customer to hold back information, he correspondingly reduces his selling effectiveness.

Giving in Order to Get

One of the facts of life is that it is human nature to try to sway people by giving them something that will please them. It is traditional in most societies to give presents of various kinds in order to create rapport or to curry favor. When a President of the United States visits a foreign head of state, he brings a gift. In 1972, when President Nixon visited the Soviet Union, he gave the Soviet Communist Party chief, Leonid I. Brezhnev, who is a car fancier, a new Cadillac worth $9,600. President Georges Pompidou of France gave Brezhnev a Citroen and a Renault when the Soviet leader made a state visit to France in 1971. A common artifact found in the ruins of many ancient civilizations is the sacrificial altar used for appeasing the gods. Certainly, the idea of giving in order to receive is a deeply imbedded human proclivity that is by no means limited to business, salesmen, or the American scene.

Because the key to selling is influencing people, it is not at all surprising that the ancient ploy of giving in order to receive is widely in evidence in selling. The nature of giving in the sales field assumes many forms, including out-and-out bribery, handing over gifts, entertaining, and reciprocity.

Bribery as such is widely condemned as a business practice; therefore, when it is done it is inclined to be disguised and indirect. The difficulty with bribery lies in its secrecy. Most buyers know that they would be fired if they were discovered accepting bribes. It often takes years to reveal—or perhaps it may never be discovered—that a buyer is under the control of an unscrupulous salesman because of bribery. For example, a salesman, whom we will call Sam Brown, called on a buyer in the electronics industry for many months without selling a thing. As a test, he occasionally quoted ridiculously low prices, yet he never got an order. All orders went to a single competitor. Brown found out that the buyer played golf at an exclusive country club because the competitor had a membership there that allowed him regularly to entertain business friends. Since it was his company's membership, only the competitor could sign checks at the club which the buyer claimed he repaid later in cash out of his pocket. For all practical purposes, the buyer had a free membership to an expensive country club where someone else paid all the bills. There was nothing Brown could do about this situation so his sales manager advised him to stop calling on this buyer. It is hard for a salesman to know when he is competing with a briber. There is no easy way to handle situations where bribing is involved. When he suspects bribery, it is best for the salesman to explain the situation to his sales supervisor and then let him decide what to do. Sometimes, when evidence will verify it, top management people of two companies can get together to catch a bribe receiver.

Gifts are only a step removed from bribery, the difference being that gifts are less apt to be passed on in secrecy. Also, they may involve items of less value. Since both bribery and lavish gift giving are either illegal or frowned on, it is not possible to make statistical comparisons about these practices, for there are no records available. The Christmas season is usually the time when business gifts exchange hands. Some companies have policies of not allowing their employees to accept any gifts. Some may limit them to a nominal amount of $5 or $10 in value. Under this policy, one witty buyer remarked to a gift-bearing salesman, it was amazing what the salesman could buy for just $10. He said he was not going to show the gift to his boss for he would hire the salesman to be the new buyer!

The salesman, or at least his company (which usually pays for the gift), is caught somewhere in the middle in the matter of gift giving. Sales departments are inclined to follow the practice of a particular industry in the matter of gift giving. Often, a month or two before gift-giving season, the salesman is asked to prepare a list of the gifts that will be required for his customers. The salesman will take into account client company policies, previous year's reactions to his gift, the playback about how competitor's gifts were received, and so on. The policy of the Internal Revenue Service is to allow a maximum business deduction of $25 per customer gift. This serves as a useful guideline in determining limits for amounts spent.[3]

Routine gifts at Christmas probably serve little purpose. A business executive who receives a superfluous desk set or personally monogrammed appointment book is hardly going to notice such a gift as his assistant is in the process of giving it away! A pair of tickets for a sports event or cultural activity that the salesman knows for certain the buyer is interested in, is much more apt to be used and remembered.

Entertainment is closely tied to gift giving, yet it is less awkward and much more accepted as a legitimate business selling practice. Industrial and resale goods salesmen usually have expense accounts that provide for certain amounts for business entertainment. The most common practice is to take the customer out to lunch or dinner. Nightclubs depend for a large share of their total sales volume on businessmen who entertain their customers. Most salesmen are limited in what they can spend for entertainment so they must learn to spend their entertainment allowances where it presumably will do the most good. Whom in the customer's company to entertain and how to entertain them must be carefully considered. Here again, the routine luncheon or nightclub visit may not be nearly as effective as the well-planned fishing trip or visit to an industrial development or research center. It would be a mistake for a salesman to assume that entertainment means only drinking and eating. Buyers often prefer to do things that are thoughtfully considered rather than frivolous and ill-planned; therefore, invitations to visit new in-

[3] An excellent reference for tax information for salesmen (what can and cannot be deducted for income tax purposes, and so forth) is the *Federal Tax Course* published by Commerce Clearing House, Inc., 420 Lexington Avenue, New York, N.Y. 10017. As an example, the following is from the 1972 edition: "Business Gifts. Deductions for business gifts are limited to $25 per individual for each year, with the following exceptions: (1) items generally distributed by the taxpayer which cost him not more than $4 and on which his name is permanently imprinted; (2) signs, display racks, or other promotional materials to be used by the donee on his business premises; and (3) awards of tangible personal property costing not more than $100 given for length of service or safety achievement" (p. 822).

dustrial installations at a company's expense may be long remembered and referred to.

Reciprocity is an accepted practice in many business fields. It is often referred to as a "you scratch my back, I'll scratch yours" arrangement. Many times reciprocity arrangements are negotiated at the higher executive levels of a company. Thus, a tire manufacturer will agree to buy an automobile company's vehicles for its sales fleet while the automobile company agrees to use its tires on their cars. The salesman probably will be coached by his company in matters relating to reciprocity so there is little purpose in discussing it here beyond pointing out that it exists.

ETHICS RELATED TO THE COMPANY

When a customer says the money spent on a competitor's product was wasted, guard against agreeing. It is best to concentrate instead on the highlights of one's own line—its advantages, its economy, its guarantee. Selling on the merits of your product, not on the demerits of the competitor, is the best policy. Agreeing that a customer was taken in by a competitor is like saying, "You certainly used poor judgment."

The salesman's relationship with the company he works for is considerably different from that of most other company employees. Some of the difference is caused by the importance of the salesman's job. *Sales are so crucial to a company that this aspect of a company's operation is kept in the limelight more than other company activity.*

The Special Pressures on Salesmen That Lead to Infractions

To the perennial question, "How's business?" the answer is always made in terms of sales. "We're up 10 percent from last year," "Sales are picking up," and "We're in a slump because of that man in the White House," are typical answers that indicate that the performance of the sales department is used by everyone in the business as the measure of its success. If the head of the accounting department is asked, "How's business?" he will not say, "Fine. We turned out 10 percent more accounting reports." If the personnel manager is asked, "How's business?" he may say, "We hired ten more people"; however, he will either say or imply that this was necessary because of increases in sales. Thus the sales department is under closer and more continual scrutiny than other departments. This means that each salesman's performance is most carefully recorded and most thoroughly analyzed. Certainly this is not the case with most other company employees. It also means that because of these pressures the salesman may be tempted to use methods of questionable ethics in order to keep his performance figures looking good.

The salesman is his company's contact with its customers. Thus all the problems of a business in its relations with customers funnel through the salesman. The pressures from customers for special considerations fall on the salesman. It is not the credit department that the customer asks for a credit extension, nor the manufacturing department that he complains to about poor product quality, it is the salesman! This means that the customer also approaches the salesman with propositions of questionable character!

The salesman performs his job mostly alone and away from the company, while other employees work on the company premises and under direct supervision. This means that the salesman can squander time and become involved in matters of questionable ethics without anyone's being aware of it.

Because of these exceptional circumstances related to the salesman's job that other company employees do not have to face, it is no wonder that questions of ethics are more prevalent in connection with the salesman's job. This, of course, makes it necessary for the salesman to concern himself more with ethics, so that he may be sure to avoid difficulties that other employees are not so apt to face.

The Salesman and Loyalty to His Company

The matter of loyalty to his company is one that each employee should think through. It is a much more serious and complicated factor than many people realize. Generally it can be said that it is a poor policy for a salesman to be negative, especially if it means condemning one's company, other salesmen, or competitors. The person who publicly condemns other people or his company mistakenly believes that he builds himself up by tearing others down. The reverse is true. People lose respect for the backbiter, especially if he attacks his own company. The idea that "the family sticks together" is one of the oldest and most widely accepted unwritten social laws. When the salesman joins a company, he in effect becomes part of the company family. When he gripes about his company to customers, they wonder why they should patronize a company whose employees are disloyal. They also wonder why the salesman works for a company that he is not prepared to support fully.

Loyalty to a company includes not passing the buck. A salesman who listens to a customer complain and says, "I'll bet that the shipping department goofed and sent it by truck instead of by air," is in effect condemning his company by criticizing one of its departments. A much better reply would be, "I can't understand what happened. The shipping department is usually quite careful about shipping special orders. I'll check it out with them right away and see whether my shipping orders were clear." Sensitive people recognize and see the injustice of a condemnation when it is made before the facts have been determined. They lose respect for anyone who condemns before he has become aware of all the facts.

Cooperation has a great deal to do with sales success. A salesman is only one unit in a company's sales system that is made up of many people who are said to back up the sales effort. In order to be successful the salesman must get full support from the people within his own organization—the advertising department, the credit department, billing and shipping clerks, and others within the sales department. Thus, he must learn to operate effectively within the system. Dr. Paul H. Nystrom, a famous pioneering professor of marketing, phrased this point most colorfully when he said: "A system in business is a harness within which men work. A tangled harness reduces teamwork, results in people working at cross-purposes, and produces friction and wasted efforts."

Misuse and squandering of company time are a form of disloyalty. The padding of expense accounts; the falsifying of reports; moonlighting (holding a second job, which may decrease the employee's efficiency); selling other products or promoting one's personal interests on company time are all methods for shortchanging the company and thus are forms of disloyalty.

Loyalty includes supporting the company in all its efforts. The salesman frequently is expected to attend sales meetings. The loyal salesman will realize that he has an obligation when attending meetings to help make them succeed. His enthusiastic participation will earn the gratitude of those who are running the meeting and will enable the salesman to get as much as he can out of the meeting, which, after all, is run for both his and the company's benefit.

Changing Jobs

The salesman is a key figure in the company. If he becomes a star salesman, he will receive job offers from other companies intent upon luring him away. As we view the free enterprise system in America, any employee owes it to himself and his family to evaluate opportunities as they present themselves. Usually, however, a good company will watch the development of its salesmen and see that their earnings are commensurate with their perfor-

Figure 10-1

Is A Salesman Entitled To Commissions On Orders Shipped After He Leaves?

What Happened: Carl O'Connor was District Sales Manager for a road-building equipment company for several years — under a series of employment agreements which provided for an annual salary plus an override on sales in excess of a quota.

The company was pleased with Carl's work and he appeared to be satisfied, until he dropped a bombshell on the boss's desk — his resignation effective two weeks hence. "I got a terrific offer from Caterpillar which I couldn't refuse," he informed his shocked superior.

On hearing that Carl was teaming up with their biggest competitor, the boss retorted: "In that case, you can forget the two weeks' notice. As far as I'm concerned, you're off the payroll effective right now!"

O'Connor cleaned out his desk, picked up a check for accrued salary and commissions, bid the office staff a fond adieu, and departed.

One month later, he phoned the company bookkeeper. "Say, Charlie, I made three sales which weren't delivered when I left. In addition, I put in a bid with the State on some equipment, and I understand they accepted the bid two weeks ago. Where are my commissions?"

"Don't quote me, Carl," the bookkeeper replied, "but the sales were completed. However, the boss gave me instructions not to pay you the commissions."

"Switch me over to him," O'Connor grated. A heated argument ensued with the company head. When the boss still refused to pay any commissions on deliveries made after O'Connor left, the e employee sued. At the trial, the company defended

▶ We always paid O'Connor *after* the goods we shipped.

▶ He wasn't with us when shipments were mad so he's not entitled to commissions.

The Decision: *Pay him the commissions on the fir three sales, but not on the bid accepted after he le* ordered the N. Y. Appellate Division. "A salesman commissions are earned when orders are procure regardless of when they may actually be filled."

As for the fact that he was always paid aft goods were shipped, the Court felt this was mere a bookkeeping practice. "The essential point is h was ultimately paid for the business he secured."

With respect to the bid that was accepted aft O'Connor left the company, since the deal wasn closed during his employ, he did not earn th commission. (102 N.Y.S. 2d 781)

TWO EXCEPTIONS: (1) If selling is only part o the salesman's job (i.e., he's required to do othe things, such as servicing accounts, supervising shi ments, installation, maintenance, etc.), his commissio isn't earned merely on the sale.

(2) There's no law prohibiting a company fro laying down a specific rule that commissions ar earned only on goods actually shipped and paid fo during the salesman's term of employment. Howeve this must be clearly spelled out — preferably in written agreement.

Reprinted with permission from *Marketing & the Law* — a newsletter published by Man & Manager, Inc., New York. Edited by Lawrence Stessin, Professor of Management, Hofstra University.

mance and that their rewards are at least comparable to those of their competitors. However, there are times (this should be done only with great reluctance and only after careful weighing of the pros and cons) when a salesman may decide to change jobs. Changing jobs usually involves one or more ethical considerations on part of both the employee and the employer. (Review Figures 10-1 and 10-2 for examples of some of the many kinds of ethical problems that can arise when a salesman switches jobs.)

In considering another job offer, the salesman must be very careful to determine what the new employer expects from him. Unscrupulous companies pirate competitor salesmen in expectation that they take their customer accounts with them. The detailed knowledge that a good salesman acquires can become quite valuable. His personal contacts, his knowledge of a territory, his understanding of the operations of the various companies that he calls on, are assets that others may be willing to pay for—but perhaps only until they themselves learn what they want to know. When the salesman decides to leave, the fair thing to do is to give ample notice so a replacement can be found and trained. The salesman who leaves an employer should conduct himself in such a way that when it comes time to say good-bye the

Figure 10–2

If An Employee You Fired Talks Against You To Your Customers, Can You Stop Him?

What Happened: Threats of revenge against an employer sometimes follow the firing of an employee. Once in a while, action follows the threats.

The Lenjo Company, selling and servicing heating equipment for office buildings and stores in the Missouri area, faced that situation. It came about when Len Maitland, sales VP, fired serviceman Carl Jones on the spot for insubordination.

Jones fired back: "You'll pay for this! I have a list of your 10 best customers — and they know me well. I'm going to call up each one and tell how you've overcharged them and installed second-hand equipment. I'll ruin your business. I know where the skeletons are hidden!"

The next day, two of Lenjo's big customers called to question Maitland on the quality of the work. They candidly admitted that Jones had been in touch with them.

Maitland got his lawyer on the telephone. "What can we do? Don't just tell me I can sue Jones for slander. By the time we get a judgment, the damage will be done!"

The lawyer thought a moment. "Let's try something else. We'll ask for an injunction to stop him," he said. A complaint and a plea for an injunction were rushed to the court. A temporary injunction was granted. Trial followed, where Jones argued:

1. This is just a slander action. No judge will ever stop a man from speaking his mind. Let them sue me for damages.

2. An injunction ordering me to stop talking violates my right of free speech. It is clearly unconstitutional.

Rejoined Lenjo:

♦ We don't claim slander. We claim he is interfering with and ruining our business. He can and should be stopped by the court.

The Answer: *Injunction upheld.* Jones is barred from ever speaking against his former employer. "In disparaging the employer's business practices, Jones was actuated by ill-will and spite — and his sole purpose was to injure the company's business," the Kansas City (Mo.) Court of Appeals said.

Since his motive was bad and it interfered with the company's contracts and sales efforts, the Court will order an injunction. This is not a case of slander (where injunctions are not granted), but of interference with business relations. (352 S.W. 2d 40)

SOME POINTERS TO REMEMBER: This recent decision granting an all-important injunction (damages alone would not have served the purpose) breaks new ground in the control of ex-employees. It is important to maintain a certain course:

1. Any threats voiced by a departing employee should be noted and recorded. Witnesses to the scene will help.

2. No action can be taken until the ex-employee does something harmful and tangible. Threats alone cannot be stopped.

3. Any suit brought should be based on interference with business and business relations.

Reprinted with permission from *Marketing & the Law* — a newsletter published by Man & Manager, Inc., New York. Edited by Lawrence Stessin, Professor of Management, Hofstra University.

employer will say "We're sorry to see you go, we wish you luck in your new job. You're always welcome, if you want to come back," and mean it.

PERSONAL-INVOLVEMENT EXERCISE 10–2

ETHICS IS NOT A MATTER OF BLACK AND WHITE—THERE ARE MANY GRAY AREAS. The purpose of this exercise is to make you aware of how widely ethical judgments can range. Judge the following situations as indicated. Results can be discussed in class to draw attention to the differences in conclusions.[4]

[4] Several of the situations that are used in this exercise were suggested in a fine article on this subject that sheds further light on matters of ethics and is well worth reading: Del I. Hawkins and A. Benton Cocanougher, "Student Evaluations of the Ethics of Marketing Practices: The Role of Marketing Education." *Journal of Marketing*, Vol. 36, April 1972, pp. 61–64.

1. A real estate salesman trying to sell a house told a prospect that it was a thirty-minute drive from the house to where the man worked. Actually, if there was no traffic and if the driver exceeded the speed limit by five miles per hour, this would be possible. With rush-hour traffic it would take closer to fifty minutes.

     —— *a.* This is out-and-out lying. The salesman should lose his license.
     —— *b.* While this is a lie, it is not so serious. The salesman should be reprimanded by the company he works for.
     —— *c.* The salesman is trying to earn a living, so if the prospect believes it, it's *his* fault.
     —— *d.* It's the responsibility of the prospect to check the facts.
     —— *e.* Other

2. A life insurance salesman developed a "scare" technique that produced good results for him. He paid nurses for the names and addresses of accident victims who were discharged from hospitals. He called on them a month after their discharge and made a sales presentation that frightened them about the uncertainties of life.

     —— *a.* This is a vicious technique that is immoral.
     —— *b.* While the method is somewhat rough, it produces sales results and helps those who have no insurance.
     —— *c.* Since this is no worse than many other pressure tactics used in selling insurance, why single it out?
     —— *d.* The salesman should be congratulated on being so ingenious.
     —— *e.* Other

3. A salesman forgot to turn in a customer's order. The customer called him about not getting his shipment. After the salesman found out that it was his mistake, he called the customer back and said that the woman on the order desk had mislaid the order but they had now found it. He had arranged to have the order sent out special delivery. The salesman reasoned that if he told the customer the truth, the customer would lose respect for him, and that future relations with the customer would be put into jeopardy. The customer had no way of knowing the name of the woman on the order desk unless he made a deliberate effort to do so, and therefore no harm would be done to her reputation.

     —— *a.* A lie is a lie. The salesman has no right to lie or to pass the buck.
     —— *b.* The customer could find out the truth if he made an effort and then the salesman would really be in trouble.
     —— *c.* If the salesman told the woman on the order desk so she would understand and cover for him in case there was a question, then it would be all right.
     —— *d.* The salesman handled the case quite well as he did.
     —— *e.* Other

4. A purchasing agent allowed a salesman whom he bought from regularly to entertain him and his wife lavishly from time to time at dinner or at a nightclub. The purchasing agent claimed that he did not allow this to influence his buying decisions in any way.

‒‒‒‒ *a.* This is common business practice, so it is all right.
‒‒‒‒ *b.* The purchasing agent is kidding himself—he can't help but be influenced.
‒‒‒‒ *c.* The practice probably influences the purchasing agent, but he's human so why shouldn't he get a few of the advantages that go with his job?
‒‒‒‒ *d.* The purchasing agent is lying and he knows it. Such a man is clearly unethical.
‒‒‒‒ *e.* Other.

5. A large manufacturer of computers insisted that salesmen dress conservatively in dark suits and white shirts and that they keep their hair trimmed short.

‒‒‒‒ *a.* Since the salesman is the company in the eyes of the customer, the employer has the right to maintain whatever image is felt to be best for the business.
‒‒‒‒ *b.* The company in a loose way has the right to coach its salesmen on how to dress, but these requirements are too stringent.
‒‒‒‒ *c.* As long as a salesman doesn't get "too far out" he should be allowed to dress and style his hair as he pleases.
‒‒‒‒ *d.* It is immoral for a company to dictate regarding matters that are as personal as dress and hair style.
‒‒‒‒ *e.* Other

6. A salesman of electrical appliances told a customer that a refrigerator was "fully" guaranteed for five years. Actually, if the customer had bothered to read the fine print of the guarantee, he would have found that the guarantee applied only if the customer registered the guarantee by filling out and mailing a questionnaire that took about twenty minutes to complete. Also, the guarantee covered parts only. Labor and house-call charges were extra and had to be paid for by the customer.

‒‒‒‒ *a.* The salesman is dishonest and should be fired.
‒‒‒‒ *b.* Customers expect guarantees to cover parts only. Therefore the salesman's statement was not misleading.
‒‒‒‒ *c.* If the company calls it a five-year guarantee, it's all right for the salesman to call it a five-year guarantee.
‒‒‒‒ *d.* It is the customer's responsibility to read the guarantee, or at least to ask the salesman to explain its provisions in detail.
‒‒‒‒ *e.* Other

7. A drug company's top salesman received a suggestion from a customer. The customer said that certain drugs should be encapsuled in gelatin. The salesman thought that the idea was so good that he did not turn the suggestion in to his company. The company manual stated that all customer

suggestions should be recorded as part of the weekly sales report. Instead, the salesman resigned to start a company of his own that encapsuled drugs in gelatin as the customer had suggested. The former salesman's own company became very successful and took quite a lot of business away from his former employer.

   —— a. The salesman was unethical. The company policies as spelled out in the sales manual are part of a moral contract. Gathering of customer ideas is part of what the salesman was paid for doing as his job.

   —— b. This is how the free enterprise system works. Someone gets an idea, and if he's clever enough to recognize its value, he's got a right to exploit the idea.

   —— c. The customer gave the idea to the salesman, not to the company.

   —— d. It is a normal business risk that a company has got to expect. All ideas are not going to be turned in; that's to be expected. There was no moral issue involved.

   —— e. Other

8. A young married graduate of a business school was being seriously considered for a salesman's job. The sales manager of the medium-sized company who was interviewing him said, "Before we decide to hire you, we'd like to take you and your wife out to dinner. Our vice-president likes to meet the wives of our salesmen because they can be a great help in influencing our customers at social events. We like to feel that a salesman's wife is his helpmate."

   —— a. It is unethical to expect a salesman's wife to help her husband in influencing customers.

   —— b. The company is right in wanting to meet the wives of their salesmen. Unless the wife supports her husband in his career, he is not going to be very successful.

   —— c. The company has a right to meet wives of salesmen, but should not expect wives to assist their husbands in their jobs.

   —— d. The company is hiring the salesman and has no right to be concerned about the wife in any way.

   —— e. Other

9. A buyer for an industrial concern let a salesman know that his wife was awfully fond of a stereo set that the consumer division of the salesman's company manufactured. The buyer laughed and said that the salesman could celebrate the receipt of his next big order by surprising his wife with one of those sets.

   —— a. The salesman should pretend that he did not understand the broad hint and ignore it.

   —— b. The salesman should pass the information on to his sales supervisor and let him decide if the company wants to give the buyer the gift that he is hinting about.

——— *c.* The salesman should let the buyer know in some gentle way that he does not approve of doing business that way.

——— *d.* The salesman should put pressures on his company to comply with the buyer's wish. After all, it isn't money out of the salesman's pocket, and it is a good way to tie the customer to the salesman and his company. Buyers do not forget favors like this.

——— *e.* Other

10. Tim Weaver, a retail sales clerk, uses a sales technique that enables him to increase his sales significantly. When customers are shopping and looking at various items, Weaver takes the item that they seem to favor and immediately starts to wrap it up. He then asks the shoppers if they need anything else. Weaver has found that most shoppers will go ahead and buy the item that has been wrapped.

——— *a.* If it works successfully, use the idea. The customer can always say "no."

——— *b.* This is clearly a high-pressure and unethical method of selling.

——— *c.* Weaver should use the method until his supervisors tell him not to.

——— *d.* Weaver cannot feel right about this in his heart and mind. Therefore, he should discontinue the practice immediately.

——— *e.* Other

11. A salesman of industrial processes was selling a piece of heat-reduction chemical equipment. The buyer asked, "Does the vapor that this machine produces pass the state's anti–air pollution specifications?" "Yes," said the salesman, "vapors are water filtered. The vapors are so pollution-free that they will pass any standards." The salesman answered the buyer's question truthfully. However, he failed to mention that while there was no air pollution problem, there could be a water pollution problem due to the filtering process.

——— *a.* Sins of omission are as bad as sins of commission. The salesman was unethical in not helping the buyer to explore fully the question of pollution.

——— *b.* The salesman was honest. He cannot be expected to bring up negative factors about his product.

——— *c.* It is the buyer's responsibility to know about what he is buying. He's a professional man getting paid for doing a job and he should know what he is doing.

——— *d.* In matters of pollution and effect of the product on the environment, all salesmen should be required to present both the positive and negative aspects of what they sell so the customer can make a balanced judgment related to their particular situation.

——— *e.* Other

THE BASIS FOR BUYING:
WHAT MOTIVATES PEOPLE TO BUY?

People buy because of complex and often obscure influences. Reasons overlap; they are often disguised. The person who makes a buying decision often cannot clearly explain why he bought what he did, or why he decided to buy from one salesman and not another. The wise salesman reviews all possible motivations for buying his product or service and then builds his sales presentation and strategy in terms of those motivations that show the greatest promise for each particular customer and situation. The use of new ideas to influence people to buy can often freshen up a salesman's selling effort. It serves a salesman well to review occasionally the basics for what motivates people. When he does this, ideas will occur to him for new approaches. There is always the danger that the old approaches will become stale. This concluding section of the book is designed to encourage the salesman to review some of the basic motivations that influence people to buy. The discussion is limited to motivations of ultimate consumers because their motivations affect the entire economy. The motivations of resale buyers and industrial purchasers differ markedly from those of ultimate consumers. For a broader discussion of motivations, consult marketing textbooks in your library.[5]

What Motivates Customers to Buy?

Motives of buyers are fundamentally of two kinds—those that are rational and those that are irrational. The buying motives of the ultimate consumer are least rational as compared with the motives of resale and industrial buyers. Regardless of whether consumers are moved to buy for rational or emotional reasons, *the salesman must always treat the motive he is appealing to as being rational, for no one wishes to appear to be irrational.* In other words, the salesman must supply the consumer with rational-sounding reasons for committing emotional acts. Thus, if an automobile salesman becomes aware that a prospect wants to get a new car in order to impress his neighbors, he should verify that the car is indeed impressive but that it also makes good economic sense to buy it. The buyer is going to have to explain to his family and friends why he bought the car. The salesman must supply him with reasons that sound wise and sensible! "This car is really a beauty, Mr. Clauson. It surely has more class than anything now in your neighborhood. Not only is it the latest in styling, but with payments of only $45.30 a month, you'll avoid those $200 and $300 repair bills that threaten anyone who drives a car with over 60,000 miles on it, like your old car."

In dealing with the ultimate consumer, the salesman must not make the common mistake of assuming that if he is selling TVs, other sellers of TVs are necessarily his biggest competitors. When he asks, "Why should I buy?"

---

[5] More detailed discussion of motivations by the author is found in Ferdinand F. Mauser, *Modern Marketing Management*. New York: McGraw-Hill, 1960.

the customer is also asking, "Should I buy a television set instead of taking a vacation? Why should I get this instead of that? Which will give me the greatest satisfaction?" Each person's amount of disposable income is limited, so there is always a question of what it should be used for. The fight among salesmen for disposable income increases as increased opportunities for spending money are devised and as incomes in this country rise.

If consumers are expected to buy one type of product in preference to another, ample reasons must be supplied to reinforce their reason for making this purchase instead of an alternative.

Personal Experience with the Product. Certainly one of the most convincing bases for buying is the past experience the shopper has had with the product. Where experience with a product has been favorable, continued purchase may be expected. Present satisfied customers usually form the bulk of the sales volume for most businesses. If customers are satisfied with the product they have had experience with, why should they change unless another product offers some added advantage?

It takes considerable ingenuity to get a satisfied user to switch to another product. Providing actual experiences with the new product is one of the few really potent devices that can cause a consumer to switch.

The salesman can exploit this basis for buying by providing potential customers with actual experience with the product he is trying to sell—for example, a demonstration ride in a new automobile, a free home trial for a sewing machine, a sample volume of an encyclopedia, and the like.

The Intended Use of the Product. In many instances, buyers have specific uses in mind for a product. A homeowner replacing a broken light switch, a student buying a necktie to go with a new suit, a farmer looking for a station wagon that has a generous amount of space for hauling farm supplies, and a waiter buying a comfortable pair of black shoes that will become part of his workaday uniform—all are examples of products sought by people with very specific needs in mind.

The retailer salesman exploits this motive by stressing how his product matches actual customer needs. The salesman of men's haberdashery should be acutely aware of the approaching season's styles and colors in shirts and suits. That way he can suggest patterns and colors that will be sought by the coming season's customers. The salesman of light switches should be able to demonstrate how his switches meet the needs of homeowners replacing old switches. If possible, he should show not only how they meet all needs as replacements but also how they provide added advantages over the old, such as noiseless switching, simplified installation, or superior styling and materials.

Investigations that a salesman can make about the actual requirements needed by customers often can be quite revealing. Frequently, and surprisingly, there can be a sharp difference between the picture the salesman has in mind as to how the product is used and the actual intent that the customer has in mind. A salesman of pickup trucks assumed that his trucks were used primarily for hauling. When he visited a few owners, he was surprised to find that the prime use was as a second car. As a result, the salesman changed his sales pitch and stressed ease of handling and comfort instead of hauling information—with improved sales results.

What Others Want in a Product. Shoppers frequently consider products in terms of what others, usually members of the family, want in a product. The mother purchases food on the basis of tastes and wishes of other members of the household. Gifts are purchased with the recipient's possible likes and dislikes in mind. Salesmen should always check to find out whether the customer is buying for himself or for someone else. When others are considered in the purchase, the sales pitch should be designed to give the purchaser assurance as to acceptance of the product by others.

Steuben glassware has successfully stressed that its product is accepted as a standard of good taste everywhere, the implication being that it can be confidently bought as the ultimate in gifts. Manufacturers of processed foods stress that their food products are liked by children or will make a mealtime hit with husbands. Whatever can be done to assure the buyer that others will applaud the contemplated purchase furthers the selling effort.

What Has Been Learned About the Product. People are influenced by and act according to what they observe, hear, and read. Therefore, it is prudent for the salesman to find out what the prospect knows about the product so he can design his sales pitch accordingly. The extent and nature of the impressions influencing people depend on the source of the information and the conviction heard in its presentation. Information that influences people in buying comes to them from many sources. Several are discussed below.

1. *Users of the Product.* Word-of-mouth information passed on by satisfied users of a product is most desirable and influential. Products also have suffered severely and even failed because of negative impressions circulated about them by former users. The user of a product is a most convincing source of information concerning it. The salesman who can have satisfied users testify on his behalf is tapping a potent source to back up his selling effort.

If possible, salesmen should regularly tune in on what people are saying about his company and its products and also about his product area in general. When the salesman is not working, it is of value for him when talking to strangers to bring the conversation around to his product area without letting the person he is talking to know that he is associated with the field. For instance, it provides insight for a salesman of automobiles to hear people talk in an unguarded manner about buying an automobile. The salesman of home improvements can learn much when he listens to people talk about plans they have for their homes or how they recently made an improvement.

It has been found that people talk favorably about products with which they experience a pleasant surprise. Thus, an insurance salesman who made personal delivery of a claim check within twenty-four hours after the claim was filed created much favorable comment from the recipient and his family. The seller of certain reference books provides neatly packaged inserts that keep the old volume up-to-date. The promptness and regularity of the service drew attention to the value of the product and caused positive comment. The salesman was able to get leads when he called back on old customers and talked to them about the good service they were getting. Follow-up attention for products already purchased usually gets positive reactions about which the users are prepared to tell others. Word-of-mouth is one of the most effective types of publicity.

2. *Advertising.* Advertising provides a great source of information. The salesman who asks a prospect about what advertising has been seen about the product being considered gets excellent clues as to what is important to the prospect.

3. *Reading (Nonadvertising).* It is safe to assume that the consumer in America is greatly influenced by reading matter. Americans are undoubtedly the world's greatest readers of magazines and Sunday supplements. A prominent feature of many successful periodicals is how-to-do-it and constructive self-improvement articles. Housewives are avid readers of women's magazines that tell them how to control their waistlines, their complexions, their hair, and their husbands. These articles generously pass out information about fashion and furniture arrangements; gardening and how best to pamper lawns; cooking and table settings to excite the most jaded of appetites; health and how to keep well while practicing girth control.

Buying decisions have been complicated by the growth of public concern about good taste. With the development in Americans of an "other-directed" personality,[6] we have become preoccupied with what other people think. Such a concern requires that material possessions exposed to the public eye reflect good taste. Home, clothing, and associates must all achieve public acceptance and, if possible, acclaim.

This puts a severe strain on the shopper who is confronted with a private dilemma about his public facade each time he is asked to reveal his taste when making a buying decision. It is true that such taste has a shallow base,[7] but it does nevertheless give rise to serious concern in the minds of many shoppers and cause them to seek assistance in choice-making. The salesman should be aware of this need and capitalize on it. Harry Henderson wrote convincingly about this in *Harper's Magazine* of November, 1953:

> My interviews with wives revealed that their (interior decorating) models and ideas come primarily from pictures of rooms in national magazines—they don't feel certain about things. "If you've seen something in a magazine—well, people will nearly always like it." So many times were remarks of this character repeated that I concluded that what many sought in their furniture was a kind of "approval insurance."

The status of advice coming from magazine articles probably ranks high, for it usually comes from a recognized authority and is presumably neutral and noncommercial. It is of tremendous advantage for the salesman to associate his product with what is written about and considered in the consumer's daily reading matter.

[6] David Riesman, *The Lonely Crowd.* New Haven: Yale University Press, 1950.
[7] Russell Lynes, *The Tastemakers.* New York: Harper & Brothers, 1954.

Thus home economists and food columnists become the darlings of home-appliance and food-product salesmen. They consider these columnists in every way possible. Health and beauty editors and people who write about color schemes and gardening are all recognized as important centers of influence by those selling products related to their domain. It is the short-sighted salesman who forgets them in his presentation plans.

4. *Comments of Friends, Experts, and Others.* People facing buying decisions often consult others before making a purchase. The salesman should carefully establish who the people are who might be consulted about his product. For example, electronic engineers generally may be found to be important centers of influence for the purchase of stereo equipment. Potential buyers of such items would certainly be inclined to consult known engineers before making a purchase commitment. If the salesman finds that the opinion of engineers looms important in the buying of his product, he should get testimony from engineers that laud his product.

Imitation. The well-known phrase "keeping up with the Joneses" is always of significance as an impetus to buy. Movie stars, community leaders, and world figures are known to have marked influence in the setting of patterns for buying, especially in the realm of fashion goods. People are often moved to emulate those they respect and admire. They also imitate because of a desire to conform. It is true that there is a desire to be different on the part of some people; however, this is not nearly so strong an influence in the mass market as conformity. If all the boys at school are wearing red hats, Johnny is going to set up pressures to buy until his green hat is replaced by a red one. Adults also have childish impulses, except they are less honest than children—they disguise them.

Imitation is a strong ally of sales success, for it can set into motion a highly desirable multiplier effect that can lead to many additional good prospects. As John Kenneth Galbraith so attractively points out, "One man's consumption becomes his neighbor's wish. This already means that the process by which wants are satisfied is also the process by which wants are created." [8]

Security, an Eternal Pursuit. Protection against insecurity is one of the fundamental and eternal quests of man. Security is actually a concern that becomes magnified as the income level of the economy rises. People pressure the government to provide more and more security. They seek to protect themselves individually by buying insurance, safety construction in tires and machines, and health preservers such as vitamins, suntan lotions, and eye-glasses.

Indirect paths to security can also get respectful consumer consideration. Sales presentations can call attention to what needs to be protected. Men and women can be reminded to protect their jobs by dressing properly. Women can be told that they will feel more secure about their husband's affections by cooking well. Students can be encouraged to buy portable

[8] John Kenneth Galbraith, *The Affluent Society.* Boston: Houghton Mifflin Company, 1958, p. 154.

typewriters and thus remove certain hazards that come from submitting handwritten assignments.

As an aside, it is interesting to note that not only individuals and families seek to guard against insecurity. Business itself is very protectionist-oriented. Advertising is used as protection against loss of competitive position. Marketing-research expenditures are made in an attempt to keep up with shifts in customer tastes. Price fluctuations are minimized through hedging. Indeed, businesses as well as individuals are very receptive to services and products that can be demonstrated to provide protection.

SOME CONCLUDING OBSERVATIONS

As a close to our study of salesmanship, we have provided two overviews of selling. One, Figure 10–3, is provided in a form from Sales and Marketing Executives—International, the professional trade association for sales managers, and Junior Achievement, Inc. It is a form that is used by local chapters of SME in their judging at an annual contest held to select the best student salesmen from schools in the chapter's area. A study of this form is educational, for it provides instructions for judges who themselves are professional salesmen and thus indicates what they look for in a sales presentation. As you examine this form, you can ask yourself, now that you have completed a course in salesmanship, how you would measure up in the eyes of such judges.

Another overview of salesmanship, as seen from a purchasing rather than a selling point of view, is found in Figure 10–4. Arnold Hartig, vice president for purchasing, Chrysler Corporation, speaks about how the salesman represents his customers to his own company.

In addition, in Figure 10–5 Hartig offers ten suggestions for sales effectiveness from the manufacturer's purchasing department's point of view. Analyze these ten suggestions and tell what you think purchasing departments attempt to accomplish.

COMPANY CHRONICLE

Charlie Springer was Elsworth's friend and a fellow salesman. Their desks were adjacent. Several times recently Elsworth had detected liquor on Springer's breath. Also, his work seemed to be deteriorating. He missed appointments and didn't follow through on things that he promised customers. Elsworth was aware of Springer's mounting problems because, since their desks were side by side, he answered Springer's telephone when he wasn't there. One afternoon Elsworth took one of Springer's calls. It was from one of Springer's customers who was very upset because of some electrical problems. The customer's house was near where Elsworth was going to make a call, so thinking to do Springer a favor since he couldn't be reached, Elsworth stopped in to listen to the customer's complaint.

ELSWORTH: Good evening, Mr. Sadler. I'm John Elsworth, the man you talked to when you called Mr. Springer this afternoon.

Figure 10–3

BEST SALESMAN CONTEST
Scoring Sheet for Judges
(See other side for Procedures)

Instructions:

A. Use grade from 0-10 for each item below.

B. Consider the factors listed before entering the grade.

C. Total the individual grades. Maximum total grade 100.

ACHIEVER'S NAME

1. _____

2. _____

3. _____

4. _____

5. _____

PRODUCT OR SERVICE

_____

_____

_____

_____

_____

	1	2	3	4	5

APPROACH: Did it include an attention-getting statement aimed at the prospect's main interest, problem or objective?

SELLING POINTS: Did the Achiever present enough sales points to arouse prospect's desire for the product or service? Did the Achiever show how the sales features would benefit the buyer? Did the salesman support his claims with examples, with testimonials, photos, sales results or letters?

DEMONSTRATION: Was the Achiever's demonstration smooth? Interesting? Convincing? Did the Achiever handle the product with respect? Dramatize any intangible?

KNOWLEDGE OF PRODUCT: Did the Achiever have a thorough knowledge of the product or service and industry?

OBJECTIONS: Did the Achiever handle objections smoothly? Were explanations convincing? Did Achiever get back to his sales story effectively?

PROSPECT PARTICIPATION: Did the Achiever seek agreement from the prospect on various points of the proposition along the way? Did he encourage the prospect to take an active part in the sale?

TIMING: Was first attempt to close made within five minutes? (Time will be announced after each interview.) Time, first attempt to close,................min.

CLOSING: Was the Achiever's closing satisfactory?

COMPLETING THE SALE: Did the Achiever write up the order effectively? Arrange for delivery? Ask for referral to another prospect? Congratulate the customer on selection? Exit effectively?

VOICE, SPEECH, AND PERSONALITY: Was voice pleasant? Was speech clear? Well-paced? Was Achiever persuasive, assuring and enthusiastic? Radiate belief in the product and its benefits?

TOTAL GRADE

PROCEDURES FOR JUDGES

In the interest of uniform competition at all levels, these procedures should be applied at Local, Sectional, Regional and National Contests.

1. *All contests* will use the standard contest materials provided by the SME and JA. These include SME Kit, Entry Blank, *Scoring Sheet,* Guide Sheet for Sales Prospects, and these Judging Procedures.

2. The mechanics of judging will be for the sales prospect to assume the role requested by each contestant. Each Achiever salesman then makes his or her sales presentation to the prospect.

   Where a panel of judges (usually three or five) is employed, the judges sit to one side, out of the contestant's line of vision, where they can see and hear the sales interview. On signal, the salesman enters the room and begins the presentation.

   Where the audience at a meeting selects the winner, arrangements will be made for the audience to see and hear the interview. Selection will be by ballot which will be counted immediately, and the winner announced before the close of the meeting.

   In both cases, the scoring sheet for Judges will be used to grade the contestants.

3. The sales prospect or customer is an essential part of the presentation. The "Guide Sheet for Sales Prospects" should be followed carefully, since the points it makes have all been proven in actual performance.

   A good method for bringing judges and prospect into a close understanding and agreement on procedures is the demonstration or "warm-up" interview. This involves the sales prospect for the Finals and a former contestant. They carry out a complete presentation while the Semi-Final prospects observe and all judges actually score the presentation. By discussion and comparison of scores, all will be oriented prior to the actual contest.

4. Each contestant will have up to five minutes to attempt to close the sale. Once an attempt is made, the length of the interview is controlled by the prospect and may be terminated at the discretion of the prospect according to previous arrangements made with the judges or the committee. The interview may be expected to end within ten minutes.

5. Because sales of intangibles, (advertising space, radio time, etc.) are not always "closed" on the first call (as opposed to an item sold to the housewife, for instance) ; an Achiever selling an intangible will have stated the objective of his call. Thus, if he is selling a market survey, his objective may be to get a firm commitment for a further appointment at which time he will have a specific questionnaire prepared covering the prospective client's particular problems. But this does not mean that he will not have to "close" this first call by getting a specific agreement from the prospect as to the purpose of the final presentation.

6. The scoring sheet for judges gives a comprehensive picture of the skill with which the salesman operates. The scoring does not rate the saleability of the product itself, because the salesman is being tested, not the product. In the interest of operating efficiency, adult Advisers suggest most products made by JA companies, and it would therefore be unrealistic to credit or penalize the Achiever for the product he is selling. Rather the emphasis in the scoring is on the factors which indicate salesmanship on the part of the Achiever. This approach to judging will provide an objective appraisal of each contestant while assuring full credit to all who make maximum use of whatever advantages they may have enjoyed in the form of product selection, sales record, or the operation of their JA Business Centers.

7. In nearly every case, selection of the winner will be obvious on the basis of adding total grades. In the very rare event of a mathematical tie, further steps are necessary.

   If the contest is one where selection is made by a panel of judges, the tied candidates should be called back and asked direct questions on selling. Select as the winner the one with the best knowledge and enthusiasm for salesmanship.

   If the contest is one where an audience of sales executives selects the winner by ballot, procedures arranged in advance by the host Sales Executives organization and J. A. Staff should be followed to break a tie. These will involve some form of re-ballot between the tied contestants, the exact form depending on the type of ballot used.

Figure 10–4

The salesman — better than anyone else — knows what is happening in the marketplace. He knows what technological developments in other industries mean to his own business. He sees how his customers' needs are changing and he knows what his customers are beginning to emphasize in the way of cost, or appearance, or quality.

By effectively communicating this to his own company the effective salesman can play a key role in helping his company pick the new products and processes and develop the additional capacity needed to take advantage of the new opportunities that will come when the market changes.

Some suppliers are in trouble because they didn't heed changes in the marketplace in, for example, the area of quality control. Rather than establish their own quality control programs they left it up to their customers to sort out and reject defective material. In other cases their salesmen have either failed or not been willing to do their own legwork to determine processing standards and specifications of their customers.

Arnold Hartig, "The Ten Commandments of Selling to the Auto Makers." *Michigan Challenge*, October 1971, pp. 23–24.

Figure 10–5

Here then are ten suggestions that can be followed by the effective salesman in dealing with a manufacturer's purchasing department:

One. Legwork with purchasing to make sure you know the ways changing conditions can influence the buying decision. As you work with manufacturing or design organizations, make sure that purchasing is aware of what you are doing.

Two. Know how your product relates to the product your customer manufactures. Be familiar with all the cost details. Have the facts that can support your proposal and that show a real value to the buyer. Get away from the idea that the important thing is not what you know but who you know. It's just not true. Purchasing decisions are based on facts — and the more facts a salesman gives, the better the decision made.

Three. Use your time efficiently and know the customer's organizations. Don't waste the buyer's time by spreading rumors, or by running down your competitors. Spend your time showing how your products can help the customer.

Four. Don't oversell your company to your customer. Don't agree to quality standards that can't be met. Don't tell a buyer you can meet a certain production schedule and then sit down with your manufacturing people to find ways to meet that schedule. Know what your company can deliver — and promise only what you know your company can deliver.

Five. Use all your influence to make sure your company can meet the customer's demands. Insist on good and adequate tooling, on reliable manufacturing processes, and keep insisting on the need for a strong quality control program in your own organization.

Six. Don't be afraid to fight. Sometimes that means telling the customer he is wrong. Sometimes it means telling your own company that it is wrong. It's never easy to fight for a position — but it's necessary if the salesman hopes to effectively serve both his customers and his company.

Seven. Keep your own organization informed of what your customer is doing by communicating all you can about the customer's problems, products, and manufacturing processes. In his way, your company will be in a better position to work on ideas that will help the manufacturer — and will lead to increased business for you.

Eight. Help your own organization build quality attitudes among its employees. Remember, your company's plant management is facing a whole new set of problems growing out of the changing character of today's workforce. Many companies are facing problems of attitude, turnover, and absenteeism on a scale never encountered before. Sometimes, newer and younger employees have the wrong idea that quality workmanship just isn't important. As a salesman, you know they are wrong. You know that quality is more important than it has ever been. And you know that it is going to be even more important in the coming years.

Nine. Get involved in community affairs. Help your company take an active part in finding answers to some of the country's serious social problems. Don't just pay lip service to this idea. For example, get your company to do whatever is reasonable to follow the lead of the automobile companies in hiring the disadvantaged people in our society. As Lynn Townsend who recently was Chairman of the National Alliance of

Figure 10–5 (continued)

Businessmen pointed out, hiring and training the disadvantaged is one way in which both large and small businesses can develop the trained manpower needed for the bigger markets out ahead.

Ten. Understand that the best way to help your customer is by keeping your own organization tuned in to the larger economic and social problems facing the country today.

Arnold Hartig, "The Ten Commandments of Selling to the Auto Makers." *Michigan Challenge,* October 1971, pp. 23–24.

SADLER: Well, I'm glad that I've at least got someone to talk to, but I want to see Springer. I've been calling him every day for two weeks. I've only been able to get in touch with him twice. Both times he promised to stop by and he never showed up.

ELSWORTH: I'm sorry to hear that. He's been having some family problems. (*Elsworth fabricated this to cover up for Springer.*)

SADLER: Well, just come down into my basement and look at the new recreation room that Springer sold me. My insurance man made an inspection and said that they can't insure the house with the wiring the way it was put in. Springer said he could save me money if his brother-in-law did the job. That was a real money-saver. Now I can't get insurance.

ELSWORTH: Springer had his brother-in-law do the job? Our company has its approved electrical contractors and Springer's brother-in-law isn't one of them.

SADLER: I know. He told me not to tell your company if I wanted to save money. They'd never know the difference. But now I've told you and have broken my promise to Springer. But I never dreamed that I wouldn't be able to get insurance.

Elsworth was shocked by all of this. He called Springer's home and his wife said he was out of town at a company convention. Mrs. Springer said she was surprised to hear from Elsworth because she thought Elsworth would be at the convention, too. Elsworth lied (again to cover up for Springer) and said that he had forgotten about Springer's being at the convention. The next morning Springer showed up at his desk looking pretty disheveled and smelling of alcohol.

ELSWORTH: Good morning. You look like something the cat dragged in from out of the rain. What's up? I talked to your wife about going to a company convention and to Sadler about that job your brother-in-law did in his basement.

SPRINGER: You've got a lot of nerve sticking your nose into my business.

ELSWORTH: You know we answer each other's phones. If you're not here and with the messes you're getting yourself into, how can I help but get involved in your affairs? I represent the company when I answer your phone, so I'm going to hear about what you're up to whether I want to or not.

SPRINGER: I know, I know. I guess I shouldn't jump on you. But give me a break, John. I'll straighten this out. There's been a couple of misunderstandings. Promise you won't tell my wife or the company about any of this?

ELSWORTH: I won't say a word to anyone. After all, it's none of my business if you want to hang yourself.

STOP & THINK

1. Review the whole sequence of events. What did Elsworth do right? What would you have done differently? Why?

2. Was Elsworth right in covering up for Springer by lying twice, once to the customer and once to his wife?

3. What loyalty, if any, does Elsworth owe his company in this matter? And the company's customer? What would you do on behalf of the company and the customer, if anything?

4. What about Springer? Elsworth claims that he is a friend. Is it none of Elsworth's business if Springer hangs himself, as Elsworth phrased it?

FIELD CHRONICLE

Elsworth was calling on a Mrs. Hollingsworth, wife of a young dentist. She wanted to add a sun porch to her home. They had purchased the neighboring lot that would be landscaped. The porch was to face and take advantage of the view. Let us tune in on Elsworth's discussions with Mrs. Hollingsworth.

ELSWORTH: We'll have a designer come out and make up a few sketches. Can you give me an idea of what you'd like the porch to look like?

MRS. HOLLINGSWORTH: Well, it should fit with the rest of the house. Yet it should look modern.

ELSWORTH: Well, your house is pretty traditional. Modern and traditional are pretty hard to blend, but we'll see what we can do.

MRS. HOLLINGSWORTH: The Manellis up the street added a sun porch. They got their idea from *Better Homes and Gardens*. I'd like something at least as nice as what they have.

ELSWORTH: Do you like their style?

MRS. HOLLINGSWORTH: I guess so, but I don't want to copy what they've got. I'd like something even nicer.

ELSWORTH: Well, *Better Homes and Gardens* has a special book of designs that has a number of sun porch treat-

	ments. Supposing I send that to you and then you can tell me what you like best.
MRS. HOLLINGSWORTH:	Oh, that's an excellent idea.
ELSWORTH:	What other features do you want on your porch?
MRS. HOLLINGSWORTH:	We want to have a fountain and small fish pond against the outer wall. Jane Freeberg wrote about how nice they are in her column. She says the sound of trickling water is soothing when you're relaxing on a sun porch.
ELSWORTH:	Well, we'll be glad to put in a tile pond and some kind of a fountain.
MRS. HOLLINGSWORTH:	Oh, Jane Freeberg says a plastic basin for a pond is better than tile. Tile springs a leak too easily.
ELSWORTH:	I'll call Jane Freeberg at the paper. I think they sell plans for what they talk about in those newspaper columns.
MRS. HOLLINGSWORTH:	Oh, that's splendid. I'll pick out the plan I like best. My husband is a nut on health, so we'll want some sun lamps out there too, to use in the winter.
ELSWORTH:	What kind of lamps will he want?
MRS. HOLLINGSWORTH:	I don't know, but I want to surprise him with those.
ELSWORTH:	Why don't you talk to one of his doctor friends in the building where his office is and see what he would recommend from a health point of view.
MRS. HOLLINGSWORTH:	Oh, that's splendid. I'll do that.

Elsworth has done a fine job of selling here because he has identified what motivates this woman.

STOP & THINK

1. What are the motivational needs of Mrs. Hollingsworth?
2. How did Elsworth cater to the things that motivate her?
3. Why doesn't this woman express any tastes or preferences of her own?

PROBLEMS

What Do You Do If the Buyer Refuses to Reveal His Motives? You are selling grocery products to resale buyers. You have about twelve items to sell on this week's round of calls. You've just made what you thought was an excellent presentation of the special deal of the week to an important account. It is important that you get your deal into this particular store. Yet, when you finish your presentation the buyer says: "No, that's not for me. What else have you got?" What do you do? There was no explanation at all to what he did not like about the deal. Think about the following alternatives and select the action you would take.

  a. You feel you've made as good a presentation as you could so you forget about it and move on to the next item.
  b. You ask the buyer why he does not like the deal before you go on to the next item.
  c. You go through the rest of your items and hope you can find a place to try to reintroduce the deal you got turned down on.
  d. Just before you're ready to leave, and after you have covered everything, you ask him to reconsider the deal he turned down.

STOP & THINK

1. What about the matter of timing your inquiry as to the buyer's motives for turning your deal down?
2. Phrase how you would ask about his motives.
3. Are there any indirect ways of getting at the reasons?

What Do You Do If You Do Not Accept Management's Recommendations? It is just after the weekly sales meeting for salesmen in grocery items. Two of the salesmen who were at the meeting stop for a beer on the way home. The following conversation takes place over the beer. Bob starts out with an obviously negative tone in his voice.

BOB   What do *you* think of the sales program for next week?
RALPH: How on earth can they expect us to push fifteen items?
BOB: If I did everything they said I should do in each store, I'd be lucky to get through 25 percent of my stores, let alone the 100 percent they expect me to cover.
RALPH: Those guys who run these sales meetings think that the store manager is waiting for us to show up and that he drops everything right away to listen to our sales pitch. Man, I can waste an hour just getting to see the manager and then I have to run around the store after him to try to get my story across. So how am I going to get through on fifteen items? If I tried to go through so many items I bet I'd get kicked out after number six in most cases.
BOB: Those guys at the home office don't know what it's like in the stores. If they did, they wouldn't be so out of their minds and ask you to push fifteen items.

How should salesmen face a situation like this? Review the following alternatives.
  a. Sit around and complain about it over a beer.
  b. Try to see things from management's point of view. (What is that point of view in this situation?)
  c. Plan a program in which you match the items with the stores you have to call on. Pick the items that fit each store best. Try to give each item some time in the stores where its chances are best. Don't cover all fifteen items in each store. Pick a realistic number to cover in each store.
  d. Do what management asks. Present fifteen items in each store. Don't stop until the manager will not listen anymore.

STOP & THINK

1. How do you explain unrealistic policies of management? Why do these things happen?
2. What is the role of the salesman in the sales meeting? Explain what these men should have done in the sales meeting.

The Ups and Downs of Salesmanship—How Do You React to Them? Two salespersons who work for food brokers were having coffee together one morning. Their conversation ran as follows:

DICK: I get awfully tired of this rat race.
MARILYN: Any job has its ups and downs.
DICK: Yeh, but I sometimes feel that I'm a failure.
MARILYN: What do you mean? I don't feel that way.
DICK: People ask me what I do and I say I work for a food broker and they don't even know what I do. If they listen long enough while I explain they say . . . oh, that's like being a salesman. I doubt if it impresses anyone. If someone says he's a teacher, or a real estate man, or a truck driver, people know what they're doing and that their job stands for something. Me? What I do—well, people could care less.
MARILYN: Just because people don't know what you do doesn't make it less important, Dick.
DICK: My wife keeps telling me I ought to get promoted. The boss is the guy who gets all the glory and has it easy.
MARILYN: I think I'll pay a call on your wife.

STOP & THINK

1. How do you react to this conversation?
2. What is success or failure in a career?
3. How important is what others, including family members, think? How do you handle their remarks?

CHAPTER REVIEW AND DISCUSSION QUESTIONS

1. In any large company there is a wide range between the sales performance of the best and the weakest salesmen. How can this range be explained, since all salesmen get the same training?
2. What can the salesman do to use his time effectively? Explain long-range versus short-range time investment and variable value of hours.
3. Explain the value of note-taking and filing. What is a "To-Do's" or

"Action List"? How does it avoid self-deception and assist in time management?

4. Power can corrupt. Sales power is no exception. Explain these statements and show why they are true.

5. Discuss the matter of gift giving. What is a proper policy in this regard?

6. Why is it a poor policy to agree with a customer who criticizes a competitor?

7. What is there about the nature of the salesman's job that makes him more susceptible to ethical infractions?

8. What are the things the salesman must consider very carefully in thinking about a job offer from another company? What considerations relate to his present employer?

9. Explain the difference between rational and irrational buying motives. Why should the salesman acknowledge the irrational motive of the customer yet treat it as being rational?

10. Review the reasons why people buy and explain what is involved in appealing to each of these motives.

EPILOGUE

If you have seriously studied this book, you have now completed a phase in your development as a salesman. We hope that what you have learned will contribute to your success both in business and in daily living. In conclusion, let us propose a toast to your good luck:

May your successes be as many as there are drops in the ocean;
May your failures be as few as the drops in this glass.
Bottoms up! [9]

[9] This is a paraphrasing of an ancient Ukrainian good-luck toast used at weddings by well-wishers in drinking to the happiness of the bride and groom.

APPENDIX A

State of Michigan, Department of Licensing and Regulation. From laws relating to the Residential Builders' Maintenance and Alteration Contractors' Licensing Act (Act 383 of 1965, as amended).

338.1508 License; fees; second examination, forfeiture, renewal, expiration; name and address change, report. [M.S.A. 18.86(108)]

Sec. 8. Application for a residential builder's, residential maintenance and alteration contractor's and/or salesman's license shall be made to the commission with the fee herein prescribed. Unless the applicant is entitled to a renewal license, he shall be licensed only after passing a satisfactory examination. The application for a salesman's license shall be submitted by the employing residential builder or residential maintenance and alteration contractor. The license fee for a residential builder shall be $35.00. The license fee for a residential maintenance and alteration contractor shall be $30.00. The license fee for a salesman shall be $25.00. In case of the failure of an applicant to pass a satisfactory examination, the license fee shall be held to his credit for a second examination for a reasonable time not to exceed 1 year. Failure to pass a second examination will automatically forfeit the license fee to the commission. Licenses of residential builders shall be renewed upon payment of a fee of $35.00. Licenses of residential maintenance and alteration contractors shall be renewed upon payment of a fee of $30.00. Licenses of salesmen shall be renewed upon payment of a fee of $25.00. All licenses issued under the provisions of this act shall lapse and expire 3 years from March 31, 1966, and on the same date each third year thereafter. All applications for renewals of licenses under this act must be made in proper form accompanied with the proper renewal fee before the date of expiration, and proper submission of said renewal application shall automatically grant said applicant permission to operate pending the actual issuance or refusal of renewal licenses. Renewal licenses may be refused for any reason which would be grounds for the revocation of said license. Every licensee shall report to the commission all changes of members and addresses of any such firm, copartnership, association or corporation holding a license under this act within 10 days after same shall occur.

338.1509 Investigation; suspension or revocation of license, reasons; civil or criminal liability; complaints, time when to be made. [M.S.A. 18.86(109)]

Sec. 9. The commission may, upon its motion or upon the complaint in writing of any person made within 18 months after completion, occupancy or purchase of a residential or combination of residential and commercial building, investigate the actions of any residential builder or residential maintenance and alteration contractor or salesman or any person who shall assume to act in such capacity within this state, and shall have the power to suspend or revoke any licenses issued under the provisions of this act or deny any pending application at any time where the licensee or applicant is performing or attempting to perform any of the acts mentioned herein:

(a) Abandonment without legal excuse of any construction project or operation engaged in or undertaken by the licensee.

(b) Diversion of funds or property received for prosecution or completion of a specific construction project or operation, or for a specified purpose in the prose-

271

cution or completion of any construction project or operation, and their application or use for any other construction project or operation, obligation or purposes.

(c) Failure to account for or to remit for any moneys coming into his possession which belong to others.

(d) Wilful departure from or disregard of plans or specifications in any material respect and prejudicial to another, without consent of the owner or his duly authorized representative and without the consent of the person entitled to have the particular construction project or operation completed in accordance with such plans and specifications.

(e) Wilful violation of the building laws of the state or of any political subdivision thereof.

(f) Misrepresentation of a material fact by an applicant in obtaining a license.

(g) Making any substantial misrepresentation, or making any false promise of a character likely to influence, persuade or induce.

(h) In maintenance and alteration contracts, failure to furnish to a lender, the purchaser's signed completion certificate executed upon completion of the work to be performed under the contract.

(i) Failure to notify the commission within 30 days of the change of name and/or the principal business location of the licensee.

(j) Failure to notify the commission within 10 days of the change of a partner, trustee, director, officer, member and/or shareholder, or the change of name of any such person.

(k) Failure to deliver to the purchaser the entire agreement of the parties including all finance and other charges arising out of or incidental to the agreement when such agreement involves repair, alteration or any addition to, subtraction from, improvement of, movement of, wrecking of, or demolition of a residential structure or combination of residential and commercial structure, or building of a garage, or laying of concrete on residential property, or manufacture, assembly, construction, sale or distribution of a residential or combination residential and commercial structure which is prefabricated, preassembled, precut, packaged or shell housing.

(l) Insolvency, filing in bankruptcy, receivership or assigning for the benefit of creditors.

(m) Failure by a salesman to pay over immediately upon receipt all moneys received by him in connection with any transactions governed by the provisions of this act to the residential builder or residential maintenance and alteration contractor under whom he is licensed.

(n) Aiding or abetting an unlicensed person to evade the provisions of this act, or knowingly combining or conspiring with, or acting as agent, partner or associate for an unlicensed person, or allowing one's license to be used by an unlicensed person.

(o) Acceptance of a commission, bonus or other valuable consideration by any salesman for the sale of any goods or the performance of any service specified in the act from any person other than from the residential builder or residential maintenance and alteration contractor under whom he is licensed.

(p) Conviction for a felony in connection with operations as a builder, salesman or a contractor.

(q) The violation of any of the provisions of this act; and

(r) Any conduct, whether of the same or of a different character than hereinbefore specified, which constitutes dishonesty or unfair dealings.

This act shall not be construed to relieve any person from civil liability or criminal prosecution under the general laws of this state, and complaints pertaining to the erection, construction, replacement, repair, alteration, additions to, subtractions from, improvement, movement of, wrecking or demolition of any building covered by the provisions of this act shall only be considered by the commission if made by written, verified complaint within 1 year after completion, occupancy or purchase of said structure by the proper authorities charged with the enforcement of the laws governing the construction of residential or a combination of residential and commercial buildings in the various political subdivisions of the state.

APPENDIX B

State of Michigan, Department of Licensing and Regulation. From laws relating to the Real Estate License Law.

The People of the State of Michigan enact:

451.201 Real estate broker or salesman; license.

Sec. 1. It shall be unlawful for any person, firm, partnership association, co-partnership or corporation, whether operating under an assumed name or otherwise, from and after January first, 1920, to engage in the business or capacity, either directly or indirectly, of a real estate broker or real estate salesman within this state without first obtaining a license under the provisions of this act.

451.208 Real estate brokers and salesmen; license, application; branch office. [M.S.A. 19.798]

Sec. 8. All applications for licenses shall be made in writing to the commission. Such applications shall also be accompanied by the recommendation of at least 2 citizens, real estate owners, who have owned real estate for a period of 1 year or more, in the county in which said applicant resides or had his place of business, which recommendations shall certify that the applicant bears a good reputation for honesty and fair dealing, and recommending that a license be granted to the applicant. Every applicant for a license shall furnish a sworn statement setting forth his present address, both of business and residence, the complete address of all former places where he may have resided or been engaged in business, or acted as a real estate salesman, for a period of 60 days or more, during the last 5 years, and the length of such residence, together with the name of at least 1 real estate owner in each of the said counties where he may have resided, engaged in business, or acted as a salesman. Every applicant for a broker's license shall also state the name of the person, firm, partnership association, copartnership or corporation, and the location of the place, or places, for which said license is desired, and set forth the period of time, if any, which said applicant has been engaged in the business, and shall be executed by such person, or by an officer or member thereof. A broker's license shall not be issued to any new applicant who is not a citizen of the United States nor to any person who has been convicted of embezzlement or misappropriation of funds. Every real estate broker shall maintain a place of business in this state. In case a real estate broker maintains more than 1 place of business within the state a duplicate license must be secured by such broker for each branch office so maintained. A broker shall be permitted to maintain, in the city which constitutes the situs of his main office, not more than 1 branch office for each 60,000 residents, according to the last federal decennial census or any subsequent federal decennial census. Any branch office maintained in excess of 25 miles from the city limits in which such broker maintains his main office must be under the personal, direct supervision of an associate broker. Every applicant for a salesman's license shall, in addition to the requirements of the first paragraph of this section, also set forth the period of time, if any, during which he has been engaged in the business, stating the name of his last employer and the name and the place of business of the person, firm, partnership association, copartnership or corporation then employing him or in whose employ he is to enter. The application shall be accompanied by a written statement by the broker in whose employ he is to enter stating that in his opinion the applicant is honest, truthful and of good reputation, and recommending that the license be granted to the applicant. Every applicant for a salesman's license shall be a citizen of the United States.

451.213   Real estate brokers and salesmen; license, suspension or revocation; investigation; grounds; liability. [M.S.A. 19.803]

Sec. 13. The commission may upon its own motion, and shall upon the verified complaint in writing of any person, investigate the actions of an applicant for a real estate broker or real estate salesman license or any real estate broker or real estate salesman or any person who shall assume to act in either such capacity within this state and shall have the power to deny, suspend or revoke any license issued under the provisions of this act at any time where the applicant or licensee in performing or attempting to perform any of the acts mentioned herein, is deemed to be guilty of:

(a) Making any substantial misrepresentation.

(b) Making any false promises of a character likely to influence, persuade or induce.

(c) Pursuing a continued and flagrant course of misrepresentation or the making of false promises through agents or salesmen or advertising or otherwise.

(d) Acting for more than 1 party in a transaction without the knowledge of all parties thereto.

(e) Representing or attempting to represent a real estate broker other than the employer, without the express knowledge and consent of the employer.

(f) Failure to account for or to remit for any moneys coming into his possession which belong to others.

(g) Changing his business location without notification to the commission.

(h) Failure of a broker to return a salesman's license within 5 days as provided in section 10.

(i) Paying a commission or valuable consideration to any person not licensed under the provisions of this act.

(j) Failing to deposit in a custodial trust or escrow account all moneys belonging to others coming into the hands of the licensee in compliance with the following requirements:

(1) All deposits or other moneys accepted by every person, copartnership, corporation or association holding a real estate broker's license under the provisions of this act must be retained by such real estate broker pending consummation or termination of the transaction involved, and shall be accounted for in the full amount thereof at the time of the consummation or termination.

(2) Every real estate salesman promptly on receipt by him of a deposit or other moneys on any transaction in which he is engaged on behalf of his broker-employer shall pay over the deposit or other moneys to the real estate broker.

(3) Under no circumstances shall a broker permit any advance payment of funds belonging to others to be deposited in the broker's business or personal account or be commingled with any funds he may have on deposit belonging to him.

(4) Every real estate broker shall immediately deposit such moneys, of what-

ever kind or nature, belonging to others in a separate custodial or trust fund account maintained by the real estate broker with some bank or recognized depository until the transaction involved is consummated or terminated, at which time the real estate broker shall account for the full amount received.

(5) Every real estate broker shall keep records of all funds deposited therein, which records shall indicate clearly the date and from whom he received money, the dates deposited, the dates of withdrawals, and other pertinent information concerning the transaction, and shall show clearly for whose account the money is deposited and to whom the money belongs. All such records shall be subject to inspection by the commissioner or his deputies and by employees of the commission. Such separate custodial or trust fund account shall designate the real estate broker as trustee, and such account must provide for withdrawal of funds without previous notice.

(k) Any other conduct whether of the same or a different character than hereinbefore specified, which constitutes dishonest or unfair dealing.

The commission may also deny, suspend or revoke such license when the applicant or licensee has been convicted of a felony within the past 5 years.

This act shall not be construed to relieve any person from civil liability or criminal prosecution under the general laws of this state.

451.217 Real estate brokers and salesmen; list of licensees, distributees, fees. [M.S.A. 19.807]

Sec. 17. Whenever funds are available for the purpose, the commission may publish a list of the names and addresses of real estate brokers and salesmen licensed under this act, together with any suspension or revocations which have been ordered or such further information with respect to this act, its administration and enforcement, as it deems proper. When such lists are published, they shall be furnished the prosecuting attorney and clerk of each county and such other public officials as may be deemed proper. Copies of the list may also be furnished by the commission upon request to any firm or individual upon the payment of a reasonable fee fixed by the commission.

APPENDIX C

MARKETING & THE LAW

Reprinted from *Marketing & the Law*—a newsletter published by Man & Manager, Inc., New York. Edited by Lawrence Stessin, Professor of Management, Hofstra University.

INDEX